*A Short Declaration
of the Mystery of Iniquity*
(1611/1612)

Classics of Religious Liberty

1. *A Short Declaration of the Mystery of Iniquity* (1611/1612)
by Thomas Helwys (ca. 1550–ca. 1616). 1998.

Classics of Religious Liberty 1

A Short Declaration
of the Mystery of Iniquity
(1611/1612)

by
Thomas Helwys
(ca. 1550–ca. 1616)

edited and introduced by
Richard Groves

MERCER

ISBN 0-86554-574-X   MUP/H429

Classics of Religious Liberty 1
A Short Declaration of the Mystery of Iniquity
Copyright ©1998
Mercer University Press, Macon, Georgia USA

Library of Congress Cataloging-in-Publication Data

Helwys, Thomas, 1550?–1616?
A short declaration of the mystery of iniquity, 1611/1612 /
by Thomas Helwys ; edited and introduced by Richard Groves.
xxxvi+156pp. 6x9" (15x23cm.) — (Classics of religious liberty ; 1)
ISBN 0-86554-574-X (alk. paper)
1. Freedom of religion—Early works to 1800.
2. Baptists—Doctrines—Early works to 1800.
I. Groves, Richard, 1943–   . II. Title. III. Series.
BV741.H39   1998
261.7'2—dc21   98-10082

CIP

Contents

Heare o King, and dispise not y counsell of y poore, and let their complaints come befsre thee.

The king is a mortall man, e not God therefore hath no power over y jmmortall soules of his subiects, to make lawes e ordinances for them, and to set spirituall Lords over them.

If the king have authority to make spirituall Lords e Lawes, then he is an jmmortall God, and not a mortall man.

O king, be not seduced by deceivers to sin so against God whome thou oughtest to obey, nor against thy poore subiects who ought and will obey thee in all thinges with body life and goods, or els let their lives be taken from y earth.

God Save y King.

Spittlefeild
neare London.

Tho: Helwys.

Helwys's inscription on a flyleaf of the copy
of Mystery of Iniquity addressed to King James I.

Preface

In 1612 Thomas Helwys, an English country gentleman whose theological and ecclesiological interests had led him to identify first with the Puritans, then with the Separatists, and finally, along with John Smyth, to help establish the first Baptist church, returned to England from exile in Holland. With him Helwys brought a manuscript titled "The Mystery of Iniquity," in which he set forward for the first time in English the notion of liberty of conscience, or freedom of religion. Shortly after settling in Spittalfield, near London, Helwys published his book. Though it was hardly a bombshell at the time of publication, it probably cost Helwys his freedom and perhaps even his life.

For more than three hundred years *The Mystery of Iniquity* was available only in its first edition. By the twentieth century only four first edition copies remained. In 1935 the British Baptist Historical Society published a facsimile edition, making Helwys's historic work more readily available to scholars and the reading public. But since the pages of the first edition were simply photographed, the difficulties of the three-hundred-year-old text remained (for example, blurred type that rendered some words or sentences unintelligible and antequated punctuation and spellings). By the late twentieth century even the 1935 fascimile copy had been out of print for decades.

I became acquainted with Helwys's work while on sabbatical at Regents Park College, Oxford University, in the summer of 1995. It was my privilege to hold in my hands and to study two of the remaining four first-edition copies, including the one in which Helwys wrote his famous note to King James: " . . . the king is a mortal man and not God. . . . " *The Mystery of Iniquity* deserves to be made available once again.

The difficulties of preparing a new edition of a work that was published in 1612, the year after the Authorized Version of the Bible (King James Version) appeared, fall under numerous headings.

First, length of sentences. Typically sentences in *The Mystery of Iniquity* are much longer than modern readers are accustomed to. For example, the opening sentence of "To the Reader" consists of approximately 300 words and is punctuated with two sets of parentheses, seventeen commas, one semicolon, two colons, and finally, mercifully, a period. Difficulties sometimes arise because the subject matter changes within a sentence.

Second, length of paragraphs. It is not unusual for paragraphs to extend several pages. In one instance in the original text a paragraph begins on page 110 and ends on page 118. Such lengthy paragraphs give no visual break for the reader. In addition, the subject matter often changes within paragraphs.

Third, punctuation. The use of punctuation marks has changed greatly in the past 375 years. For example, the original text of *The Mystery of Iniquity* contains few, if any apostrophes. Colons often are used where a period would be used today. In several instances a question mark appears in the middle of a sentence.

Fourth, archaic spellings. The list of words that have changed in spelling since Thomas Helwys's time would be too long to serve any practical purpose.

Fifth, archaic verb endings (-*est*, -*eth*) and pronominal forms (*thee, thou, ye, thine*).

Sixth, archaic words. For example, *coopes, mainprise, enowe, war* (meaning overcome), *botches*, and *pight*.

Seventh, words that are still in use but are not regularly used. For example, *gainsay* (to dispute or to deny), *divers* (various), *despoil* (to pillage, strip of belongings, possessions or value).

Eighth, words that continue in use but with different meanings. For example, *instant* (urgent), *challenge* (to exercise), *equal* (fair), *despite* (spite).

Ninth, capitalization. Consistently, Helwys used uppercase initial letters for *Archbishops, Lord Bishops, Canons, our Lord the King, Temple, Tabernacle*, and *Beast* (as in *First and Second Beast*), to mention only a few; but rarely for *Lord* when referring to God or Jesus, or *Word* when used in the Word of God.

Tenth, words that were rendered difficult or impossible to decipher given the state of the printed text.

Eleventh, parenthetical statements. Frequently, Helwys set off statements within parentheses that likely would be set off by commas today.

Twelfth, sentences beginning with "and," a convention not in vogue in modern writing.

My first concern was simply to make available a text that is accessible to modern readers, both physically and in terms of readability. The 1935 fascimile edition, while preserving the exact appearance of the original text, is largely inaccessible to readers both physically—it has long been out of print—and in terms of readability: a photograph only reproduces the difficulties of the original. Beyond that, my concern was to retain as much of the letter and spirit of Thomas Helwys's own writing as possible.

The most conservative approach to such a task would be simply to reprint the text as it appeared 375 years ago, but in modern type. That is the approach, for example, of the following excerpt from "A True Confession" (1644) as it was reproduced in Lumpkin's *Baptist Confessions of Faith*.

[xi] A TRVE CONFESSION OF THE FAITH, AND HVMBLE ACKNOVVL-
EDGMENT OE THE ALEgeance, vvhich vve hir Maiesties Subjects, falsely
called Brovvnists, doo hould tovvards God, and yeild to hir Majestie and
all other that are ouer vs in the Lord. (p. 82)

Given the presentation of *The Mystery of Iniquity* in its seventeenth-century form, this minimalist approach would provide the reader with a text that is more accessible than the first edition or the fascimile edition. But portions of the text would remain obscure, and the reading of the whole would still be exceedingly difficult.

A looser, but still conservative, approach would be one which placed a priority on preserving the original text even while adapting it to a modern setting. This is how I would describe the approach that was taken by the team that produced the New King James Version of the Bible. Noting that language is constantly in flux, the translators "sought to keep abreast of changes in English speech." Thus, "where obsolescence and other reading difficulty exist, present-day vocabulary, punctuation, and grammar have been carefully integrated" (preface, New King James Version of the Bible).

The approach I have taken falls somewhere between these two conservative models. I have made what I consider to be only moderate concessions to the "changes in English speech." The most noticeable changes I have made in the text are: (1) to break up unnecessarily lengthy sentences; (2) to replace archaic verb endings and pronoun forms with modern ones; (3) to introduce modern punctuation; (4) to substitute modern spellings for archaic ones; (5) to use uppercase initial letters only for proper names, titles of God or Jesus, or the Word of God.

I have introduced no modern words into the text. When archaic words appear, their meanings are explained in footnotes. Words which are still in use, though not widely used, are left as Helwys wrote them, as are words that continue in use though with changed meanings. I have printed in bold those renderings of which I am confident but not certain. When I have been completely perplexed, I replaced the word in question with **(uncertain)**.

Finally, regarding quotations from scriptures. When Helwys included a scripture reference along with a biblical quotation, I left the reference in the body of the text. Many times, however, he quoted scriptures without references. In these instances, I have traced the references and placed them in footnotes. I have made few changes in Helwys's quotations of scripture.

I am grateful to Paul Fiddes, principal of Regents Park College, Oxford University, and Sue Mills, librarian/archivist, Angus Library, Regents Park College, for their support during my sabbatical at Oxford. I am grateful also for the encouragement offered to me by Leon Macbeth, Southwestern Baptist Theological Seminary; Bill Leonard, Wake Forest University Divinity School; and Edwin Gaustad, University of California, Riverside. I am especially grateful to the members of Wake Forest Baptist Church, Winston-Salem, North Carolina, for their continuing support and for the sabbatical which made this study possible.

Finally, I wish to thank Rosemary, my wife, for typing the manuscript and for exhibiting such extraordinary patience and support.

Winston-Salem, North Carolina   *Richard Groves*

Introduction
Historical Background

The Church of England in the Sixteenth Century

The second half of the sixteenth century was an unsettled time for religion in England. In 1534 Henry VIII broke with Rome and declared himself head of the church. But the church that Henry was head of remained essentially Roman in character and practice. Henry's son, Edward VI (1547–1553), took the Church of England in a decidedly Protestant direction. Images were removed from churches, altars were replaced by tables in the naves, clergy were allowed to marry, vestments were simplified, the laity was allowed to receive the wine in communion, and a new prayer book was approved by the parliament. Just a month before his death Edward issued the Forty-Two Articles Act which adopted a Protestant view on every contested issue. Dissenters, like Hooper and Knox, who had fled to Europe during Henry's reign, returned to England under Edward.

Protestantism had barely taken root in the Church of England when Mary (1553–1558) succeeded Edward and took immediate action to move the church toward Rome. Monasteries were refounded, Catholic services, ritual processions, and repressive legislation were reintroduced. Once more Protestants, as many as 800, fled to Europe for safety. Many of the English exiles became prominent church leaders under Elizabeth. Fifteen became bishops; others returned as heads of university colleges or deans of cathedrals.

In 1556 the Genevan Book of Order was published by a committee of four, headed by John Knox. It was a genuine alternative to the English Book of Common Prayer, from which it differed in allowing for greater participation by the congregation and excluding "anything that seemed reminiscent of the Catholic liturgy."[1] Four years later the Geneva Bible was published. It was an immediate success, going through sixty editions in the next fifty years. The Geneva Bible became an important source for the Puritan critique of the Roman church. For example, its marginal note on Revelation 4:3 identified the locusts which come out of the bottomless pit as, "Heretics, false teachers, worldly, subtle prelates with monks, friars, cardinals, patriarchs, archbishops, bishops, doctors, bachelors, and masters."[2]

Elizabeth, Mary's sister, came to the throne in 1558. The religious pendulum had swung toward Protestantism, then toward Catholicism under her predecessors. She was intent on finding a middle way. Many assumed Elizabeth would move in a more Protestant direction. After all, she had been taught by Protestant tutors. And she revered Henry, her father. Protestant exiles in Europe began making plans to return to England. Underground churches preached openly against Catholicism. Crucifixes were torn from church walls.

Initially, Elizabeth gave indications that she would indeed favor Protestantism. When the bishop of Winchester praised Mary in his funeral address for refusing the title supreme head of the church, Elizabeth had him arrested. In 1559 Parliament approved an Act of Supremacy and in 1563 reaffirmed the Act of Uniformity. The former named the Queen as Supreme Governor, repealed principle Marian statutes, and revived most of Henry's statutes regarding the organization and administration of the church. The latter authorized what came to be known as the Elizabethan prayer book, laid down penalties for those who refused to use it, and for those who wrote or spoke against it. All references to the pope were removed.

But the Act of Uniformity disappointed Protestants in mandating that "such ornaments of the church and of the ministers shall be retained and be in use, as was in the Church of England, by authority of Parliament, in the second year of the reign of King Edward the Sixth. . . . "[3] This meant that the vestments that men like Hooper had criticized so strongly were now required once again. In addition, the Act of Uniformity enforced attendance at parish churches.

---

[1]H. G. Alexander, *Religion in England, 1558-1662* (London: University of London Press, 1968) 43.

[2]Ibid.

[3]Ibid., 59.

When the Oath of Supremacy was offered to the Marian bishops all but two refused to sign. They were deprived of their positions. Elizabeth replaced the deprived bishops with people of her own choosing, most notably Matthew Parker, archbishop of Canterbury. More than 200 lower clergy also refused to sign.

The implementation of the Supremacy and Uniformity acts was accomplished by the Royal Injunctions, which covered almost every aspect of church life. Clergy were required to be licensed by a bishop in order to preach. Preachers were expected to preach on the Royal Supremacy at least four times a year. In churches that did not have a licensed preacher official homilies were to be read. All books or pamphlets were to be authorized by the church.

In 1563 the Thirty-Nine Articles, which were similar to the Forty-Two Articles of 1553 though on some points even more explicitly Protestant, were approved as the doctrinal test for clergy.

Puritans

It was during the reign of Elizabeth and in reaction to her "settlement" that the Puritans came into prominence. Though a contemporary referred to them as "a backwater in the national life,"[4] the Puritans were represented among the bishops, in Parliament, among clergy and laity. They were energetic propagandists and pamphleteers. The Puritans had no intention of leaving the Church of England. Their aim was to reform it from within.

Patterson distinguishes two phases of Puritan movement.[5] In the first phase (1559–1570) the focus was on liturgical concerns. Those who returned from exile when Elizabeth became queen were intent on securing control over the national church and reducing its worship to "purer" forms. They disliked a number of ceremonies retained in the Elizabethan prayer book: "with this ring I thee wed" (weddings); "receive ye the Holy Ghost" (ordination); the wearing of vestments by clergy; making the sign of the cross (baptism); wearing of the surplice in church and cap and gown in daily life; kneeling at communion; the burial service, and observance of holy days.

---

[4]M. W. Patterson, *A History of the Church of England* (London: Longmans, Green, and Company, 1909) 303.

[5]Ibid., 303-307.

In its second phase, beginning in 1570, the focus shifted from liturgy to the proper form of church government. Patterson stated the issue succinctly: "Parity of ministers was their cry, the overthrow of the Episcopacy was their aim. . . . The divine right of Presbyterianism was matched against the Anglican divine right of Episcopacy."[6]

For the moment power was in the hands of those who considered the Puritans as great a threat to the church as the papists. Archbishop Parker issued his Advertisements of 1566 which declared that in cathedrals and collegiate churches the clergy must wear copes at communion and surplices at other services, and that in parish churches the surplice should be worn at all services. Most Puritans conformed but many did not. Those who did not conform were imprisoned and deprived.

In 1583 Parker was succeeded by John Whitgift, who was a Calvinist theologically but not ecclesiastically. Whitgift, who was called the "Canterbury Caiaphas" in the Marprelate tracts,[7] remained at Canterbury throughout the reign of Elizabeth. Patterson says that "the most characteristic feature of his episcopate was the determined stand he made against Puritan efforts to undermine the Church of England. He suppressed prophesyings, he enforced on the Puritans, on the pain of suspension, complete conformity to the Prayer Book. . . . "[8] In 1593 Whitgift secured the banishment of Nonconformists.

Separatists

Understandably, Puritans were dissatisfied with Elizabeth's settlement of the religious situation in England, some more than others. Some despaired of reforming the Church of England. Possibly as early as 1580 a group led by Robert Browne (ca. 1553–1633) determined to separate from the church rather than attempt to change it. Their cry was, "Reformation without tarrying for any."

The Separatists did not recognize the historic church as a church at all, because "it was contaminated by the presence within its fold of evil livers;

---

[6]Ibid., 307.

[7]A series of satirical tracts, secretly published, which attacked the "covetous popish bishops" in a "railing rollicking stule," possibly associated with John Penry.

[8]Patterson, A History of the Church of England, 297.

they thought that the true church ought to consist of 'saints' alone."[9] Drawing on the writings of Separatist leaders Henry Barrow and John Greenwood, B. R. White enumerates four arguments in support of the Separatist contention that the Church of England was in a state of total apostasy. First, its members were not normally people who had been converted, that is, they had not made a personal confession of faith and were not committed to a life of obedience to God. Second, the ministry of the parish churches was not patterned on the apostolic model of presbyters and deacons. Third, the worship of the parish congregation was based on a book that, in their opinion, derived from Rome rather than from scripture. Fourth, the members of the parish church had no part in the governing of their own congregation. Stated positively, the Separatists understood the church to be a covenantal community of faith, whose members were bound together by obedience to Christ, whose will was made known in scripture.[10]

Because they favored a congregational form of church polity and rejected both episcopal and presbyterian forms of government, the Separationists ran afoul of both Presbyterians and Anglicans. Browne himself was forced to flee to Holland. Henry Barrow, John Greenwood, and John Penry, were imprisoned and executed. Ernest Payne claims that Penry was the first to advise both Puritans and Separatists to emigrate to the American colonies in the hope of finding freedom there.[11]

After the deaths of Greenwood, Barrow, and Penry, the Lower Trent Valley became an important center of Separatist activity. There the company of Separatists was divided into two congregations, one meeting in Scrooby, led by William Brewster and John Robinson, the other meeting in Gainsborough, led by a Cambridge man named John Smyth.

Smyth had studied under Francis Johnson, a leading Puritan, while he was at Cambridge. In 1594 Smyth was appointed fellow of Christ's College and ordained by the bishop of Lincoln. By this time Smyth was already leaning toward Puritanism. In order to avoid taking a living, which would have meant that the bishop might attempt to harry him into conformity, Smyth became city lecturer in Lincoln, a position that was supported by

---

[9]Ibid., 309.

[10]B. R. White, *The English Separatist Tradition* (Oxford: Oxford University Press, 1971) 71.

[11]Ernest A. Payne, *The Free Church Tradition in the Life of England* (Londond: SCM Press, 1944) 34.

town funds or private persons. Two years later he was driven from that position for "his personal preaching at men in the city."[12] For a while Smyth supported himself as a physician. But in 1606 he separated from the Church of England and became pastor of the group of Separatists at Gainsborough.

Under pressure for violations of the Conventicle Act (1593)—that is, for their unsanctioned worship assemblies—the Smyth congregation joined other English Separatists who had gone into exile in the Netherlands. In 1604, when hopes were dashed by a new set of canons and discipline for the government of the Church of England, more than 300 had fled to the safety of Amsterdam, Leyden, and other cities and villages in Holland. One group was led by Francis Johnson (Smyth's old tutor) and another was led by John Robinson. At first the various Separatist groups clustered in Amsterdam. But after a few months the Scrooby group, numbering about one hundred, moved to Leyden. As we shall see later, the Gainsborough group divided over ecclesiological differences, with half following John Smyth and joining the Dutch Mennonites, and half following Thomas Helwys and returning to England to establish the first Baptist church on English soil. The Scrooby congregation, discouraged by news from England, opened negotiations with the Virginia Company hoping to settle in North America. In 1620 William Brewster and members of his congregation from Leyden, along with Puritans and Separatists they picked up at Southampton, sailed aboard the Mayflower for America.

King James 1

James I (1566–1625), who became king in 1603, had been brought up in Scotland where episcopacy had been abolished, and the state church had become Calvinist in theology and Presbyterian in form. James's background might have led some to think that he would be more inclined to a presbyterian form of church polity than to an episcopalian form. (Indeed, later James sent two representatives of the Church of England to the Synod of Dort [1619] which condemned Arminianism.) But such was not the case.

---

[12]Michael R. Watts, *The Dissenters, From the Reformation to the French Revolution* (Oxford: Clarendon Press, 1978) 41.

Consistent with his claim that "the chiefest of kingly duties [is] to settle affairs of religion," in 1604 James called a conference of religious leaders at Hampton Court shortly after assuming the throne. The purpose of the conference was to deal with Puritan complaints. Those complaints were set forward by John Reynolds, president of Corpus Christi College, Oxford: "That the doctrine of the church might be preserved in purity, according to God's Word. That good pastors might be planted in all churches to preach the same. That the church government might be sincerely ministered, according to God's Word. That the Book of Common Prayer might be fitted to more increase of piety."[13]

Regarding the matter of church government, John Reynolds proposed a presbyterian form of polity. A summary of the meeting indicates that at this proposal "his Majesty was somewhat stirred . . . thinking that they aimed at a Scottish presbytery which, saith he, as well agreeth with a monarchy as God with the devil. Then Jack and Tom and Will and Dick shall meet, and at their pleasure censure me and my council, and all our proceedings: then Will shall stand up and say, it must be thus; then Dick shall reply and say, nay . . . but we will have it thus."[14] James implored the Puritans not to bring the matter up again for seven years, "and if then you find me pursy and fat and my windpipes stuffed, I will perhaps hearken to you. . . ."[15]

Though the Puritans could point to certain concessions James made at the Hampton Court Conference, his own view was revealed a few months later in a "proclamation enjoining uniformity." The conclusion of the conference, he said, was "that no well-grounded matter appeared to us or our said Council why the state of the Church here by law established should in any material point be altered."[16] Specifically, "no apparent or grounded reason was shewed why either the Book of Common Prayer or the Church discipline here by law established should be changed. . . ."[17]

---

[13]J. R. Tanner, ed., *Constitutional Documents of the Reign of James I A.D. 1603–1625 with an Historical Commentary* (Cambridge: Cambridge University Press, 1930) 62.

[14]Ibid., 67.

[15]Ibid.

[16]Ibid., 71.

[17]Ibid.

Though the Hampton Court Conference had an immediate impact on church life in England, especially among Puritans, the decision to publish a new translation of the Bible had the most long-lasting and far-reaching consequences. The proposal was made by Dr. Reynolds, but James approved the idea. The new translation was destined to be associated with his name for centuries to come.

Leon Macbeth says that "much of James's reign was spent in making good his threat to harass and exile those who refused to conform to the Church of England."[18] Underhill claims that, "In 1604 no fewer than 300 Puritan clergy were ejected, while the Separatists were constantly persecuted by the ecclesiastical authorities for breaking the laws of attendance at public worship."[19] But in 1610 George Abbot, a Puritan sympathizer and head of the Calvinist party at Oxford, succeeded Bancroft as archbishop of Canterbury, and the rigorous enforcement of uniformity came to an end. Ironically, it was Abbot who was responsible for the executions of Bartholomew Legate and Edward Wightman, "the last heretics ever burned in England."[20]

Both Legate and Wightman were executed on the express order of King James. The king personally interrogated Legate on several occasions.[21] Five years earlier one of Legate's brothers, Walter, also a Separatist, had been executed by drowning. A third Legate brother, Thomas, died in 1607 after spending five years in Newgate prison. Bartholomew Legate was burned in Smithfield on 18 March 1611 or 1612, for Arianism, preaching that Jesus was a "meere man." Edward Wightman, a draper in Burton-on-Trent, was accused in February 1610, and tried in December 1611, on a variety of charges, among them, claiming to be the Holy Ghost, and writing a letter to the king in which he said that he (Wightman) had been called to deliver the world from the heresies of the Nicolaitians, that is, the three creeds of Christendom. Wightman was tried and convicted by the bishop of Coventry. He recanted when the fire was lit. But a month later he recanted his recantation and was burned at the stake. Iviney claims that Wightman was a

---

[18]Leon MacBeth, *The Baptist Heritage, Four Centuries of Baptist Witness* (Nashville: Broadman Press, 1987) 100.

[19]Edward Bean Underhill, *Tracts on Liberty of Conscience and Persecution, 1614–1661* (London: J. Haddon, 1846) 33.

[20]Patterson, *A History of the Church of England*, 328.

[21]Leonard Levy, *Treason against God. A History of the Offense of Blasphemy* (New York: Schocken Books, 1981) 183-86.

Baptist, because he was also charged with saying that "the baptizing of infants is an abominable custom; that the Lord's Supper and baptism are not to be celebrated as they are now practiced in the Church of England; and that Christianity is not wholly professed and preached in the Church of England, but only in part."[22]

Though both Legate and Wightman stood apart from many Separatists in some of their beliefs, and though they were the last two persons to be executed in England for their religious beliefs, nonetheless their executions served as a powerful reminder that dissent would not be tolerated. Ironically, 1611 was also the year of the publication of a new translation of the Bible which was destined to be associated forever with the king who had executed Legate and Wightman.

In the year Edward Wightman was burned at the stake, Thomas Helwys returned from exile in Holland.

Thomas Helwys

Thomas Helwys (ca. 1550–ca. 1616) was aware of the danger inherent in returning to England. While still in the Netherlands, he had written, "Let none think that we have not sat down and in some measure thoroughly considered what the cost and danger may be. . . . " After thoroughly counting the cost, he and the other members of his tiny band of Baptists, possibly as few as ten, made their fateful decision.

Perhaps Helwys thought his connections could protect him. His father, Edmund, had been a country gentleman who had sold land in the counties of Lincoln and Northampton and had taken a lease on Broxtowe Hall, an estate near Nottingham. An uncle, Geoffrey Helwys (1541–1616), was a merchant in London who had been an alderman and sheriff of London. A cousin, Gervase Helwys (1561–1615), had been knighted along with scores of others by King James in 1603, when the new king was enroute from Edinburgh to London, and later became lieutenant of the tower in London. Ironically, Gervase held that position while Thomas was a prisoner in Newgate. Gervase was implicated in the death of Sir Thomas Overbury (1581–1613) and was beheaded on Tower Hill, 20 November 1615.

---

[22]Joseph Iviney, *A History of the English Baptists*, 4 vols. (London: B. J. Holdsworth, 1811) 1:124.

Thomas himself had been educated at Gray's Inn in London, one of four inns of court which were intended chiefly for the profession of the law but also provided general education for the sons of nobility and gentry. Gray's Inn was the largest and most fashionable of the four. Thomas Cromwell had studied law there. William Burghley, high treasurer of England, and church leaders Bancroft and Launcelot Andrews also studied there. During the time that Helwys studied at Gray's Inn, Francis Bacon represented the district in Parliament. Indeed, Bacon had speculated in a building within the Inn.

On board ship from Holland Thomas Helwys carried with him a manuscript he had written while in exile. The title of the manuscript, "The Mystery of Iniquity," was taken from 2 Thessalonians 2:7, which reads in the King James Version: "For *the mystery of iniquity* doth already work: only he who now letteth will let, until he be taken out of the way." Like other writings by Separatists during the period, "The Mystery of Iniquity" was preoccupied with identifying apocalyptic figures from scripture with contemporary movements, notably the Roman Catholic Church and the Church of England. Unlike any other work of its time, it also contained the first exposition in English of the notion of liberty of conscience.

Helwys came by his theological interests honestly. In 1589 his father, Edmund, wrote "A Marvel Deciphered," a treatise on Revelation 12. Burgess described the work as a "patriotic tract called forth by Protestant feeling engendered by the Spanish attack on England. The writer makes a veiled allusion to Queen Elizabeth as foreshadowed by the woman clothed with the sun . . . and to the pope as the dragon that made war on her."[23] Edmund died on 2 October 1590, while Thomas was studying at Gray's Inn, leaving bequests to "twenty poor villagers in Basford, Bilburrowe, and Bulwell." His will contained a personal confession of faith.

Ominously, Helwys completed his study at Gray's Inn in 1593, the year that fifty-six members of a Separatist church in London were arrested and joined their leaders, Henry Barrowe (ca. 1550–1593) and John Greenwood (d. 1593), in prison. The lay members were later released but Barrowe and Greenwood were executed in April. John Penry (1559–1593), another Separatist, was executed in May.

---

[23]Walter H. Burgess, *John Smyth the Se-Baptist, Thomas Helwys, and the First Baptist Church in England with Fresh Light upon the Pilgrim Fathers' Church* (London: James Clark and Co., 1911) 110.

After completing his studies, Helwys returned to Broxtowe Hall and assumed the life of a country gentleman. On 3 December 1595, he married Joan Ashmore. Over the next twelve years they had seven children. Together they entered into the life of the Puritan community. Champlin Burgess says that "their house became a hospitable center and place of call for the Puritan clergy of the district. Helwys himself was deeply interested in questions of religion, and his doors were open to those able to discuss with him the pressing problems of the day. Here Richard Bernard called on his way home from conferring with Arthur Hildersham; here John Smyth, when he was sick nigh unto death, found a haven of refuge."[24] Smyth and Helwys become close friends. Joan and Thomas Helwys became members of Smyth's Gainsborough congregation. The flight of the Smyth group to Holland was probably funded by Thomas Helwys. Several years later, John Robinson, responding to Helwys's criticism of his (Robinson's) decision to remain in the Netherlands, said, "The truth is that it was Mr. Helwiss who above all . . . furthered this passage into strange countries; and if many brought oars, he brought sails."[25]

The nineteenth-century Baptist historian Joseph Iviney says that Smyth and Helwys were excommunicated from the Church of England "on account of their objecting to the validity of infant baptism."[26] Burgess claims that "the High Court of Ecclesiastical Commission for the province of York took active proceedings against members of the Gainesborough and Scrooby churches in the autumn of 1607."[27]

Helwys left his wife and seven children in England when he fled to Holland, possibly thinking that they would not be touched or perhaps that he would send for them later. But in 1608 Joan Helwys was brought before the ecclesiastical commissioners and sent to prison for "refusing to take an oath according to law." She was brought back to court a few months later. It is not known how her case was decided. The law called for banishment, in which case she could have joined Thomas in Holland, but there is no record that she did so.

---

[24]Ibid., 115.

[25]Burgess, *John Smyth the Se-Baptist, Thomas Helwys, and the First Baptist Church in England*, 107: quoting Robinson in *Of Religious Communion*.

[26]Iviney, *A History of the English Baptists*, 1:122.

[27]Burgess, *John Smyth the Se-Baptist, Thomas Helwys, and the First Baptist Church in England*, 116.

The Smyth group settled in Amsterdam in a mass of buildings attached to the Great Bakehouse owned by the Mennonite Jan Munster.

In the interplay between Smyth and the other Separatists in Holland it became clear that Smyth differed from the other leaders on significant ecclesiastical and liturgical matters. He differed with Johnson on the use of scripture in worship. Smyth did not believe an English translation should be used in worship; the Greek and Hebrew should be translated by the preacher on the spot. He believed that it was less likely the Spirit would be quenched in this way. Further, Smyth held that the Greek and Hebrew scriptures were inspired by God, but that the translations were not. He also objected to sermons being read and hymns being sung from a book. He believed that only church members should be allowed to make contributions to the church. Smyth also questioned the practice of the Johnson group of giving power to the elders but not to the members.

In Holland the English refugees found a measure of religious liberty unknown in their own land. W. T. Whitley says that the town authorities adopted "the plan of Rhegius, that if Anabaptists would keep their errors to themselves they should be left alone."[28] Most importantly, the Smyth-Helwys group came into contact with Mennonites, "who maintained on principle that the sword should not be used to uphold religion. They declared that Christ alone was king over the church, and that freedom in religion should be allowed to all who observe civil order."[29] This seed found fertile soil in the mind and conscience of Thomas Helwys. But B. R. White insists that the newly arrived Smyth-Helwys group remained separate from the Mennonites on one important point. They "believed that the civil government was not only a 'holy ordinance of God' but also that civil governors may be members of the church of Christ" and that "it is lawful in a just cause to take an oath by the name of the Lord."[30]

It was while they were in Amsterdam that Smyth and the others in his group arrived at the conclusion that baptism on profession of repentance and faith was the sole requirement for membership in the church. This elim-

---

[28]W. T. Whitley, *A History of British Baptists* (London: Charles Griffin and Co., 1923) 33-34.

[29]Wilbur K. Jordan, *The Development of Religious Toleration in England*, 4 vols. (London: George Allen and Unwin, 1932) 1:291.

[30]B. R. White, *The English Baptists of the Seventeenth Century* (London: Baptist Historical Society, 1996) 22.

inated the practice of infant baptism. It also seemed to require that their tiny church be reconstituted, not on a basis of mutual covenant between its members, but by the baptism of all professed believers. Smyth baptized himself (se-baptism), then he baptized Helwys and the others "out of a basin."

Shortly, however, Smyth began to question whether he had been correct in not seeking baptism by the Mennonites. The issue was whether there was a legitimate church at hand. He believed that if a legitimate church were available, one should seek baptism there. If not, it would be permissible for believers to baptize one another. Believing that he had made a mistake, Smyth began making overtures toward the Mennonites (Waterlanders), hoping to make application for membership. Helwys disagreed with Smyth's desire to join the Mennonites, believing that their views were similar to the Catholic concept of apostolic succession. Helwys's group, consisting of Helwys and possibly ten others, excommunicated Smyth and declared themselves to be "the true church."[31] Smyth and thirty-one others (fourteen men and seventeen women) applied for acceptance into the Mennonite church in Amsterdam, presenting the Waterlanders with a confession in twenty propositions as part of the application. Smyth expanded the confession to one hundred propositions for his followers. Helwys wrote to the Mennonites opposing the application of Smyth and his congregation. With his letter of opposition, he sent a confession in nineteen propositions to more or less match Smyth's twenty propositions. In 1611, this was expanded to twenty-seven articles as "A Declaration of Faith of English people remaining at Amsterdam in Holland."

John Smyth died of consumption in August 1612. After his death, his congregation made a second attempt to unite with the Mennonites and was accepted 21 January 1615. Subsequently, the group lost its identity as a separate community.

Separated from Smyth, Helwys devoted himself to writing. Burrage claims that Helwys "seems to have been the leading thinker of his party"[32] and that he wrote four books over two years, including the confession of faith. After the confession, Helwys's second writing, a brief piece of twenty-four unnumbered pages, was "A short and plain proof, by the word and

---

[31]Underhill, *Tracts on Liberty of Conscience and Persecution, 1614–1661*, 39.

[32]Champlin Burrage, *The Early English Dissenters in Light of Recent Research* (Cambridge: Cambridge University Press, 1912) 1:251.

works of God, that God's decree is not the cause of any man's sin or condemnation: and that all men are redeemed by Christ; as also that no infants are condemned." It was dedicated, on 2 June 1611, to Lady Bowes in whose house at Coventry he had heard Smyth debate with other Puritans on their duty to separate. His third work, "An advertisement or admonition unto the congregation which men call New Fryelers (Free Willers)," was written to address issues between himself and Mennonites. Helwys's fourth and last writing was "A Short Declaration on the Mystery of Iniquity" in 1611/1612.

In Amsterdam Thomas Helwys became convinced that his flight from persecution had been a mistake. "Thousands of ignorant souls in their own country were perishing for lack of instruction," he wrote. He and his little band of Baptists returned to London where they founded a church in Spittlefields outside the city walls. If it can be said that John Smyth founded the first English Baptist church, "though not on English soil," it can be said that Thomas Helwys founded in 1612 the first Baptist Church on English soil. One of his first tasks was to publish the book he had brought with him from Amsterdam.

When the copies of The Mystery of Iniquity came from the printer, Thomas Helwys wrote a note inside the cover of one copy. Evidently, it was his intention that it would be read by King James. The note said:

Hear, O king, and despise not the counsel of the poor, and let their complaints come before thee.

The king is a mortal man and not God, therefore has no power over the immortal souls of his subjects, to make laws and ordinances for them, and to set spiritual lords over them.

If the king has authority to make spiritual lords and laws, then he is an immortal God and not a mortal man.

O king, be not seduced by deceivers to sin against God whom you ought to obey, nor against your poor subjects who ought and will obey you in all things with body, life, and goods, or else let their lives be taken from the earth.

God save the king.

Helwys signed his note, "Tho. Helwys. Spittalfield near London." It is not known whether King James received the book or, if he received it, read it. It is widely assumed, however, that the book and the note sealed Thomas Helwys's fate.

Helwys was arrested in 1612 and placed in Newgate Prison in London. There is no direct documentary evidence related to Thomas Helwys during the final period of his life. However, a pamphlet titled "The Discovery of a London Monster called the Black Dog of Newgate," sheds light of what life was like there. The poem was published in 1612 by "Robert Wilson . . . to be sold in his shop at the new gate at Gray's Inn." It describes the coming of a priest to visit the prisoners.

> See in yon hall are divers sorts of men,
> Some weep, some wail, some mourn, some wring their hands,
> Some curse, some swear, and some blaspheming. Then
> My heart did faint, my head hair upright stands.
> O Lord, thought I, this house will rend in sunder,
> Or else there can be no hell, this hell under.
> Thus wond'ring, I on sudden did spy
> One all in black came stampling up the stairs.
> Who's yon? I ask. And thus he made reply,
> Yon is the man does mitigate our cares.
> He preached Christ, and does God's word deliver
> To all distressed, to comfort men forever.
> Then drew I near to see what might betide,
> Or what the sequel was of that I saw:
> Expecting good would follow such a guide,
> As preached Christ, and taught a God to know.
> A hundred clustered nying the pulpit near,
> As if they longed the Gospel to hear.[33]

Champlin Burrage suggests that Thomas Helwys may have been the author of a revealing handwritten document that was found in the library of the House of Lords, though he offers no reason for claiming that "the handwriting may be that of Thomas Helwys." On the scrap of paper is written, "A most humble supplication of divers poor prisoners and many others the king's majesty's loyal subjects ready to testify it by the oath of allegiance in all sincerity, whose grievances are lamentable, only for cause of conscience." The supplication is addressed to the "Right Honorable assembly of the Commons-house of Parliament" and is signed "By his majesty's faithful

---

[33]W. T. Whitley, *Thomas Helwys of Gray's Inn and Broxtowe Hall, Nottingham* (London: Kingsgate Press, 1935) pages unnumbered.

subjects most falsely called Anabaptists." The petitioners claimed that they had been kept "many years in lingering imprisonments, divided from wives, children, servants, and callings, not for any cause but only for conscience toward God, to the utter undoing of us, our wives, and children." Burrage notes that "the words 'rejected by the committee' are written in a scrawly hand at the close of the petition."[34]

John Robinson seems to have assumed that Helwys was alive in 1614 when he wrote his response to Helwys's charges in *The Mystery of Iniquity*. In 1616 Geoffrey Helwys, Thomas's uncle, bequeathed ten pounds to Joan Ashmore Helwys. In the will she is referred to as Thomas Helwys's widow.

A Summary of The Mystery of Iniquity

Book I

Relying almost exclusively on apocalyptic biblical passages, Helwys attacked both the Roman church and the hierarchy of the Church of England. He argued that the Roman church is the "abomination of desolation" spoken of by Daniel, the "mystery of iniquity" and the "man of sin" spoken of by Paul, and the first beast of the Revelation. He was especially critical of its "strange exaltation of power and pomp." Before the "bloody sword" of the beast even secular rulers bow in subservience. Helwys was offended by what he considered to be the excessive and extravagant use of titles in the Roman church. He referred to such titles as "spiritual names of blasphemy," because they rightly belong to God and to Christ. But Helwys was most offended by the power Rome exercised to "bind men's consciences," by taking "the Word of God from the people that they might not have it so much as in their own language, neither may they meddle with the spirit of knowledge and understanding of it. . . . "

The Church of England, Helwys argued, is the second beast of the book of Revelation, for it attempts to compel people to worship the image of the first beast. The liturgy and the vestments—"your surplice and cross and churchings and burials . . . your chantings . . . your whole conformity"—

---

[34]Burrage, *The Early English Dissenters in Light of Recent Research*, 1:255ff.

were far too Roman for Helwys's Separatist/Baptist tastes. The ecclesiastical court system—"your canons and consistories . . . your courts, offices, and officers"—were reminiscent of Rome's heavy-handed treatment of dissenters. He spoke powerfully of "the silenced at home and the banished abroad." The titles used in the Church of England seemed but an echo of those he so despised in the Roman church. Helwys could not withhold his sarcasm when speaking of "your Common book" which required that "some prayers be said after the curate be paid his dues, some on the north side of the table, some in one place, some in another," and which instructed priests "what to pray, when to pray, and where to pray, and what to put on when they pray." Finally, he attacked the pomp and power of the Church of England, declaring, "The apostle Paul was better worthy of double maintenance than you and all the priests in all your provinces and dioceses. Yet he labored with his hands. . . . " Remarkably, Helwys proposed that the king confiscate all the "goodly palaces and possessions" of the church and require that the church survive on "a voluntary, liberal distribution." Sounding very much like the free church tradition which followed him, Helwys wrote, "Oh, that we might live to see all them that preach the Gospel to live off the Gospel, that is, off the free liberality of the saints."

Book II

The second book contains Helwys's defense of the notion of freedom of conscience, a concept Helwys recognized was likely to be considered heretical. Nonetheless, he dared to present his case to the public and, more specifically, to King James, for book II throughout is addressed directly to the king. "In a good cause," Helwys asked, "why should we fear to stand before kings, seeing their thrones are established by justice?"

Following Paul in Romans 13, Helwys believed the state is divinely ordained. That being the case, he argued, citizens are bound to obey, "not only for fear but for conscience' sake" (Romans 13:5). Even if the king should act unlawfully "(which God forbid), he is in these things to be submitted to."

There is a limit to the powers of the state, however. The king does not have "power to command men's consciences in the greatest things between God and men." "Let this (earthly) kingdom, power, and honor fully satisfy your lord the king's heart," Helwys pleaded. "And let it suffice the king to have rule over the people's bodies and goods, and let not our lord the king give his power to be exercised over the spirits of his people."

One of Helwys's greatest concerns was the use of the sword of the state to insure conformity in the kingdom of heaven. In Christ's kingdom, he argued, "no earthly power can be helpful." If Christ's sword, which is his Word, "will not prevail to bring men under obedience to his own laws, what can our lord the king's sword do? It is spiritual obedience that the Lord requires, and the king's sword cannot smite the spirits of men."

At a time when it was customary for the religion of the people to be determined by the religion of the monarch, Helwys boldly declared that people "should choose for themselves their religion, seeing they only must stand themselves before the judgment seat of God to answer for themselves, when it shall be no excuse for them to say, We were commanded or compelled to be of this religion by the king or by them that had authority over them." Though anti-Catholic feeling was high under James, Helwys dared to extend the right to choose one's own religion to "them of the Romish religion." "For we do freely profess that our lord the king has no more power over their consciences than over ours, and that is none at all." But Helwys went even further. He extended freedom in religious matters to all persons. "For men's religion to God is between God and themselves. The king shall not answer for it. Let them be heretics, Turks, Jews, or whatsoever, it appertains not to the earthly power to punish them in the least measure."

Book III

In books III and IV Helwys dealt with what he called "false professions of Christ," Puritanism and Brownism. He found the Puritan desire to reform the Church of England from within rather than separate from it disingenuous at best. His sarcasm crackled. You claim "that there is a way of reformation," he said, "wherein you would be, if you might have leave or license to enter thereinto, which seeing you cannot obtain, you justify it lawful to walk in an unreformed profession of religion upon this ground because you may not have leave by act of Parliament to reform."

The foundation of Helwys's criticisms of Puritanism was his conviction that, despite their critique of the Church of England, the Puritans had not separated themselves from the second beast. They continued to seek and to accept church appointments. This Helwys found hypocritical. "All the power you have to administer is by the authority of the bishop's bull, which you have in so great contempt." In the final analysis, he said, "you have no ministry but from Rome." In response to the Puritans' defense that they had not separated from the church out of a concern for the peace of the church, Helwys argued that with their "books of open contempt" and their "tedious Parliament suits," they could hardly have devised "more unpeaceable courses." If the Puritans really cared about the peace of the church, they would separate from it. In truth, he said, it was not the peace of the church the Puritans were concerned about; it was their own peace.

Helwys's criticism of the Puritans provided him an opportunity to set forward his congregational understanding of church polity in juxtaposition to presbyterianism which they preferred over the Church of England's episcopalian form of government. In the early church, he said, election, or the calling of a pastor, was the responsibility of the congregation itself. "How blessed and comfortable a thing were it, for a holy people so to elect their pastor that should lead them, and feed them with the wholesome word of doctrine and exhortation, and watch over their souls in the Lord." Likewise, ordination "was performed and done in the presence of the church or congregation by fasting and prayer and laying on of hands. . . . " This, he claimed, is in sharp contrast to the manner in which Puritan clergy "by suit and service, by riding and running, by attending and waiting, by capping and curtseying, and at last by prostrating yourselves on your knees at the feet of an archbishop or lord bishop, receiving your ordination from him. . . . "

Regardless of the topic Helwys was dealing with, he was never far from liberty of conscience, the notion that provided the intellectual power that energized his theology. Thus, when he criticized the Puritans for preferring a presbyterian form of church government over an episcopalian form, saying that "they are all one condition in their degrees, and not any one of them more pleasing to God than another," his real complaint was that both forms of polity had one goal, namely, "to rule over men's consciences by their own laws and decrees."

Book IV

In the concluding book Helwys dealt with the second "false profession of Christ," Brownism, the Separatists who took their name from Robert Browne (ca. 1553–1633). If dealing with the Puritans provided Helwys an opportunity to set forward his notion of the congregational form of government, his critique of the Brownists, chiefly John Robinson (ca. 1575–1625), provided an occasion for him to present his views on baptism.

The Separatist position was that a church is essentially a body of people who voluntarily enter into relation with one another on the basis of a covenant. Helwys said that there is "no way to join and come to Christ, but only to 'amend their lives, and be baptized.'" Baptism, not covenant, is the unifying foundation of the church.

Helwys quarrelled with Robinson over the nature and meaning of baptism. Robinson had argued that in its "essential causes," the matter of baptism is water, and the form is washing in the name of the Trinity. Helwys responded by saying that the matter of baptism is water and the Holy Spirit, that is, being purified "from an evil conscience" as well as being washed in water. Further, Robinson had said that "a lawful person by whom, a right subject upon which, and a true communion wherein it is to be administered" provide the "appurtenances" in which baptism is "clothed." Helwys answered angrily that the Holy Spirit, a lawful minister, a right party to be baptized, and a true communion or congregation in which the baptism is to be take place are no mere "appurtenances" to baptism; they are the "essential parts thereof."

This was no mere haggling over words. Robinson's position allowed room for infant baptism; Helwys's did not. "How does this baptism belong unto infants?" he asked. "Can there be amendment of life for the remission of sins in infants? Can infants be buried into the death of Christ to walk in newness of life? Can infants put on Christ by faith? If they can do none of these things . . . may they not be baptized."

Just as he had criticized the Puritans for maintaining their ties to the Church of England, Helwys criticized the Brownists for retaining their baptism at the hands of Anglican priests. To his way of thinking, the Separatists had not really separated. "It is time to leave off talking of separation," he said, "and to separate indeed." Helwys could not resist noting that Browne himself, after living in exile in Holland, returned to England, conformed, and lived out the remainder of his days as a rector. Helwys said that Browne had not been able "to keep his face towards Jerusalem and the land of Canaan, (and) has fainted in the way, and rebelled in the wilderness, and returned to his so much formerly detested Babylon and Egypt."

Appendix

Helwys concluded his book with a brief but passionate attack on other Separatists for remaining in the safety of the Netherlands rather than returning to an uncertain future in England with him. Though hardly more than an appendix, this final section of *The Mystery of Iniquity* reveals Helwys's heart and soul, his passion for the Gospel, and his great courage.

Helwys was especially critical of unnamed "deceitful-hearted leaders" who remained in exile in order "to save their lives" and to "make sure not to lose them for Christ." He accused some of his fellow exiled Separatist leaders of fleeing to the Netherlands for their own profit, and in order to draw "people after them to support their kingdom." He argued that the disciples "did not understand our Savior Christ as these men do." He cited passage after passage from the Acts of the Apostles, Paul's letters, and Revelation, in which early Christians were encouraged to endure persecution and suffering rather than to flee from it. He spoke passionately, powerfully, and eloquently of the Christian duty to be faithful even unto death. "For the disciples of Christ cannot glorify God and advance his truth better than by suffering all manner of persecution for it, and by witnessing it against the man of sin with the blood of their testimony." Seeing those words in his own handwriting, even Helwys was struck by their power, and admitted, "It had been better, we confess, to have been part of a book than such an addition."

Helwys was under no illusion regarding the danger that awaited him and his small band of Baptists once they set foot on English soil. But he was convinced that neither he nor the other English Separatists could witness faithfully to the Gospel while living safely on foreign soil. He concluded his book by calling on his fellow expatriots to "come and lay down their lives in their own country for Christ and his truth." Then, praying for "wisdom and strength, and help from the Lord, 'who is able to establish us that we may stand, and by weakness to confound mighty things'" (1 Corinthians 1:27), Thomas Helwys said amen.

Significance of The Mystery of Iniquity

Church historians are in virtual agreement that Thomas Helwys's *The Mystery of Iniquity* must be granted a place in history on the grounds that it contains the first exposition in English of the notion of freedom of conscience or religious liberty. When toleration was the liberal idea of the day, Helwys called for "universal religious liberty—for freedom of conscience for all."[35] At a time when his fellow Baptist John Smyth, or Smyth's followers, claimed that "the magistrate is not by virtue of his office to meddle with religion, or matters of conscience . . . but to leave *Christian* religion free,"[36] Helwys argued that religious liberty must be available to everyone: "Let them be heretics, Turks, Jews, or whatsoever, it appertains not to the earthly power to punish them in the least measure."

Historians have not been favorably impressed either with Helwys's literary abilities or the quality of the book as a whole. Underhill said that the book "bears evidence in its style and matter that Helwys was greatly overwrought."[37] Champlin Burgess says that Helwys was "very well versed in the Scriptures, but he lacked the sense of proportion which a wider range of reading would have given." Perhaps condescendingly, Burgess says that, "He meant well but his work suffered because he had not undergone the discipline of a thorough literary training." He characterizes Helwys's style as "exuberant and rambling. It is sometimes difficult to disengage his meaning from his tangle of words."[38] H. Wheeler Robinson agreed with the negative assessment of *The Mystery of Iniquity* as literature: "None could call it literature in the high sense of Milton's classical definition; we certainly cannot claim for Thomas Helwys that he was a 'master spirit' in his realm, or that his style 'embalms' his thought with literary grace."[39] Eighteenth-century Baptist historian Thomas Crosby damns Helwys with faint praise: "Helwys had not, as the former [Smyth], the advantage of a learned education, but appears by his writings to have been a man of good-natured parts, and not without some acquired."[40]

---

[35]Underhill, *Tracts on Liberty of Conscience and Persecution, 1614–1661,* 47.

[36]W. L. Lumpkin, ed., *Baptist Confessions of Faith* (Valley Forge PA: Judson Press, 1959) 140; emphasis mine.

[37]Underhill, *Tracts on Liberty of Conscience and Persecution, 1614–1661,* 276.

[38]Burgess, *John Smyth the Se-Baptist, Thomas Helwys, and the First Baptist Church in England,* 203.

[39]H. Wheeler Robinson, *The Mistery of Iniquity by Thomas Helwys of Gray's Inn and Broxtowe Hall, Nottingham* (London: Kingsgate Press, 1935) iii.

[40]Thomas Crosby, *The History of the English Baptists,* 4 vols. (London: by

Nonetheless, critics like Underhill acknowledge that when Helwys addressed the subject that was the passion of his life, religious liberty, "we come upon some of the most dignified and eloquent passages in all the writings of Helwys. He is here lifted up by the very greatness of his theme."[41] Burgess said that "his writings contain some passages which rise to the level of eloquence because of the intensity of feeling and depth of conviction from which they spring."[42] Robinson says The Mystery of Iniquity "is a layman's book, both in authorship and appeal. It has the passion, and to some extent, the method of the prophet Amos."[43] He claimed that "this little book is 'the precious life-blood' of a brave and earnest spirit, and that it has been 'treasured up on purpose to a life beyond life.'"[44]

Robinson's suggestion that The Mystery of Iniquity has been "treasured up on purpose for a life beyond life" suggests that the book may have had little influence at the time of its writing. Indeed, there is scant evidence that it had a significant impact in Helwys's own time. It can be assumed that his successor as pastor of the tiny congregation at Spittalfields, John Murton, read the work and was duly influenced by it. It is certain that John Robinson read it, at least the part about him, because two years later he wrote a response (Of Religious Communion). Otherwise, there is no evidence that The Mystery of Iniquity was an influential book of the period.

Burgess argues, however, that though "the work of these several pioneers of religious liberty (Smyth, Helwys, Busher) may not have shown a great harvest in their lifetime, it was destined to bear good fruit in after days. The advocates of civil and religious liberty in the time of the Commonwealth looked back to the works of these valiant champions of religious freedom and found in them a storehouse of argument for promoting the same good cause in their own time, and at length the principles they enunciated were applied in the law of the land."[45]

---

the author, 1738) 1:269.

[41]Underhill, Tracts on Liberty of Conscience and Persecution, 1614–1661, 277.

[42]Burgess, John Smyth the Se-Baptist, Thomas Helwys, and the First Baptist Church in England, 203.

[43]Robinson, The Mistery of Iniquity by Thomas Helwys, v.

[44]Ibid.

[45]Burgess, John Smyth the Se-Baptist, Thomas Helwys, and the First Baptist Church in England, 296.

In 1935 the British Baptist Historical Society published a facsimile copy of *The Mystery of Iniquity*, the first time the book had been reproduced in any form since its publication in 1612. In a preface H. Wheeler Robinson offered four reasons why the book deserved republication. As we prepare this new edition of Helwys's classic work, those reasons are as persuasive now as they were then.

> (1) the light it throws on religious conditions and controversies . . . at the time when our Authorized Version of the Bible was published;
> (2) the human interest of a book which apparently cost the author his life;
> (3) its defense of the distinctive position of the founder of the first Baptist church in England;
> (4) its insistence, for the first time in England, of the right of universal religious liberty.[46]

To these should be added, first, that in Thomas Helwys's *The Mystery of Iniquity* one finds some of the earliest expositions of doctrines which Baptists have brought together in a distinctive theological cluster: believer's baptism, a congregational form of church polity, the right of the individual to read and interpret scripture for him/herself, and the separation of church and state.

Second, one senses the bitter nature of the intra-Separatist disputes. Helwys's characterizations of people who were closest to him theologically are often harsh. He called even other Separatists infidels and unbelievers, while acknowledging their contempt of him. He referred to John Robinson as a "malicious adversary of God's truth."

Third, in *The Mystery of Iniquity* one can see the hermeneutical method of a lay-scholar in action. It is a method which shows great familiarity with and respect for the authority of the scriptures, and which strikes the reader at times as quite sophisticated.

---

[46]Robinson, *The Mistery of Iniquity by Thomas Helwys*, iii.

A Short Declaration
of the Mystery of Iniquity

Jeremiah 51:6

*Flee out of the midst of Babylon, and deliver
every man his soul. Be not destroyed in her
iniquity, for this is the time of the
Lord's vengeance. He will render
unto her a recompense.*

Hosea 10:12

*Sow to yourselves in righteousness; reap
after the measure of mercy. Break up your
fallow ground, for it is time to seek
the Lord, till he come and rain
righteousness upon you.*

Anno. 1612

To the Reader

The fear of the Almighty (through the work of his grace) having now at last overweighed in us the fear of men, we have thus far by the direction of God's Word and Spirit stretched out our hearts and hands with boldness to confess the name of Christ before men, and declare to prince and people plainly their transgressions, that all might hear and see their fearful estate and standing, and repent, and turn unto the Lord before the decree comes forth, and before the day of their visitation be past, and that the things that belong to their peace be altogether hid from their eyes. And whereas in this writing we have with all humble boldness spoken unto our lord the king, our defense for this is we are taught of God especially to make supplications, prayers, intercessions, and give thanks for our lord the king.[1] And we are taught that the gracious God of heaven (by whom the king reigns) would that the king should be saved and come to the knowledge of the truth. And therefore we the king's servants are bound especially by all the godly endeavors of our souls and bodies to seek the salvation of the king, although it were with the danger of our lives. For if we saw our lord the king's person in danger, either by private conspiracy or open assault, we were bound to seek the king's preservation and deliverance, though it were with the laying down of our lives, which, if we did not, we should readily and most worthily be condemned for traitors. How much more are we bound to seek the preservation and deliverance of the soul and body of our lord the king, seeing we see him in such great spiritual danger as we do. And if any shall be offended at us for so doing, they therein love not the king. And if our lord the king should be offended at us his servants for so doing, the king therein loves not himself. And if all men and the king should for this be offended with us (which God forbid), yet herein we are sure our God will be well pleased with us, in that we have with our best strength and faithfulness obeyed him who commands us and teaches us to admonish all men every-

---

[1] 1 Timothy 2:1-2.

where to repent. And this is our sure warrant, and our assured hope and comfort. Now as we have (according as we hold ourselves bound) thus far confessed Christ's name before men by writing, so we shall (the Lord assisting us) be ready, as we hold ourselves bound to confess Christ before men by word of mouth, not fearing (through God's grace) them that kill the body and after that are not able to do any more. In this duty to God and his people, we must needs confess we have hitherto greatly failed, but we will now be ready, the Lord strengthening us, rather to be sacrificed for the publishing of the Gospel of Jesus Christ, and for the service of your faith, than to fail as we have done both in our duties to God and you. This we readily vow to God and promise to you. And to will to do this good is present with us, but we find no means **in us** to perform this duty and service. And we see a law in our flesh strongly rebelling against the law of our minds. But our assured trust and confidence is that God's grace alone is sufficient for us to make **in us** every way able unto these things, unto the which of ourselves we are no way able. Yet we will say with the Apostle Paul, "If God is on our side, who can prevail against us? And who shall separate us from the love of Christ? Shall tribulation? Or anguish, or prosecution, or famine or nakedness, or peril, or sword? No, the Lord we trust in these things makes us conquerors."[2] And "though our outward man should perish"[3] or suffer many afflictions (which we were most foolish, **if** we should not wait for), yet the people of God look unto the truth we witness, and consider with holy and wise hearts whether we have not good warrant, yea, direct commandment to do that we do, though we be **unfit** and unworthy for such a service. Shall we hear the Lord say, "Come out of her my people"?[4] and shall the Spirit of God that commands him that hears say, "Come," and shall we not say come? Shall the Word of the Lord command to call up archers against Babel and all that bend the bow to besiege it round about, and let none escape, and to recompense her the double (Jer.50:29; Revelation 18), and shall we spare our arrows, though they be weak? And shall the Spirit of God say, "All you who are mindful of the Lord keep not silence," (Isaiah 62:16)[5] and shall we hold our peace because we are not eloquent? No, no, we have too long rejected our duties herein, and

---

[2]Romans 8:31, 35, 37.
[3]2 Corinthians 4:16.
[4]Revelation 18:4.
[5]Isaiah 62:6?

now through God's grace we dare no longer do so. And therefore do we thus cry unto you, the people of God, saying, "Babylon is fallen, she is fallen,"[6] "Come out of her, come out of her," for if you still partake with her in her sins, you shall certainly be partakers of her plagues. And therefore we say, "Let him that is athirst come. And let whosoever will, take of the water of life freely."[7] And we call unto all valiant archers that bend the bow to come to the siege against this great city. And we pray all that are mindful of the Lord not to keep silence, nor to give the Lord rest, till he repair, and until he set up Jerusalem the praise of the world. And our continual prayers to the Lord are, and shall be, that the Lord will enlighten your understandings, and raise up all the affections of your souls and spirits, that you may apply yourselves to these things, so far as his Word and Spirit does direct you, and that you may no longer be deceived and seduced by those false prophets who prophecy peace to you when war and destruction is at the door, which the Lord give both you and them to see, that you may all flee unto the Lord for your deliverance and salvation. Amen. Tho. Helwys

---

[6]Revelation 18:2, 4.
[7]Revelation 22:17.

The declaration with proof that these are the days of greatest tribulation, spoken of by Christ (Matthew 24), wherein the abomination of desolation is seen to be set in the holy place.

That there has been a general departing from the faith and an utter desolation of all true religion.

That the prophecy of the first beast (Revelation 13) is fulfilled under the Romish spiritual power and government.

That the prophecy of the second beast is fulfilled under the spiritual power and government of archbishops and lord bishops.

How kings shall hate the whore and make her desolate.

What great power and authority, what honor, names, and titles God has given to the king.

That God has given unto the king an earthly kingdom with all earthly power against the which none may resist but in all things obey willingly, either to do, or suffer.

That Christ alone is king of Israel, and sits upon David's throne, and that the king ought to be a subject of his kingdom.

That none ought to be punished either with death or bonds for transgressing against the spiritual ordinances of the New Testament, and that such offenses ought to be punished only with spiritual sword and censures.

That as the Romish hierarchy say in words they cannot err, so the hierarchy of archbishops and lord bishops show by their deeds they hold they cannot err, and herein they agree in one.

The false profession of Puritanism (so-called) and the false prophet is thereof discovered.

Their two deceitful excuses for their undergoing of all those things they cry out against made manifest.

The false profession of Brownism (so-called) plainly laid open with their false prophets and with their false supposed separation from the world.

The vanity of their most deceitful distinction between a false church and no church (whereupon their whole false building stands) made evident.

Some particular errors in Mr. Robinson's book of justification of separation laid open.

That no man justifying any false way or any one error, though of ignorance, can be saved.

The perverting of those words of our Savior Christ (Matthew 10), "When they persecute you in one city, flee into another," contrary to all the meaning of Christ plainly showed.

Book 1

What Godly reader can, without mourning affections, read the great destruction and overthrow of Jerusalem with the house and people of God prophesied by the prophet Jeremiah? And what heart is not much affected to see the exceeding great sorrow of the prophet, when he utters the prophecy thereof, and declares the sins of the people? (Jeremiah 9) And when all these things were come to pass (according to the Word of the Lord), and that the prophet saw it with his eyes, who could not yet sit down and lament to hear the most grievous lamentations that he pours out, for that so great desolation and destruction, wherewith the Lord had destroyed and made desolate that his own city, house and people? (Lamentations 1–3) Nay, they that gave no regard to the words of the Lord spoken by the prophet concerning these things (Jeremiah 37:2), yet when they saw the prophecy accomplished, then deep sorrow took hold upon them. Then "the elders of the daughter Zion sat upon the ground and kept silence, and cast dust upon their heads, and girded themselves with sackcloth, and the virgins of Jerusalem hanged down their heads to the ground." (Lamentations 2:10) And whoso reads cannot deny but there was just cause of all this sorrow. And therefore well might the prophet say, "Behold and see if there be any sorrow like my sorrow." (Lamentations 1:12) And if it cannot be denied but that the hearing and seeing of this prophecy of so great desolation fulfilled was just cause of this great sorrow, where are then the eyes and ears of men that they might hear and see far greater tribulations and desolations than these, prophesied by a greater prophet than Jeremiah, and even now fulfilled in the fierce wrath of judgment by the Most High, and that in the sight of all men? And yet who considers of it? Who takes up a lamentation for it? Are men utterly void of mourning affections? Or are they destitute of understanding in the cause of sorrow? Or do men think the danger is past? Surely, one of these must needs be the cause, or else men's hearts would abound with sorrow, and their cries would pour out floods of tears, and they would utter with their tongues and pens lamentations of great woe.

Now, if it can be showed by the word of truth that deep error of darkness does possess the two last, that is, that which through ignorance think in themselves there is no such cause of sorrow, and those that through ignorance do think that the danger is already past, then the first that cannot mourn must fall under the sharp censure of great hardness of heart, and insensible deadness of all affections.

We, in the humility of our souls, confess that this work is too great for our abilities. But our strength is of the Lord, who is able to make us sufficient for these things, if we by faith in Christ depend upon him, the which our faith being so full of infidelity it must needs follow that our strength is full of weakness, which would beat us to the ground for undertaking this or any such work of the Lord. But that the Word of God compels us, which commands us to show ourselves faithful in little (Matthew 25:19-30), from which ground (by the grace of God) we have been drawn to do that little we have formerly done, and undertake (through the Lord's gracious assistance) now to do that we shall do, beseeching, and trusting of his mercy toward us herein, that all the praise may be given only to the glory of his name.

First, then, to show to them their error that through ignorance do not see there is great cause of lamentation and woe, we require them to turn their ears to the prophecy of that great prophet Christ Jesus (in) Matthew 24:4-28 and Luke 21:8-31 where he foretells that when men shall see the abomination of desolation spoken of by Daniel the prophet set in the holy places, then shall be great tribulation such as was not from the beginning of the creation to this time, nor shall be, and except those days be shortened, there should no flesh be saved. Has the like prophecy ever been heard of? Or can there be any desolation like to this desolation, wherein no flesh shall be saved? No, from the beginning of the world there has not been the like, nor shall be, says our Savior Christ. Who can remain ignorant of these days and times, and what ignorance is it not to know that these are even the days and times here prophesied of? Have not wars and rumors of wars been heard of? Has not nation risen against nation, and realm against realm? Have not there been famines and pestilence and earthquakes in divers places? And have not many been offended, and betrayed one another and hated one another? And have not many false prophets arisen? Does not our Savior Christ say these are the beginnings of sorrow? Now, all these things being come to pass, which are the beginnings of sorrow, it must needs be that the days of the height of sorrow are now come. And do not men now see the abomination of desolation set up in the high places? Is it not deep error of ignorance, then, for men not to see that there is now the greatest cause of sorrow and lamentation that ever was? And next to show in few words the error of them that think the danger of the days is past. Let them look upon the words of our Savior Christ, when he speaks of the shortening of the days. He says in Matthew, "Then if any say, Lo, here is Christ, or lo, there is Christ, believe it not."[1] And in Luke, "Take heed, be not deceived, for many will come in my name, etc."[2] Is not this instant[3] these days? Were there ever so many saying, "Lo, here is Christ, lo, there is Christ"? And were there ever so many false professions of Christ and false prophets, showing great signs and wonders, if it were possible to deceive the very elect? Who can then deny but that these are deepest days of danger, whereof Christ gives such warnings to take heed? Therefore, easily may they here **see** their error into whose hearts that imagination has once entered to think that these dangers here prophesied of are past. Why then, if the end of these sorrows be not past, and the beginnings be past, as is shown, then must it needs be confessed that the days of greatest tribulation are present. But who considers these things? Or who regards the words of the great prophet? If men did consider and carefully behold these things, what heart could conceal sorrow enough, and what head could contain tears, or tongue have sufficient words to express and utter the sorrows fitting these days? If Jeremiah complained for want of tears, and could not be satisfied with sorrowing for the slain of the daughter of Zion that perished by the sword and **famine** (which was but bodily death), how much more cause have men now to sorrow to see men poisoned with bitter waters, killed with fire, and smoke, and brimstone, stung with scorpions, hurt with serpents (Revelation 9:5; 8:11) and cast into the great winepress of the wrath of God (Revelation 19:20), which is the everlasting destruction of soul and body in hell, to suffer all the plagues, torments, and judgments of wrath forever? Was the famine of bread, and the sword of Nebuchadnezzar, and the seventy years captivity a full sufficient cause to make Jeremiah's eyes fail with tears, his bowels swell, his heart turn within him, and his liver to be poured upon the earth?[4] And are not all the woes uttered

---

[1]Matthew 24:15, 21-22.
[2]Luke 21:8.
[3]Urgent, current.
[4]Lamentations 2:11.

by the seven angels from the sound of seven trumpets, whereof an angel fleeing through the midst of heaven, said with a loud voice, "Woe, woe, woe, to the inhabitants of the earth, from the sounds remaining of the trumpets of the three angels, which yet must blow their trumpets,"[5] and have not these three last angels blown their trumpets? And does not the sound thereof yet sound in our ears? And are not all the woes thereof yet in the sight of our eyes? Are not all these woes thereof (which are woes of everlasting death and destruction) sufficient to break men's hearts all to pieces? What stony hardness of heart possesses men in these days that their hearts do not melt for these woes?

A main and general reason of all this is because this prophecy is of spiritual desolations, destructions and woes, and cannot be understood but with spiritual hearts, nor seen but with spiritual eyes. And the hearts and eyes of men are natural and carnal, and therefore these things cannot affect them. (1 Corinthians 2:14)

Another special reason is because men do not consider how far these things concern themselves, but every nation, and every people, and every man puts these days far from them, as no way pertaining to them. If we therefore could prevail (oh, that we might prevail) by all the fear and love of God to persuade men, and by the compassionate pity of the salvation of their own souls move them with deepest consideration to consider how nearly those things concern them, lest they be under these woes and be not aware thereof, which men may easily be by reason of the great ignorance that is in all men, particularly in the understanding of the prophecy of this book of the Revelation, which most men (though otherwise accounted mighty in the Scriptures) do pass by, seldom or never touching them in their teachings or writings, being tainted (we doubt not) with their own insufficiency therein, which if they would acknowledge, it were commendable (their acknowledgement we mean, not their ignorance). But yet their **course** is much more commendable than all theirs that have busied themselves to bring forth so many imaginary expositions of that holy writ. We say imaginary expositions because they are for the most part but according to the vain imaginations and fancies of men's minds, without the warrant of the Word and Spirit.

---

[5]Revelation 8:13.

We confess in humility to our own shame we are better able to reprove this than to correct it, acknowledging unfeignedly and groaning daily under the burden of our own great ignorance and blindness in the understanding of the prophecy of that book. All this may further provoke us with you, and you with us to take heed lest we be under any part of this desolation and woe, under which whosoever is, and remains, he must perish, as by the grace of God we shall make evidently appears from the scriptures. Therefore, let all people and nations and tongues take heed and beware.

And first to proceed in this cause, we will endeavor to prove by the witness of the undoubted word of truth that all nations and peoples upon the earth that have or do profess Christ (for of them only is this prophecy) have been under this abomination of desolation. The words of the prophecy thereof by Daniel makes it most plain where he says, "In the middle of the week he shall cause the sacrifice and oblation to cease, and for the overspreading of the abomination he shall make it desolate." (Daniel 9:27) Agreeable to this prophecy is that Revelation 11 where it is said that the two witnesses of God (which are the Spirit of truth and the Word of truth in a testimony of the apostles [John 15:26, 27; Acts 5:32]) which are "two olive trees and two candlesticks standing before the God of the earth, having power to shut heaven that it rain not, and to turn the waters into blood, and smite the earth with all manner of plagues as often as they will. . . . Their corpses shall lie in the streets of the great city, spiritually called Sodom and Egypt, three days and a half. . . . And after three days and a half, the spirit of life from God shall enter into them, and they shall stand upon their feet." And with these two prophecies agree also the prophecy (in) Revelation 12:14, "of the woman fleeing into the wilderness into her place, where she is nourished for a time, and times, and half a time." Let us compare these prophecies together. Daniel says the sacrifices and oblations cease in the midst of the week, which are three days and a half. John says (Revelation 11) the two witnesses (the Word and Spirit of truth) lie killed in the streets three days and a half. And (in) Revelation 12 the woman, which is the kingdom of Christ, "the heavenly Jerusalem, the mother of all the faithful" (Galatians 4), flees into the wilderness for a time, times and half a time, which may with good warrant according to these prophecies be expounded to a day, two days and a half. Thus then we conclude. The true sacrifices, and oblations of the people of God, the Word and Spirit, and the heavenly Jerusalem, the spouse of Christ, ceasing, lying dead in the streets, and being fled into the wilderness, it must needs follow that there was an utter desolation of all the holy things and all the means of salvation.

For further confirmation of this, see the words of the apostle (2 Thessalonians 2:3) speaking of the last day, where he says, "That day shall not come except there come a departing first." It were much weakness in any to think that this is not spoken of a general departing, in that there were many particular departings in the apostle's time. But here he speaks of a departing from the truth, and an exalting of an adversary, the "man of sin, to sit in the temple of God, as God, showing himself that he is God," "whom the Lord shall consume with the Spirit of his mouth and abolish with the brightness of his coming."[6] These words show to the understanding of the most simple that is an utter departing, in that there must be a coming again for the abolishing of this wicked man. And here may be discovered, by the way, the damnable heresy of those men which are twice dead, and plucked up by the roots, and those are they who have fallen from grace, which were once dead and have been quickened by the Word and Spirit of God and are dead again, which now hold and say that the man of sin sits and rules in the church of Christ. In this place it is showed that the Lord's mouth consumes the man of sin, and the brightness of Christ's coming abolishes him. Now we confess, if there can be a church of Christ where the Spirit of the Lord's mouth is not, and where his brightness shines not, in such a church the man of sin may sit and rule as God, and these men are only fit subjects for such a kingdom. But let the children of God learn to know and profess that in the church of Christ there is the Spirit of the Lord's mouth, and his shining brightness, which consumes and utterly abolishes the man of sin, and therefore they cannot both rule in one house. Now, for the bare words about which they contend, thus much we say (not to them, but to such as may be in danger to be seduced by them). These are the words. The apostle (speaking of the man of sin, who exalted himself against all that is called God, or that is worshipped) says thus, "So that he does sit as God in the temple of God, showing himself that he is God."[7] Now, as it is said, he sits as God showing himself that he is God, even so does he sit as in the temple of God, showing it to be the temple of God. This exposition is agreeable to the ground of the scriptures, and according

---

[6]Revelation 11:4, 6, 8, 11.
[7]2 Thessalonians 2:4, 8.

to the proportion of faith, for the scriptures teach us everywhere, and we believe, that Christ is the head of the church, and as he "walks in the midst of the seven golden candlesticks,"[8] and as he sits in his church being God. And the man of sin cannot sit with God, as God, in the temple of God. Therefore we say unto these men, as our Savior Christ said unto Satan, hence from us. It is written (2 Corinthians 9:15-16),[9] "What concord has Christ with Belial? And what agreement has the temple of God with idols?" etc. And I Corinthians 10:21: "You cannot drink the cup of the Lord, and the cup of devils. You cannot be partakers of the table of the Lord, and the table of devils." But seeing these men can find no better a pretense to follow, and to help to heal the deadly wound of the head of the beast, than by pretending that they have found him sitting in the temple of God, they looking with the same eye may find also in the same place that he shows himself that he is God. And if they will abide by the letter of the scripture herein likewise, then have they found a new temple, and a new God most fitting for them, because that their temple, and God, and they shall all perish together. We mean those only that have been enlightened with this truth, that Christ and the man of sin cannot rule and reign, or dwell together in one house. And now have they found (as they most blasphemously affirm) Christ and the man of sin exalted both in one temple.

In all this we have not digressed from the matter in hand, in that we have showed that by the departing the man of sin was exalted, and therefore the departing was general, and the man of sin his exaltation general, as does further appear by the words of Daniel 9:27, where he says (speaking of the sacrifice), "and for the overspreading of the abominations, he shall make it desolate." Answerable to this prophecy is that prophecy in the book of Revelation 13:7, where it is written. "And it was given unto him (speaking of the beast that had seven heads and ten horns) to make war with the saints and to overcome them. And power was given him over every kindred and tongue and nation." Who can deny but this is general, even a general desolation when the saints are overcome, "and when all that dwell upon the earth (as follows verse 8) shall worship the beast." All our particular knowledge of the fulfilling of this prophecy will make it more evident. And who does not know and see that this prophecy is fulfilled in

---

[8]Revelation 2:1.
[9]2 Corinthians 6:15-16.

that Romish mystery of iniquity, "who yet sits upon many waters, with whom have committed fornication the kings of the earth, and the inhabitants of the earth are drunken with the wine of her fornication"? (Revelation 17:2) We doubt not but many will agree with us in this understanding. And we that wish unfeignedly the salvation of all, and that they would come to the knowledge of the truth, do earnestly desire that those that are overwhelmed in this mystery of iniquity and under the power of this deceivableness of unrighteousness, would but consider which way it can be avoided but that this prophecy is fulfilled in that great exaltation of the man of sin in that Romish profession. And if they would come to the scriptures, and particularly to the book of Revelation, they should be forced either to deny the prophecies of this book to be true, or else they must needs yield that they are fulfilled in that their profession. For how shall they be able to point out upon the face of the whole earth any one part of this prophecy fulfilled, but it shall be found in and from them? For which way should they go about to show the man of sin, being the mystery of iniquity (in the deceivableness of unrighteousness), to be exalted, sitting as God, and as in the temple of God, sitting upon seven kings and ten kings, giving their power thereunto? If these prophecies be not fulfilled in that their Romish professions, then is it not nor ever was it begun, nor fulfilled in any false profession of Christ upon the earth, which cannot be because we see here the apostle to the Thessalonians says, "The mystery of iniquity does already work."[10] And in that this prophecy of Christ also is come to pass (Matthew 24), where he says, "Many will come in my name saying, 'Lo, here is Christ,' etc." This proves that the abomination of desolation is set up already in the high places. The prophecy then being fulfilled, it must needs be fulfilled according to the due proportion thereof, in exaltation and power, which must of necessity be in that Romish church, as if they were not altogether blind they might see, by looking upon that church at Rome which the apostle Paul wrote to, and by comparing that church in Rome and this church of Rome together. They shall see a strange exaltation of power and pomp, such as there is no prophecy of scripture for to be in the church of Christ, a spiritual power setting up a pope or bishop by virtue of his office with a triple crown, kings and princes bowing to him, and serving him, and (by virtue of his office) carrying a bloody sword, and his hands full of blood.

---

[10]2 Thessalonians 2:7.

This is part of his outward pomp and power. Also, bearing spiritual names of blasphemy, as to be head of the church, and bishop of the universal flock, taking upon him to have power to cast soul and body to hell, and to send to heaven whom he will, to make spiritual laws and decrees what he will, and to bind men's consciences to the obedience thereof.

If this be not he who sits as God, showing himself to be God, if this be not the abomination of desolation set by where it ought not to be, where should it be found? Can the earth afford a greater exaltation of the man of sin than this? And does it not reach from hell to heaven? What heart would not tremble to see and hear of such high blasphemy and sin against God? If it were not the Lord of Hosts that shall judge these things, there could not judgment great enough be found. But these sins of highest pride toward God, and greatest cruelty toward his saints, "shall go up into heaven, and God shall remember all these iniquities, and reward them double";[11] whereas although the Spirit of God bids the heavens "rejoice, and the holy apostles, and prophets, because God has punished and revenged for their sakes." (Revelation 18:20) Yet who can but with compassionate hearts lament to see so many souls perish daily and continually under this destruction? For all the souls upon the earth that exalt, give power, and submit themselves to this man of sin, and so die, they perish to everlasting destruction, although they do it ignorantly. A hard doctrine will this seem to the most. But the mouth of the Lord has spoken it. The apostle in this place of 2 Thessalonians 2 proves it without a contradiction, where it is said (verse 10) "that the man of sin his coming is in all deceiveableness of unrighteousness among them that perish." First, then, here is proved that the mystery of iniquity prevails by deceiveableness. Now, men are deceived by being ignorant of the deceit. And they that are thus deceived through ignorance are they that perish, for (says the apostle) this deceiveableness is effectual or prevails among them that perish. And verse 12: "That all they might be damned which believe not the truth, but had pleasure in unrighteousness," speaking of this deceivableness of unrighteousness by the man of sin. For further proof thereof take the voice from heaven (Revelation 18:4), which says, "Go out of her, my people, that you be not partaker of her sins, and that you receive not of her plagues." Here is no exception, ignorant or not ignorant. If they come not forth at the voice of the Lord's call, but still

---

[11]Revelation 18:5-6.

remain and abide there, they shall surely be partaker of her plagues, "and her plagues come at one day, and they are death and sorrow, and famine, and burning with fire," and "in one hour shall she be made desolate." (Verses 8 and 19) Whose soul would not mourn to hear so many great princes and states, and people abroad, and to see nobility, gentry, and people at home perish, and ready to perish daily under this so great and swift destruction? It were to be wished that all good and holy means were used for their information and instruction herein, with love and meekness, by the sword of the Spirit, which sword only is to be used to compel men's consciences to submit to the truth that is the Spirit of the Lord's mouth, whereby he will consume the man of sin.

If by this we have said we can neither persuade them to be careful of their own estates (which is fearful) nor persuade any other to be more careful of them and more compassionate of their estates, yet this much have we gained toward the cause in hand, that it being proved that the mystery of iniquity, and the abomination of desolation is exalted to the highest in that Romish profession. Then we doubt not but it will be yielded that all nations (acknowledging Christ) have been **overspread**, and under the power of that Romish profession. And so are all these prophecies fulfilled in our eyes, which have been produced to prove that there has been an utter desolation of Christ's power and authority, and the power and authority of the man of sin exalted. And it has been proved that all that submit themselves to that power of the man of sin, do, and must perish, except they repent. Therefore according to our first words we exhort all peoples and nations, and tongues to take heed and beware, lest they be under the words of everlasting destruction prophesied of in this book of the Revelation, and they themselves be not aware thereof.

And seeing it is proved that all peoples and nations and tongues have been under it, let them that think they are come forth, look how they are come forth, lest they be deceived, or lest coming forth they have looked back again, to whom our Savior Christ says, "Remember Lot's wife." (Luke 17:32) We doubt not but we shall have the ready consent of divers nations and peoples to approve of our understandings and applications of this prophecy of the exaltation of the man of sin to be fulfilled in the See of Rome. And we need to make no question, but therein we are of one judgement in the truth. For it is impossible that the heart of man should devise a mystery of iniquity or deceivableness of unrighteousness above it, in that there is in it the height and power of all pride and cruelty, reigning and ruling over men's consciences as God, under a most glorious show of godliness, whereby all nations have been made drunk with the wine of that cup of fornication, and whereby the whole power of Christ (in his laws, statutes, and ordinances) has been and **yet** is abolished utterly. And in the streets of this great city (we mean no particular place, but the whole mystery of iniquity, spiritually called Sodom and Egypt) have the corpses of the two witnesses of the Lord (his Word and Spirit, in the doctrine of the apostles) **(uncertain)** dead. For who does not know that they have altogether taken the Word of God from the people that they might not have it so much as in their own language, neither may they meddle with the spirit of knowledge and understanding of it, but from **(uncertain)** as they thought (and yet do think) good to deliver it to them, and that must stand for the Word and Spirit of God without trying. And this may suffice for a plain and general discovery of that Babylon, Sodom, and Egypt (spiritually so-called), and of that beast with seven heads and ten horns, and the **(uncertain)**, seeing there are so many excellent discoveries written thereof.

And shall we now sit down as though our danger were past in finding out the first beast, and so make the prophecy of God (Revelation 13:11) of no effect, which so plainly sets forth and describes a second beast, of no less danger than the first beast? Shall we so betray the cause of God, and the souls of thousands and ten thousands of men? God forbid. And will any of you that freely approve of all the findings out and discoveries of the first beast not with willingness consent to the finding out of the second? Far be it from you to have so little love of God's truth and the salvation of men. Well we will do our endeavors to discover the second beast, leaving it to the consciences of whomsoever it may most concern to judge whether we deal faithfully or no, and we will forejudge ourselves to deal most weakly. (In) Revelation 13:1-18 it is written, "I saw another beast coming up out of the earth, which had two horns like the lamb, but he spoke like the dragon and does exercise the power of the first beast, saying to them that dwell on earth that they should make an image of the first beast, and causes as many as would not worship the image of the beast should be killed, and made all to receive a mark in their right hand, or in their foreheads, and that no man might buy or sell, save he that has the mark or the name of the beast, or the number of his name."

Which way now (in finding out the second beast) shall we be able to look beside that great hierarchy of archbishops and lord bishops? Are not you they that pretend (in meekness and humility) the word and power of the

Lamb, who says, "Learn of me that I am meek and lowly, etc.,"[12] but exercise the power of the beast, and speak like the dragon? Have you not made and set up the image of the beast? Is not your pomp and power like his? And has there not been much like cruelty used by that power? Does not the blood of the dead cry? And have not the imprisoned groaned under that cruelty? And do not the silenced at home, and the banished abroad daily complain? May not all these cry, "How long, Lord, how long? When will you revenge?"[13] Are not your canons and consistories, and all the power that belongs to them, with all the rest of your courts, offices, and officers, are not these parts of the image? Are they not like the beast? Will you say they are like the Lamb, or like his apostles? It cannot be that you should say they are. The fear of the Almighty would astonish you. And if you cannot possibly prove that power, that pomp, that cruelty, those canons and courts with the belongings and belongers thereunto to be like the Lamb, then let the terror of the Almighty possess you, and make you afraid to use and possess all those things under the pretense of the power of the Lamb. Have you not souls to save? Pity yourselves and perish not. There is mercy with the Lord if you will fear him. What will it profit you to enjoy these things for a little while (as many of your predecessors have done before you), even a little while, and then be condemned and fall under the fierce wrath of God? Had you not much better, a thousand times better, yea, ten thousand times better, and more, too, be ministers of Christ "abounding in labors, in weariness and painfulness, in watchings often, in hunger and thirst, in fastings often, in cold and in nakedness,"[14] that you may say (at your last ends) not as apostles but as the apostle says, "We have fought a good fight, and have finished our course. And we have kept the faith. Henceforth is laid up for us the crown of righteousness."[15] But if this be your fight (as it has been the fight of divers of your predecessors), to cause as many as would not worship the image of the beast (your hierarchy) should be killed, and to make all, both small and great, rich and poor, bond and free, to receive a mark in their right hand, or in their forehead, and that no man may buy or sell save he that has the mark of the beast, or the number of his name, if this be your fight it is evidently the fight of the

---

[12]Matthew 11:29.
[13]Habakkuk 1:2.
[14]2 Corinthians 6:5.
[15]2 Timothy 4:8.

second beast, and not the fight of the apostle Paul. And there is no crown of righteousness laid up for such a fight.

And do you not all these things, when you force and compel men to submit to your whole conformity, which is the perfect image of the beast? Not to speak of your surplice, and cross, and churchings, and burials and **coops**,[16] and chantings, and organs in your cathedrals? And how many more such abominations we cannot reckon up, neither need we, seeing so many writings are full of them. But whosoever shall look upon them with an eye of less than half uprightness shall easily see them to come out of the bowels of the beast, and to be the deformed image of his ugly shape.

To let all these pass (the beast whereof shall be called to account in the day of the Lord), we come to your Common Book, not meddling with every particular of it, but with the most general. By what power do you make prayers and bind men to them, and appoint the order of them in time and place, whereof two you appoint to be read every evening without alteration, some prayers to be said after the curate be paid his due, some on the north side of the table, some in one place, some in another? Will you see a special ground of these four abominations in appointing your priests what to pray, when to pray, and where to pray, and what to put on when they pray, because you made so many priests, and have so many yet among you, as neither know what to pray, where, nor when to pray, nor what to put on when they pray, insomuch as if you did not allow them a sum of made prayers, they had been, and yet would be, altogether without prayers? And this does the mystery of iniquity with the deceivableness of unrighteousness hide from the simple, and from the great and wise, by your made order of prayers. For take your Common Book from them, and then would the impudent be ashamed of such a ministry. Oh, that ten of the best and chief of a thousand of those your priests might be debarred from your book, and be set in a congregation of very partial hearers of their side to show their best abilities for the office of the ministry. Baal's priests were not more discovered (1 Kings 18) than they would be, for the fault was in their God in that he had no ear to hear, but your priests' fault would be found in themselves in that they would have no one word to speak to God's glory, nor to edification. How can you but know this as well as you know your right hand from your left? How will you answer this when you come before

---

[16]Prisons.

the righteous judge? Shall you be able to stand in his presence? The Lord give you hearts to repent, otherwise how shall you think to escape the fierce wrath of the Lord? Did the Lord bring evil upon the house of Jeroboam—"and swept it away, as a man sweeps away dung till all be gone," and "the dogs eat him of Jeroboam's house that died in the city, and the fowls of the air eat him that died in the field"—because he set up calves to worship, and make priests of the meanest of the people, which were not of the sons of Levi? (1 Kings 14:10, 11; 12:31) And do you think to escape with less judgments that set up the image of the beast, and such a blind priesthood to support it? For you know that it is blind ignorance that supports the mystery of iniquity. And therefore, shall the Lord by the brightness of his coming abolish it. What shall we say of your bareheaded and barefooted white sheet penance, whereunto (to mock the Almighty) is joined a written repentance?

Thus do you devise men's prayers, and devise men's repentances, and they must say and repent as you by your power appoint them. Have you power also to appoint the Lord to accept these prayers and repentances? Or do you not care whether the Lord accepts them or no, so that you be submitted to therein? Then do you seek your own worship and not the Lord's. Judge yourselves, and let all judge between the most holy Lamb, and the most polluted beast, and confess and testify whether these things be of the Lamb, or of the image of the beast.

The like of these things are without numbering, and there would be no end made if we should follow them. But we will draw to an end, hoping that they that see these will see all.

Yet let us speak some things of your excommunication by the power whereof are cast out those that most seek to serve God in sincerity, and if the most wicked fall under it, they may be remitted (submitting to the power) by paying large fees, especially if they be rich and simple or mean of degree. And whosoever withstands the power of this forty days, then upon a writ of signification he is to be cast into prison, without bail or **mainprise**.[17] Is this learned of the Lamb or of any of his apostles? We read that the apostles suffered such violences and tyrannies. But the Word of God teaches not the disciples of Christ any such administrations. And this

---

[17]The action of procuring the release of a prisoner by becoming surety for his appearance in court at a specified time. Compare *bail*.

is not the meekness of the Lamb, but the image of the cruel power of the beast.

The power of this excommunication is of another special use of profit, in that by the power thereof are brought in all duties, tithes, and court fees. What horrible profanation of the holy ordinance of Christ is this, to make it an instrument to compel men to bring in exacted fees and duties and tithes. We read (1 Corinthians 16) that Paul appointed in the churches gatherings for the saints, and (1 Timothy 5) giving direction for the relief of widows. He also gives a special charge for providing for the elders and especially for those that labor most. "The elders," says the apostle, "that lead, go before, or rule well, let them be had in double honor, especially they that labor in the Word and doctrine."[18] First, here is shown the power whereby they must lead, go before, or rule, that is, by the Word and doctrine. The apostle proves by two reasons from the scriptures that such elders are worthy of double honor, because the scriptures say: 1. "You shalt not muzzle the mouth of the ox that treads out the corn."[19] 2. "The laborer is worthy of his wages."[20] And here is showed what the apostle means by honor, that is, maintenance. But all this is from a voluntary, liberal distribution, as is showed (in) 2 Corinthians 9:13. How unlike is this to your ruling power, and to your double honor and maintenance. Here is no imprisoning by power, nor excommunication for fee, tithes and duties. We confess our lord the king may give you what his pleasure is, but it were to be wished that all those goodly palaces and possessions with all the privileges and prerogatives belonging to them were preserved for the maintenance of the king's state and dignity. And they were more befitting for the king and his posterity to support them in their due pomp and royalty than to support the pride and pomp of such as pretend to be ministers of the Gospel. The apostle Paul was better worthy of double maintenance than you and all the priests in all your provinces and dioceses. And yet he labored with his hands, although he had the care of more and more worthy churches than are now upon the earth, that would willingly have administered unto him, but he would make the Gospel free. Oh, that we might live to see all them that preach the Gospel (if they stand in need) to live off the

---

[18]1 Timothy 5:17.
[19]Deuteronomy 25:4.
[20]Luke 10:7.

Gospel, that is, off the free liberality of the saints. Those pastors would not devour the flock, but feed it. And we may pray that the Lord would put into the heart of the king to take into his own hands all those possessions and tithes, wherewith those devouring shepherds (that destroy the flock) feed themselves. That day shall be the most happiest day to the whole land that ever was since it was **(uncertain)** a land. And that in these four things. First, it would overthrow that high pride and cruelty of the image of the beast and mystery of iniquity. Secondly, it would make a way for the advancement of the kingdom of Jesus Christ in the sincere and humble profession thereof. Thirdly, it would enrich the crown and fill the king's coffers, upheaped with such a yearly revenue as no peace nor war should ever be able to make them half empty. And all this may be done by a holy, good, just, and lawful means. Fourthly, it would enrich the whole land above measure, and that in disbursing the land of all those courts with all the suits and services that belong unto them, the taxations, fees, and penalties whereof are without number. And the king would stand no need of taxes or subsidies, although we would not wish the king's people to withdraw the showing of their loyal love to our lord and king in those things.

Oh, what a full and ready consent would there be in the king's people to these things. How profitable would it be unto them. The Lord persuade his heart to it, seeing it would be for God's glory, his own benefit, and the so great good of his whole land. And it would be the greatest and chief benefit of all to them to whom it may seem the greatest loss. For they should be disburdened of those things which although they be pleasant for a season yet they will be most bitter in the day of account, which will come, let them be sure. And it would make them live moderately off that they have, and use good and honest endeavors to support themselves. And there would be true comfort in such gain.

Lastly, to make it appear plainly enough that this hierarchy of archbishops and lord bishops is the image of the beast, let all behold the names of blasphemy which it bears, and they are these, so far as we know the number of them:

Archbishops
Primates
Metropolitans
Lords Spiritual
Reverend Fathers
Lords Grace

What names of blasphemy are here. They are the titles and names of our God, and of our Christ. What words of detestation were sufficient to be uttered against such blasphemous abomination? Who is able to keep silence? If men (professing Christ) will not speak, the stones shall speak, rather than the Lord will be without witness. Shall men be afraid to speak for fear of loss of goods, of lands, or for fear of imprisonment, banishment, or death? No, no, let them take all, life and all. Let them shed blood until they have enough. And let the servants of God rejoice in the saying of the angel of the waters, "Lord, you are just, which are and which was and which shall be, because you have judged these things, for they shed the blood of saints and prophets. And therefore have you given them blood to drink, for they are worthy." (Revelation 16:5-6) This has the Lord fulfilled upon all those that are dead and have not repented of this abomination. And this will the Lord fulfill upon all that are alive, if they repent not. Is it not sufficient to despoil and rob Christ of all his power? But you will also take from him the titles of honor due to his name. To pass by your derived Grecian names, which we (to speak the truth) are not able to our own satisfaction to declare the interpretation of (and that no way lessens the iniquity of them, but rather shows it more, that you should get you names of such hidden blasphemy that simple men cannot understand without an interpreter), let us speak with fearfulness of that name, which you might all tremble to hear of, and that is lord spiritual, the very attribute of the God of all spirits. For he only is the Lord spiritual and the spiritual Lord. And give us leave to show you how you are hedged in, that all subtle sophistry shall not help you out. Bear you not this title by reason of your spiritual power and authority? And do you not by your spiritual power and authority make spiritual canons and decrees? And are not all your courts spiritual courts? And do you not require spiritual obedience in all these things? Is not your title and power a differing title and power from all other lords? See how the style does hedge you in, which goes thus, "All the lords spiritual and temporal," so that you cannot say you are spiritual lords because of your profession, for you will not deny but the temporal lords are spiritual lords in profession as well as you. Therefore, must it needs be that you are spiritual lords because of your spiritual power, and spiritual power is over the spirits of men. So then as temporal lords have power over men's bodies, so must spiritual lords have power over men's spirits. But there is only one spiritual Lord, which is the Father of Spirits, and therefore whoever takes this title and this power upon themselves, they take upon them the name, title, and power of God. And this is the man of sin that sits as God, showing himself to be God, which herein the second beast does according to, or in the image of the first.

Do you think that God has forgotten to be just, and are his just judgments gone forever? Can you see and condemn in your words and writings the exaltation of the man of sin in the Romish profession, and can you not see and condemn it in your own? To such the apostle Paul says, "O thou man that condemns them that do such things and does the same, thinkest thou that thou shalt escape the judgment of God?" (Romans 2:3)

And for that double degree of Reverend-fatherhood which you take to yourselves, some of you being Most Reverend and some Right Reverend Fathers, how might we find out under what condition you bear this name? It is plain that you bear not that name because you have begotten all that people in Christ, for most commonly you are their Reverend Fathers in God before they ever heard your voices. Then must it needs be in you a name by inspiration, seeing it is not by operation or work. So are you inspired with a Reverend Fatherhood upon the instant time of your entrance before you have wrought any work among that people. When you shall meet Christ in his coming, what will you answer him for the breach of his straight commandment herein, where he says, "Call no man father upon the earth, for there is but one, your Father which is in heaven."[21] Are you not exalted above your brethren by this name? Then you are they of whom Christ speaks of in this place, and whom he will bring fallow, (Matthew 23:9-11) for thus taking upon you the name of God, and exalting yourselves above the brethren. And if you have not sold yourselves to work wickedness (which God forbid), and if you think it robbery to make yourselves equal with God,[22] let your hearts tremble, and your hands shake to subscribe to such names of blasphemy. And let your ears tingle when you hear them uttered and read in your presence. And observe but what magnificence is upon you when you sit upon your high places and hear yourselves thus entitled, and remember that he sits over you that will tread you under foot for thus robbing him of his honor, if by repentance you make not your peace with him.

Now for the next name of blasphemy (that is within our capacity to speak of), it is the title of Lords Grace. This is your household title. We

---

[21]Matthew 23:9.
[22]Philippians 2:6.

mean that it is a title that may not be omitted in all ordinary occasions. Does not this attribute belong only to the Lord of Grace? And will you have this prerogative with him? Now, although this title be used (in what sense we know not) in the styles of some civil magistrates, wherewith we meddle not, yet we know all your titles of degree you bear by a spiritual prerogative. And therein consists the mystery of iniquity. And therefore are all your names of honor and prerogative (whereby you challenge superiority) names of blasphemy, and directly against the express commandment of Christ, who by his commandment (that were worthy to be obeyed) charged his disciples that they should in no wise seek superiority in his kingdom, neither in name nor power.

"The lords of the Gentiles bear rule one over another, and are called gracious lords, and bear names of honor. But it shall not be so among you. He that will be greatest shall be least in my kingdom." That is, he that will be exalted in name or power by being a disciple of my kingdom, he shall be the least. (Luke 22:25-26)

But the words of our Savior Christ are not at all **regarded** herein. The man of sin will have a kingdom where there shall be mighty power and authority one over another's conscience, appointing and compelling men how they shall worship their God, and to imprison, to banish, and to cause to die them that resist. And the man of sin will have in his kingdom names of most high honor, yea, even the names, titles and attributes of God, and thus does he sit as God does in name, title, and power. And this prophecy is now fulfilled, as he that has an eye may see, and he that has an ear may hear. For let any man but hear the prophecy of this book of the Revelation, and he may see it fulfilled in the first and second beast as evidently as if Christ should send one from the dead and declare it to him, and say this is the first beast and this is the second. And they that will not believe him in his Word, neither would they believe him if he should send one from the dead. (Luke 16:31) And now all that do agree with us in judgment concerning the first beast, that it is plainly to be seen in that Romish profession, and that it is impossible that the man of sin should be exalted in a higher measure of exaltation, we call you all forth for witnesses before God and men, whether it be not as plainly to be seen that the second beast, that has two horns like the Lamb, pretending or making show of the word and power of the Lamb in humbleness and meekness, but speaking like the dragon, and exercising the power of the first beast, and making the image of the first beast, we call you all to witness whether the second beast be not as plainly to be seen in the hierarchy of archbishops and lord bishops, and whether it be possible that there should be made so **lively** an image of the first beast as is in this hierarchy in all titles and names of blasphemy, in all pomp, and in all power throughout, beginning at their book-worship, with the conformity belonging to it, and so going through all their offices, and officers, courts, canons, and decrees. If all these be not the image of the first beast, conceived in his bowels, and brought out of his bosom, let heaven and earth witness, and let all the men upon earth deny if they can, and show any other image of the first beast. And therefore all you whom this may most concern, either deny this prophecy of God, and wipe it out (which if you do, God will deny you, and wipe you out of the book of life), or else confess it to be fulfilled in and among you, and give glory to God, and cast away your abominations, and take heed of hardness and hearts that cannot repent, which heap up as a treasure unto themselves wrath against the day of wrath. Oh, why should you for the pleasure of unrighteousness (for a very few days, little do you know how few) utterly destroy your own souls and perish, yea, and destroy the souls of all that submit to you in the least of these things, except they repent?

And if you will yet justify yourselves in these things and make show of yourselves to be the servants of the Lamb and not the servants of the beast, then stand forth and defend your kingdom and cause with the spiritual sword of the Lamb, which is the Word of God, and convince your gainsayers, and stop their mouths therewith, and so shall you approve yourselves bishops in deed. And if you can prove by God's Word that we ought to say prayers as you command us, we will both sing and say as you bid us. And if you can prove your names of blasphemy and titles of degree, your pomp, and all your cruel spiritual power, good. By that warrant, we will yield it you all and not diminish you of the least title thereof. What need you fear to bring it to trial? You have learning enough, you have partakers **enowe**,[23] if you had but half a good cause, which battle if you will fight, we say to you as Michaiah said to Ahab, when he would go up to Ramoth Gilead: "Take it in hand, go by and prosper."[24] But we will tell you also with the same prophet that if you stand in this cause, "The Lord has determined evil against you." (2 Chronicles 18:16, 22)

---

[23]Enough.
[24]2 Chronicles 18:14.

But in all this let us persuade you in fear to God and shame to men to cast away all these courses we shall now mention. Do not, when a poor soul by violence is brought before you to speak his conscience in the profession of his religion to his God, do not first impose the Oath Ex Officio.[25] Oh, most wicked course. And if he will not yield to that, then imprison him close. Oh, horrible severity. If he will not be forced by imprisonment, then examine him upon divers articles without oath, to see if he may be entrapped any way. O, grievous impiety. And if any piece of advantage (either in word or writing, or by witness) can be gotten, turn the magistrate's sword upon him and take his life. Oh, bloody cruelty. If no advantage can be found, get him banished out of his natural country, and from his father's house. Let him live or starve, it matters not. Oh, unnatural compassion without pity. Let these courses be far from you. For there is no show of grace, religion, nor humanity in these courses. This is to lie in wait for blood, and to lay snares secretly to take the simple to slay him.

And to conclude this point in hand, let it be truly observed whether those that are of the Romish profession (servants of the first beast, coming in question before this hierarchy) have not found much more favor than those that have stood most for reformation. And has there not been gnashing of teeth and gnawing of tongues, with all extreme perverseness and contempt against the one, when there has been good, mild, and even carriage towards the other? Which good carriage toward them, we disapprove not, nor envy not, but could wish that the wholesome word of doctrine with all the cords of love were applied and used unto them for their information and drawing them from their blind errors. But we mention it to this end, to show what uprightness there can be to God or the king in this. For first, it is not possible but this whole hierarchy will confess that those which seek reformation have much more light of **truth** and gifts of knowledge for the building up of a people unto God than the other, and that the first and they are all of one judgment concerning the doctrines of the scriptures in the fundamental points of religion (as they speak). And yet there is no comparison between their patient enduring them of the Romish profession, and their impatient not enduring of the other. Is this uprightness

---

[25]The Oath Ex Officio—An oath employed by the High Commission "by which the accused was compelled to answer questions and incriminate himself." M. W. Patterson, *A History of the English Church* (London: Longmans, Green, and Co., 1909) 315.

to God? Secondly, touching the king and state, the children in the streets know the treachery and the infidelity that has been found in divers of the one profession. And they themselves know the ever untouched fidelity of the other. What uprightness is this to the king and state? The evident reason of this may appear to the wise. And may not this appear to be it, that the Romish profession is but chiefly an enemy to the kingdom of Christ, and but dangerous in some of them to the kingdom of the king, approving of archbishops and lord bishops, and could wish they were cardinals. But those of all sorts that seek reformation are most chief enemies to the kingdom of archbishops and lord bishops, and would have them humble and faithful pastors to feed the flock, and therefore in no wise are to be suffered, howsoever true they be to God and their king. And does not all this show the affinity and nearness between the first and second beast?

But lest any should stumble at this part of the prophecy (Revelation 13:12), where it is spoken that the second beast causes the earth and them that dwell therein to worship the first beast, and therefore the Romish beast being the first, this hierarchy cannot be the second, in that it does not cause men to worship the pope of Rome, we pray it may be observed how it is showed (2 Thessalonians 2:7, 9, 10) that the mystery of iniquity is a working power of Satan, which working power (according to the degrees hereof) is set forth unto us in the book of the Revelation after divers manners, and described to us in divers shapes or similitudes, and named unto us after divers names. And in the height of the exaltation thereof, this power is set forth and described to us under the two names and similitudes of the first and second beast, both which exercising one power (though in divers likenesses) do bring all, both small and great, under the subjection of that one power, "both their hearts being set to do mischief, and talking of deceit at one table." (Daniel 11:27) And so does the second beast cause all to worship the first, in that it is all one power building up one kingdom. And the pope's person is not the mystery of iniquity, for then, when the pope were dead, the mystery of iniquity and the beast were dead, until another pope were set up. And if the pope's person were the man of sin, then the Lord (by the Spirit of his mouth) should abolish and consume the pope's person, but there is no such prophecy of scripture. And then should the prophecies of the fall of Babylon be understood of the overthrow and consuming of the earthen or stone walls, and timber houses of a city. But this were too carnal an understanding, to conceive that the Spirit of God's mouth which shall consume the man of sin, spoken of 2 Thessalonians 2, and shall shake assunder the city, "which spiritually is called Sodom and Egypt."[26] It were too carnal to understand this to be of earthly houses and cities, and fleshly persons. They are not the matter and substance that shall be abolished by the brightness of this his coming, here spoken of, as we doubt not but will easily appear to the wise, though some have been, and are, much mistaken herein.

And that we may come to the true understanding of this part of the prophecy, "and he did great wonders (speaking of the second beast) so that he made fire come down from heaven in the sight of men," (Revelation 13:13) and to see how it is fulfilled in the second beast, we must remember (as we have formerly said) that this is a spiritual prophecy of a spiritual mystery of iniquity, which none may deny. And then does it appear that these wonders wrought (by making fire come down from heaven) are lying spiritual wonders, and the fire is a false spiritual fire, the which (even as the true spiritual fire, which is the Holy Ghost) does truly work wonderful powerfully upon the hearts and affections of them that believe the truth, even so this false fire (which is the spirit and power of Satan) does work effectually upon the hearts and affections of those that receive not the love of truth, and that after a wonderful manner of deceiveableness of unrighteousness, so that men are strongly persuaded and believe that it is the true fire from heaven, even the Spirit of God. And this fire has the hierarchy of archbishops and lord bishops made come down from heaven, especially in their former times when men had their word and power, with their prayer book, and all their cathedral abominations in such admiration, and with such zeal were **(uncertain)** unto them. And as yet some are to this day zealously persuaded of the holiness and goodly order of these things, all which (in the beast that has two horns like the Lamb) made such a glorious show being compared to the former things, as men were **ravished** in their spirits, and thought (and yet some **[uncertain]** do think) that their hearts and affections were kindled with fire from heaven. By this false fire (which is by an effectual working power in all deceiveableness by unrighteousness) even hereby has and does the first and second beast work all their signs and lying wonders, and which men (through great ignorance) have and do look for some strange sights from heaven to know the two beasts by. Their hearts have been and are (with the pleasures of unrighteousness) stolen away. This can

---

[26]Revelation 11:8.

all (that are of any understanding) who may now remain under the power of the second beast easily discern, how by a wonderful fiery blind zeal all those that are under the power of the first beast are misled. But they cannot discern their own estates, which are one and the same under the second beast, who is more deceivable, because of his two horns like the Lamb. And therefore men had need more carefully to look unto themselves, lest they be still deceived, except men will rest in security and perish to destruction, which all must do that obey the power, either of the first or second beast, as is with all evident plain showed in Revelation 14:9, 10, 11, where it is written, "If any man worship the beast and his image, and receive his mark in his forehead or in his hand, and whosoever receives the print of his name, he shall drink (says the Spirit of the Lord) of the wine of the wrath of God, which is poured into the cup of his wrath, and shall be tormented with fire and brimstone, and they shall have no rest day or night."

What will prevail with men, if neither the forewarning prophecies, nor threatening judgments of the Lord will move them to consider and flee the fierce vengeance that is already come? Does our Savior Christ tell that the abomination of desolation shall be set up in the holy places? And does the apostle Paul show that the man of sin exalts himself and sits as God in the temple of God? And does the prophecy of the Revelation so duly set down and declare the manner of the working of the mystery of iniquity according to the several decrees thereof, until it come to that height of exaltation before spoken of by Christ, and by the apostle in the similitude of the first and second beast, who bears the names of blasphemy in taking upon them the names and attributes of God, as is before shown, causing all that dwell upon the earth to worship the beast and his image, and so sits as God in the high places, and in the temple of God, which is in the hearts of men? (1 Corinthians 3:16 and 2 Corinthians 6:19). And do we see all these things fulfilled before our eyes, and will not he that reads consider? And does our Savior Christ show the greatest judgments of the Lord to be upon men in those days, in so much as no flesh shall be saved, and except those days should be shortened no flesh should ever be saved? And does the apostle Paul show that because men will not receive the love of the truth, the Lord shall send them strange delusions that they should believe lies, that all might be damned which believe not the truth, but have pleasure in unrighteousness? And does the Spirit of God in the Revelation of John say that all who worship the beast and bear the least mark of the beast and his image shall drink even of the mere wine of God's wrath out of the cup of his wrath?

And will not all this move the hardened hearts of men to look about and carefully to search out the prophecies of scripture concerning these things, and compare them with these times, and seek and find out how they are fulfilled, which (through the grace of God) every faithful heart, seeking, shall now easily discern, seeing the first angel (Revelation 16) has poured out his vial, so that noisome and grievous sores do appear upon the men which have the make of the beast and upon them that worship his image? Yea, (glory and honor and praise be given to our God) the first angel has also poured out his vial upon the throne of the beast, and his kingdom does already war[27] dark. Who does not see this that looks but with any seeing eye after religion? Do not now, more than ever, the noisome botches[28] of many gross absurdities appear in the bewitched understanding of those men that bear the mark, and worship the beast and his image? And is not the palpable darkness of blind ignorance openly discovered upon the throne of the beast? And does not the beauty of this image fade? Is not the baptizing by midwives quite vanished? And does not bishoping of young and old much decay? Does not the dully reading of injunctions and homilies grow to forgetfulness? And are not profane perambulations well laid aside? And do not holy evens and days, and ember weeks[29] almost pass out of mind? And is not the book itself become much out of use? Has not whole conformity received a blow? And will not any halting subscription serve the turn? Oh, that the spiritual lords of this spiritual kingdom could see that the smoke of the burning thereof is already **deeply** begun and does highly ascend, that they themselves might help to heap coals upon the throne thereof, and flee from the burning therewith.

Let them not forecast to preserve it, nor seek to deliver it out of the hand of the Almighty. They may more easily pull the prey out of the lion's mouth, or "draw out leviathan with a hook"[30] than prevent the mighty One that has judged these things (Revelation 18), "who is clothed with a garment dipped in blood, and his name is called the Word of God, and who has

---

[27]Overcome.

[28]Patchwork, hodgepodge.

[29]Ember day—a Wednesday, Friday, or Saturday following the first Sunday in Lent, Whitsunday, 15 September, or 13 December, and set apart for fasting and prayer.

[30]Job 41:1.

upon his garment, and upon his thigh a name written, The King of Kings and Lord of Lords." (Revelation 19:12,16)

Thus have we (according as we foretold of ourselves) set down these things with great inability, but yet with all fidelity according to our consciences in the best measure of understanding concerning the second beast, who has caused to make the image of the first. And we desire the godly wise that seek salvation by the Lamb, that they will compare the beast (which we all agree to be the Romish hierarchy) and his image (which how can it be imagined, but the hierarchy of archbishops and lord bishops must needs be), compare them together in their spiritual pomp, spiritual names of blasphemy, spiritual power, and cruelty, and cast but a partly indifferent eye upon their administrations in their offices, officers, courts, canon, and decrees, and then let the Word and Spirit of God direct them to judge righteously of the beast and his image, to know them that you may not submit to the spiritual power of the beast and his image, neither receive his mark in your forehead nor in your hand, or the least print of his name. For it you do, your portion is to drink of the cup and wine of God's wrath, and to be tormented with fire and brimstone before the holy angels and in the sight of the Lamb. The word of the Lord has spoken it, and his word is true and not lying.

Book 11

But shall we now think we have fully discharged ourselves to God and men in speaking generally unto all, and shall we not in humility particularly call upon those servants of the Lord of whom he has especially prophesied that they shall "hate the whore and make her desolate and naked and shall eat her flesh and burn her with fire"? And this shall be done, saith the Lord, by the kings of the earth (Revelation 17:16), of whom we could be content not once to speak for fear of offending, but therein is infirmity in us and no faithfulness to God nor them. The wise king (that knew right well the power and authority of a king) advises "not to stand in an evil thing before the king for he will do whatsoever pleases him." (Ecclesiastes 8:3) But in a good cause why should we fear to stand before kings, seeing their thrones are established by justice? (Proverbs 16:12) Our cause then being good, for it is the cause of God, as all shall confess, thus much is it that we do in all reverent humility beseech of all kings and princes that they will perform this service unto the Lord according to this prophesy prophesied of them, in the performance whereof the Lord requires their fervent zeal, which they ought to show by their perfect hatred and detestation of the whore, by which zealous hate they are to be provoked to "make her desolate and naked, and to eat her flesh and burn her with fire." And after the manner and with these great and fervent affections shall these kings that obey the Lord in this work serve him. In all this we beseech that we may not be understood as though we mean that kings should do this by their temporal sword of justice, no, nothing less. The Lord requires no such means in this business, for he has testified by prophesy, as we have formerly showed (2 Thessalonians 2), that "he will abolish and consume the man of sin, the mystery of iniquity," which is this beast and whore and city, "by the spirit of his mouth and by the brightness of his coming."[1] And therefore this prophesy may not be understood that kings ought to do this by their temporal power, but by

---

[1] 2 Thessalonians 2:8.

the Word and Spirit of the Lord in their testimony, with all holy zeal. And this cannot be done except they first take all their power and authority from the beast. For no man can serve two masters, but he shall please the one and displease the other.[2] Kings cannot serve the Lamb and the beast, but they must needs hate the one and love the other. And this is most plainly set down in this prophesy (Revelation 17), for in verse 13 and verse 17 it is said of kings that they shall have "all one mind and be of one consent with the beast and shall give their power and authority unto the beast and shall fight with the lamb until the words of God be fulfilled." And in verse 16, "They shall hate the whore and make her desolate, for God has put in their hearts to fulfill his decree." Thus we see these kings prophesied of by the Spirit of the Lord to do this great work of God. When they shall take it in hand, they shall not halt between two opinions,[3] they shall be neither hot nor cold,[4] but they shall be most zealous for the glory of God and shall no longer retain any friendship with the beast (always our meaning is spiritual). Now then those kings and princes that will in this service obey the most high God and advance his glory that has so greatly advanced them to high honor and dignity, let them take all their power and authority from the beast and withdraw all the affections of their hearts and souls and turn again to hatred and an utter abhorring of the beast and whore. And so shall they make it manifest to all the world that they are true lovers of the Lamb and perfect haters of the beast, and that they are they in whom this prophesy is fulfilled. Oh, that kings and princes would strive to go one before another in giving honor to God therein.

And amongst all the rest of the great and mighty kings and princes of the earth, loyalty, nature, and grace does bind us with desires of exceeding dutiful and reverent affections to wish and desire that our lord and king might be with the foremost in this great and acceptable service of the King of Kings and Lord of Lords, which were a worthy service, most well beseeming our lord the king for whom the king of heaven has done so great things. And if our lord the king will do this service for his God, then must he not by his power support the beast nor his image which are one and the same power. And seeing our lord the king has seen the deep iniquity of the per-

---

[2]Matthew 6:24.
[3]1 Kings 18:21.
[4]Revelation 3:15.

emptory ruling presbytery, let him much more see the high iniquity of the proud, ambitious, cruel, ruling prelacy, which is a power set up in the place of God, bearing the names of high blasphemy. Oh, let it be far from our lord the king to give his power "which God has given him to punish evil-doers and to reward them that do well" (1 Peter 2:14) let it be far from our lord the king to give this power to the beast or his image, for that advances the mystery of iniquity and smites down the mystery of godliness. God has not communicated his own power to kings and princes for this end.

And seeing we have begun to speak to our lord the king, let us declare what power and authority God has given to him, whereunto his subjects ought of conscience to obey.

Our lord the king has power to take our sons and our daughters to do all his services of war and of peace, yea, all his servile service whatsoever. And he has power to take our lands and goods of whatsoever sort or kind, or the tenth thereof to use at his will. And he has power to take our "menservants and maidservants and the chief of our young men and cattle," and put them to his work, and we are to be his servants. (1 Samuel 8:11-18) In all these things our lord the king is to be submitted unto and obeyed.

Also, he has power to make all manner governors, laws and ordinances of man (1 Peter 2:13-14). Thus does God give our lord the king power to demand and take what he will of his subjects, and it is to be yielded to him, and to command what ordinance of man he will, and we are to obey it. And in all these things we acknowledge before God and men we ought to be subject "not for fear only but also for conscience' sake" (Romans 13:5). We meddle not with any conditions or contracts made between the king and his people, whereby our lord the king (in favor) may or does abridge himself of his prerogative and so make himself subject to his own covenants or conditions, which our lord the king ought to keep, though it be to his disadvantage, if they be not merely unlawful. But we speak only of that power which God has given to the king, all which our lord the king ought to use lawfully. But if he should do otherwise (which God forbid), he is in these things to be submitted unto. (Ecclesiastes 8:3-4; 1 Peter 2:18-24) And "whosoever resists, resists the ordinance of God and shall receive to themselves condemnation." (Romans 13:2) Thus has God given our lord the king all worldly power which extends to all the goods and bodies of his servants. And does our lord the king require any more? We know he does not. Then let not our lord the king now be angry that we his servants speak the second time unto him. Does not the king know that the God of Gods and Lord of Lords has under him made our lord the king an earthly king and given him all earthly power, and that he has reserved to himself a heavenly kingdom, "a kingdom that is not of this world" (John 18:36,37), "neither are the subjects of his kingdom of this world"? (John 17:14) And yet this King was in the world and his subjects are in the world (verse 12);[5] and that with this kingdom our lord the king has nothing to do (by his kingly power) but as a subject himself; and that Christ is King alone, only high priest and chief bishop; and there is no king, no primate, metropolitan, archbishop, lord spiritual, but Christ only, nor may be, either in name or power to exercise authority one over another. (Luke 22:25, 26; Matthew 23:11, 12) And will our lord the king not withstanding all that Christ has done for him in giving him such a kingdom, with such great dignity and power therein, will the king not withstanding enter upon Christ's kingdom and appoint (or by his power suffer to be appointed) laws, lords, lawmakers over or in this kingdom of Christ, who (we may be bold to say with warrant) if he were upon earth in the flesh, he would be subject to our lord the king in his earthly kingdom? For so he was to Caesar. (Matthew 17) He paid him tribute, and he commanded to "give unto Caesar things that were Caesar's."[6] Yea, he would not meddle with anything that belonged to the king, not so much as to command the two brothers to "divide the inheritance,"[7] nor to judge the woman "taken in adultery."[8] Far be it from the heart of our lord the king to give his earthly power to any to rule as lords over the kingdom and heritage of Christ, which he has reserved to himself to rule and govern only by his Word and Spirit, where no earthly power may be admitted in that it is no earthly kingdom.

Behold now we have begun to speak unto our lord the king, and we are but dust and ashes, and our lord the king is but dust and ashes as well as we. Therefore, let not our lord the king be angry that his servants speak the third time unto him. We know our lord the king may do "whatsoever pleases him and who shall say unto him, What doth thou?" (Ecclesiastes 8:3, 4) Yet though he should kill us, we will speak the truth to him. "It is the king's honor to search out a thing" (Proverbs 25:1).[9] And we know the

---

[5]17:11.
[6]Matthew 22:21.
[7]Luke 12:14.
[8]John 8:1ff.
[9]Proverbs 25:2.

king is a wise man and a man of understanding. Thus then we speak to him. Will the king challenge to himself to sit upon the throne of David and to judge Israel? We, the king's servants, mean, will the king have the same power over the church and house of God that the kings of Israel had under the law, who sat upon David's throne? Will and ought the king to make a covenant and cause all to stand to it? And must all stand to it? And will and ought the king to compel all that are found in his dominions to serve the Lord as the king commands? (2 Chronicles 34:32, 33) And will and ought the king to slay all that come not to the Passover? (Numbers 9:13) If our lord the king has this power then he ought to execute it, and then he sits upon David's throne. And then the king of Spain has the like power to compel all in his dominions to serve God as he commands. And so every king sits upon David's throne, and all kings are therein to be obeyed. For will not our lord the king that is a man of understanding yield that Queen Mary, the king's noble predecessor, had the same power and authority by her sword of justice over her subjects that our lord the king has, and that her subjects were bound to obey her in all things and submit to her sword of justice as well as our lord the king's subjects are to obey him and submit to his sword of justice? For all earthly kings have one manner of power and sword. (Romans 13) If our lord the king by his discerning judgement sees this, then our lord the king will easily see that as Queen Mary by her sword of justice had no power over her subject's consciences (for then had she the power to make them all Papists, and all that resisted her therein suffered justly as evil doers) neither has our lord the king by that sword of justice power over his subject's consciences. For all earthly powers are one and the same in their several dominions. And if our lord the king will have any other power it must be a spiritual power, and then that must be with another sword, even a spiritual sword. For an earthly sword is ordained of God only for an earthly power, and a spiritual sword for a spiritual power. And offenses against the earthly power must be punished with the earthly sword, and offenses against the spiritual power with the spiritual sword. And with this sword the King of Kings makes our lord the king mighty through him to "cast down holds, casting down the imaginations and every high thing that is exalted against the knowledge of God, and bringing into captivity every thought to the obedience of Christ," (2 Corinthians 10:4-5) who is "the fruit of David's loins, concerning the flesh," and only "sits upon David's throne forever," (Acts 2:30; Luke 1:32, 33; and Isaiah 9:7) "and upon his kingdom to order it and to establish it with judgment and with justice, the rod of whose power is sent out of Zion, who is ruler in the midst of his enemies, whose people shall come willingly" (Psalm 110:2, 3) and requires not any earthly power to build up his church, as he showed when he declared that "all power was given him in heaven and in earth." He bids his disciples, "Go therefore and teach all nations, baptizing them in the name of the Father, etc." "He that shall believe and be baptized shall be saved, but he that will not believe shall be damned." (Matthew 28:19; Mark 16:16) "Who when he ascended upon high he led captivity captive and gave gifts unto men. He gave some to be apostles, etc., for the repairing or gathering together of the saints." (Ephesians 4:5, 12) Here is showed unto our lord the king that which we know he is not ignorant of, that Christ only sits upon David's throne to order it. And we the king's servants show it that the king might not be deceived by deceivers who would persuade the king that he has the same power over the church of Christ that the kings of Israel had over the church of the Old Testament, to this end, that they might use the king's earthly power to rule over and build up (as they pretend) the spiritual tabernacle, temple and church of Christ, which if the king shall suffer them to do, he shall sin against God in entering upon the kingdom of Christ, who only is the king of Israel (John 12:15), "whose power and sword are spiritual, whose tabernacle, temple and house is holy, made without hands," (2 Corinthians 3:17; 1 Peter 2:5; Hebrews 9:11) and therefore has given spiritual "gifts unto men, for the gathering together of the saints for the work of the ministry, and for the building up of the body which is his Church," and does not will nor require to have people commanded and compelled by an earthly sword or power as in the days of Hezekiah and Josiah, kings of Israel. For that was an earthly or "carnal commandment." (Hebrews 7:16) And they had a worldly tabernacle made with hands and worldly ordinances and carnal rites (Hebrews 9:1, 2, 10). And therefore were the ordinances or laws commanded to be kept by a worldly power, and the tabernacle to be build by hands. But now we have a tabernacle "which the lord pight[10] and not man" (Hebrews 8:2), and that carnal commandment is changed (Hebrews 7:12). And we have a commandment "after the power of endless life" (verse 16) unto the obedience of which law no earthly king's power can cause or bring any man to obey in any one thing, and the which tabernacle not made with hands no earthly

---

[10]Pitched.

power which consists only of the strength of hands can cause to be built in any one part thereof. But all this is to be done only by the King of Israel's power, who has all power given him in heaven and in earth, whose power is all-sufficient to bring under obedience all his subjects whereunto no earthly power can be helpful, whose sword is his Word, "which is lively and mighty in operation and sharper than any two-edged sword," (Hebrews 4:12) and therefore needs not the help of any king's sword. If his sword will not prevail to bring men under obedience to his own laws, what can our lord the king's sword do? It is spiritual obedience that the Lord requires, and the king's sword cannot smite the spirits of men. And if our lord the king shall force and compel men to worship and eat the Lord's Supper against their consciences, so shall he make his poor subjects to worship and eat unworthily, whereby he shall compel them to sin against God, and increase their own judgements.

Oh, let not our lord the king suffer such evil to be done by his power. Little does our lord the king know how many thousands of his people have been compelled through trouble and for fear of trouble to worship and to eat the Lord's Supper unworthily, and so to worship and to eat and drink to their own damnation, who, although they perish in their own sins, yet their blood will be required at their hands that have compelled them so to sin against their consciences. And the Lord in mercy give the king a heart to look into it that it be not laid to our lord the king's charge if he shall suffer them to exercise such power by his authority. And we bow ourselves to the earth before our lord the king in greatest humbleness, beseeching the king to judge righteous judgement herein, whether there be so unjust a thing and of so great cruel tyranny under the sun as to force men's consciences in their religion to God, seeing that if they err, they must pay the price of their transgressions with the loss of their souls. Oh, let the king judge, is it not most equal[11] that men should choose their religion themselves, seeing they only must stand themselves before the judgement seat of God to answer for themselves, when it shall be no excuse for them to say we were commanded or compelled to be of this religion by the king or by them that had authority from him? And let our lord the king that is a man of knowledge yet further consider that if the king should by his power bring his people to the truth, and they walk in the truth and die in the profession of

---

[11]Fair.

it in obedience to the king's power, either for fear or love, shall they be saved? The king knows they shall not. But they that obey the truth in love, whom the love of God constrains, their obedience only shall be acceptable to God. (1 Corinthians 13) Thus may our lord the king see that by his kingly power he cannot cause or make men bring an acceptable sacrifice to God. And will the king make men (whether they will or no) bring an unacceptable sacrifice to God? And shall the king herein think he does please God? God forbid. If the king will please God in such service, then must he seek to "convert sinners from going astray," (James 5:20) "and turn men to righteousness," (Daniel 12:3) not with his sword of justice but "by the foolishness of preaching." For that is the means whereby God has appointed to save them that believe. (1 Corinthians 1:21, 27) "For God has chosen and appointed the foolish things of the world, the weak things, the vile things, the things that are despised, and things which are not, to confound and bring to naught things that are." And these things has God chosen to set forth Christ, the power of God, and the wisdom of God. Here is not the absolute **authentic** word of command nor the mighty, powerful, punishing sword of our lord the king required to this work of the publishing of the Gospel of Jesus Christ. And let the king call to mind that which no doubt the king has often read in the Gospel According to Luke (9:52, 56), that when the Samaritans would not receive Christ, and that his disciples said, "Will you that we command fire to come down from heaven and consume them," Jesus rebuked them and said, "You know not of what spirit you are. The Son of Man is not come to destroy men's lives but to save them." Whereby the king does see that Christ will have no man's life touched for his cause. If the Samaritans will not receive him, he passes them by. If the Gadarenes pray him to depart, he leaves them.[12] If any refuse to receive his disciples, he only bids them "shake off the dust of their feet for a witness against them."[13] Here is no sword of justice at all required or permitted to smite any for refusing Christ. Then let not our lord the king suffer his sword of justice, which God has given him with power from himself to defend and rule with authority, and keep in all obedience his own people, and people of God, unto the king's own laws and statutes, which appertain to the well-governing and ruling of the king's state and kingdom,

---

[12]Luke 8:37.
[13]Luke 9:5.

which is worldly and must fade away. Let not our lord the king suffer this sword to be used to rule and keep in obedience the people of God and of the king to the laws, statutes, and ordinances of Christ, which appertain to the well-governing and ruling of the kingdom of Christ, which is heavenly and endures forever, the sword of whose kingdom is spiritual, by the power of which sword only Christ's subjects are to be ruled and kept in obedience to himself, by the which sword our lord the king must be kept in obedience himself, if he be a disciple of Christ and subject of Christ's kingdom. And this takes away (without gainsaying) all the kingly power and authority of our lord the king in the kingdom of Christ. For he cannot be both a king and a subject in one and the same kingdom. The king's understanding heart will easily discern this.

Then let our lord the king in all happiness and prosperity sit in his own princely throne of that mighty kingdom of Great Britain, which God has given to the king and to his posterity. And the Lord give the king a most wise heart to rule and judge his people. And the Lord give all his people faithful hearts to love and obey him. And let all those the king's enemies that would not that he should reign over them be slain before him.

And let our Lord Jesus Christ in power and majesty sit upon David's throne, the throne of the kingdom of Israel, which his Father has given unto him. And let Christ according to his own wisdom judge his people Israel. And let our (lord) the king be his subject, the which our lord the king yielding himself to be. The king must needs grant that as he is an earthly king he can have no power to rule in this spiritual kingdom of Christ, nor can compel any to be subjects thereof, as a king, while the king is but a subject himself. For there may be but one king in Israel.

And let not our lord the king be now angry, and his servants will speak but this once. Will our lord the king, being himself but a subject of Christ's kingdom, take upon him by his kingly power to make primates, metropolitans, archbishops, and lord bishops to be lords in the kingdom of Christ and over the heritage of God? And will our lord the king do this against the whole rule of God's Word, wherein there is no one tittle to warrant our lord the king thereto? Will not our lord the king be supplicated by the humble petition of his servants to examine his power and authority therein? Far is it from the hearts of us the king's servants to move the king to depart from the least tittle of his right that belongs to his royal crown and dignity. And far be it from the king to take from Christ Jesus any one part of that power and honor which belongs to Christ in his kingdom. Let our lord the king pardon his servants for meddling in this matter. For we profess ourselves bound upon the peril of our souls to be faithful subjects both to Jesus Christ our King and to our lord and king. And therefore it stands us upon to know what belongs unto Christ our heavenly king and unto our earthly king. And Christ our spiritual King has freely spoken unto us, and commanded us to "give unto our king that which is our king's."[14] And will not our lord the king say as freely unto us, "Give unto God that which is God's"? We doubt not but our lord the king will say so. Why then we appeal unto our lord the king that is our earthly king. And let the king speak according to the true judgment of his heart. Will the king say that it belongs to him to make spiritual lords over the house of God? And will the king warrant his saying to be good? And if the king warrant it only by his princely prerogative, may we thereupon give unto the king this power in submitting ourselves to such spiritual lords and to their power? Were not this to take from our spiritual Lord and King that which is even his own name, title, and power, and give it to another? What greater evil can be committed against Christ than to take his honor and power from him and give it to earthly men, who should fear and tremble before him in giving to him glory and honor and not taking from him? Let not our lord the king be partaker in such great evil to suffer a power and name of blasphemy to be set up so directly against the express commandment of Christ, who forbids all lordly titles and ruling power one over another in his kingdom. We dare not but think it is done ignorantly, both by our lord the king who suffers this, and by them that administer in this greatest evil. We the king's servants say this greatest evil in that it is the abomination of desolation set by in the high places which are the days of "greatest tribulation that ever was or shall be, the which days except they should be shortened no flesh should be saved."[15]

And if it shall not yet appear unto our lord the (king) that this hierarchy of archbishops and lord bishops is this abomination of desolation set in the high places, then we beseech the king upon our knees, by his highest honor and renown, by his truest justice and most righteous judgement, by his most godly prince-like care of the salvation of all his subjects, and lastly and above all, by his chiefest love unto God and to his holy truth, that our lord the king will with his royal consent give way that this cause may come to an

---

[14]Matthew 22:21.
[15]Matthew 24:22.

equal[16] trial. But thus far: that the king will but take and hold his sword of justice from this hierarchy, that they may not smite the faithful, true, and loyal subjects of the king therewith neither to death, nor to imprisonment, nor to banishment, for speaking or writing only against their kingdom. And let our lord the king (by the humble supplication of us his servants) be entreated to leave them to defend their spiritual power and names by the sword of the spirit, which ought to be the weapon of their warfare, if they be spiritual lords as they pretend. And then shall our lord the king see this cause truly decided to the king's honor and great comfort. For the king knows that this hierarchy, with all their learned dependency, if their cause be good, they cannot lose it for want of learning, in that they have wisdom and learning, if it be according to godliness, sufficient to convince the whole earth. And if they can with all that mass of learning maintain their primacy and prelacy, archbishopry and spiritual lordships, then may our lord the king let them enjoy it with comfort. But if they cannot, with all the spiritual weapons and armor they have, uphold it, then let it fall and go into the bottomless pit, from whence it came (Revelation 9:2) and whither it must go, though all the kings on earth should strive to uphold it. (Revelation 20:1,2,10) Let not our lord the king therefore give the least support thereunto by the power of his sword. The Lord grant that we may find favor in the king's eyes in this so just and equal a cause, which is that we may but try the power of these (called) spiritual lords, and that by earthly power they may not force men to yield to their spiritual authority. How can it but seem equal in the king's sight that spiritual lords should have no more spiritual authority than they can get and maintain by spiritual power? And if the hierarchy themselves think it unequal that the doctrine of their power should be tried, and be not most willing and ready thereunto, but shall by policy and secret intimations **shift it off**, then shall our lord the king that is wise easily discern that their "deeds are evil" and "they hate the light neither come to the light lest their deeds should be reproved." (John 3:20) "But they that do truth come to the light that their deeds may be made manifest that they are according to God." Thus shall our lord the king and all the world have a full trial of them, whether their deeds are wrought according to God, or no. For if they will now come to the light of God's Word in the sight of all men and manifest their deeds to be wrought according to God,

---

[16]Fair.

then have they approved themselves. But if they do not, then has our
Savior Christ here condemned them with his own mouth. And let our lord
the king also condemn them in his own wisdom. Shall we need to be
importunate with our lord the king in this cause of his poor people which
concerns the condemnation of all their souls? What need we, seeing our
lord the king knows that "a king that judges the cause of the poor rightly,
his throne shall be established forever." (Proverbs 29:14) Then let our lord
the king hear the cause of the poor, and the rather in that the king's most
noble predecessor has before justly adjudged the same cause and freed his
people so far of the bondage wherein they were. King Henry VIII, that
prince of great renown, freed his people from the bondage of the first beast,
especially in these two great and main particulars: in causing the scriptures
to be set over and printed for the people in their own language, that so they
might hear the word with their own ears; and also that their worship should
be in their own tongue, that they might speak to God with their own
tongue, and not in a strange tongue, as they did.

Let heaven and earth judge, and let our lord the king judge, and let all
the king's people judge, whether this was not the depth of all darkness,
when men might not know what God speaks to them, nor know in their
public worship what they speak unto God. Let our lord the king judge
whether ever there was such spiritual cruelty upon the earth, when the poor
people of God for whom Christ died were debarred from the presence of
God in their public worship, and might neither hear God nor speak to God
with their own outward ears and tongues, but as the ministers of the man
of sin appointed and in a strange tongue as they taught them. We know our
lord the king sees that here the abomination of desolation was set up in the
high places, as also the corpses of the two witnesses of God prophesied of
Revelation 11:8 (which are the Word and Spirit of God) lay dead in the
streets of that great city, there being no true use at all of them, and the
people being deprived of the life of them, for the Word was a dead letter
to them, and the Spirit a dead spirit.

The king's predecessor of famous renown thus freed his people from
that bondage of the first beast. But there is risen up a second beast which
exercises the power of the first beast, and now our lord the king's people
cry to the king with the sighs and groans of their spirits (and would cry also
with a loud voice but for fear of the beast) and humbly beseech the king that
he would put too his helping hand to free his people from the bondage of
the second beast, that their souls may not perish to everlasting perdition,

which all must do which are under the bondage of the same, and so continue we. And now let the king hear with an ear of compassion, and see with an eye of pity, the cruel spiritual bondage that his poor people are kept under by the second beast in these particulars.

The king's people have the Word in their own language and may pray in their own tongue. But they must not understand the Word but as the lord bishops will have it understood. And they must not pray nor administer in the holy things but as they appoint. Now let the king with a godly, wise heart consider in what woeful spiritual bondage God's people and the kings are kept by this hierarchy. Now plainly would our lord the king see the cruel spiritual tyranny hereof, if the king would make it but his own cause. Would not the king think it a most cruel tyranny if the king should be by force compelled to understand and believe the scriptures as the hierarchy of Rome would have him, and to worship God and administer in the holy things as the hierarchy would appoint? And if the king would not so do, that then that hierarchy would have power to put the king in prison? And if that would not serve the turn, to procure or cause the king's life to be taken from him, or at least to banish the king from his kingdom and nation? Would not our lord the king think this great tyranny and cruel bondage? We know the king would, for which cause the king and his predecessor have cast off this bondage. Then let the king see that the king's people are under this same bondage. For if they will not understand the scriptures and worship God as the hierarchy of archbishops and lord bishops command and appoint, they straight send a pursuivant,[17] apprehend them by violence and force, imprison them, sometimes divers years, many times not suffering so much as their wives to come at them, and if their lives cannot be gotten, then procure their exile or banishment. The Lord give the king a heart to pity his people herein. The king is ignorant of these dealings, and none dare tell the king thereof, the prelacy have been so mighty and so cruel.

And will it please the king to view the cause of his people (being true and faithful subjects) yet further? What does it profit the king's people to have the Word of God to hear, and read it, seeing they are debarred of the Spirit of God to understand it, but according to private interpretation, by the lord bishops as though they had the Spirit and could not err? Oh, that our lord the king who is a man of excellent wisdom would but bend his wisdom

---

[17]An officer of arms ranking below a herald but having similar duties.

to behold how that herein (wherein the whole power of the beast consists) this hierarchy of archbishops and lord bishops does nothing differ from the first beast. For the first beast keeps both the Word and Spirit from the people. And they keep the Spirit of God in bondage, and then is the Word of God of no effect, debarring the people of God thereof, tying them to their spirits in the understanding of the scriptures which none may try whether they be of God or no, but must believe and obey, or else go to prison, and if will not yield either be hanged or banished.

Judge, O king, is this a rule of direction and ordinance of the Lamb who commands bishops to be "gentle, towards all men, apt to teach, suffering evil men patiently, instructing them with meekness that are contrary minded, proving if God at any time will give them repentance, that they may acknowledge the truth, and come to amendment"? (2 Timothy 2:24-26) By these fruits may our lord the king and his people know the bishops of the Lamb, who is lowly and meek, and bids learn so to be of him. (Matthew 11:29) But to pull men that are contrary minded out of their houses by pursuivants, to cast them into prison and cause them to be there at excessive charges, utterly undoing them, their wives, and children, and bringing them to all outward misery, and causing them to be banished from under their natural prince (to whom they are most true subjects), forth of their native country, and from their father's homes and all their friends and familiars, will not our lord the king say that these are the bishops of the beast, who is "like a leopard, and his feet like a bear's, and his mouth as the mouth of a lion," (Revelation 13) of whom they learn to be proud and cruel? And all these evils and many more have come upon the king's people because they will not understand the scripture by the spirit of the lord bishops and pray in their worship to God by the direction of their spirit.

Will our lord the king hear the earnest complaint of his people herein and grant redress that as the king's people, by the means of the king's most noble predecessor enjoy that blessed liberty to read and hear the Word of God in their own language and to pray in their public worship in their own tongue, that so by our lord the king's means the king's people may enjoy this blessed liberty to understand the scriptures with their own understanding and pray in their public worship with their own spirits? Then if men err, their sin shall be upon their own heads, and the king's hand shall be innocent and clear from their transgression, which it cannot be if the king shall willingly suffer his power to be used to compel men to pray and understand by the direction of the lord bishops' spirit. And if the king shall give his power to the lord bishops but to compel men to eat meats "which through our Lord Jesus Christ are all clean, yet to him that judges them unclean to them they are unclean" (Romans 14:14), in which case if a man freely of his own accord do eat and doubt "he is condemned, because he eats not of faith," why then, if a man in this case be forced by the king's power (whether he will or no) to eat when he doubts, and so he be condemned (verse 24), is not this "to wound the weak conscience, and to sin against Christ"? (1 Corinthians 8:12) And can our lord the king's hand be innocent herein when by the king's power men shall be compelled to sin? Oh, that the king would then see that if he may not give his power to rule men's consciences in the least things that are indifferent, much less has the king power to command men's consciences in the greatest things between God and men.

This being so, we the king's servants (with all the humility and reverence that can or may be given to any earthly prince) do out of our true loyalty, obedience, and faithfulness of our hearts, thus speak to the king. Let it suffice our lord the king and let it not seem a small thing, that the God of Gods has made our lord the king a mighty earthly king over divers nations and has given our lord the king an earthly power to make laws and ordinances (such as the king in his own wisdom shall think best, and to change and alter them at his pleasure) to rule and govern his people by, and to appoint governors and officers to execute the king's will. And all the king's people are bound of conscience to God and duty to the king to obey the king herein with their goods, bodies and lives in all service of peace and war. And whosoever shall resist the king herein, they resist the ordinance of God and shall receive judgment from God, besides the punishment with the sword of justice which God has given to the king to punish evildoers that transgress the king's laws. And God has also honored the king with titles and names of majesty that are due but himself (Psalm 82:1,6; Daniel 5:18) and has commanded honor to be given to the king (1 Peter 2:17). And God has commanded all his people specially to pray for the king. (1 Timothy 2:2) Let this kingdom, power and honor fully satisfy our lord the king's heart, and let it suffice the king to have all rule over the people's bodies and goods, and let not our lord the king give his power to be exercised over the spirits of his people. For they belong to another kingdom which cannot be shaken (Hebrews 12:22,23,28), differing from all earthly kingdoms. For our lord the king knows that the chief of earthly kingdoms are compared to "gold, silver, brass, iron." (Daniel 7:37,46) But this is the kingdom which the God of heaven has set up, which shall "never be destroyed; and this kingdom shall not be given to another people, but to the holy people of the most high God and all powers shall serve and obey him." (Daniel 2:44; 7:27) Therefore in this kingdom let our lord the king give us his servants leave again to tell the king that he must be a subject in this kingdom, and that our lord the king has no power nor prerogative (as a king) to make laws. For in this kingdom, "there is but one lawgiver, who is able to save and to destroy." (James 4:12) Neither has our lord the king power to appoint officers in this kingdom and much less to make spiritual lords over this kingdom to bring all men's spirits in subjection to their spirits in the understanding of the scriptures and worshipping God.

Wherein lest we may seem to speak untruly to the king, we humbly beseech our lord the king that it may be lawful for his servants, with his princely favor, to show the king some few particulars out of a multitude. And first, we show the king that whereas our Savior Christ (Matthew 18:15,20) gives a rule of direction to admonish a brother, if he sin, not speaking particularly of some sins, but generally of all or any one sin, as we the king's servants understand with all the understanding that God has given us, the lord bishops say this is not to be understood generally of every sin against God but particularly of some, and herein must be subject to the spirit of their understanding and that rule of Christ must be no sure nor perfect rule. Next, let us show the king that if there be such a sin committed as the bishops judge to be a sin, according to their rule (which let the king give his servants leave to suppose to be adultery) and that it proceeds or comes to this degree, that it must be told to the church, which we understand to be the whole congregation, more or less, the lord bishops by their spirit of understanding say, "Tell the church," that is to be understood, tell the ordinary, which is either the bishop's chancellor, or the archbishop's official. They are they that have power to bind in earth, and it shall be bound in heaven. And their fees being paid them, they have power to loose on earth, and it shall be loosed in heaven.[18] Oh, that the king's ear would but hear half the depth of this iniquity. And the king's servants know the king's heart would never endure it that his people's consciences should be thus wounded and their souls destroyed by being compelled to submit to such spirits of understanding. Furthermore, let our lord the king know that

---

[18]Matthew 16:19.

the Holy Ghost testifies (Acts 14:23) saying that "they had ordained elders by election in every church, and prayed and fasted." This we understand was the whole congregation's fasting and praying, and election, and that the church has power to appoint or ordain or lay on hands, if there be no elders, as they did. (Acts 13:2, 3) But all this (say the lord bishops, by the spirit of our understandings) does belong to us, and the patron. And the people have nothing to do, but must be content to have such a pastor as we appoint, though they never heard him, knew him, nor saw him, and although the congregation afterward should like never so well of him. Yet the lord bishops they have power to take him away from them, and to deprive him, and silence him, and punish them if they hear him, although he be never so well approved among them. Thus must the king's peoples be compelled to understand the scriptures, for the abandonment of their power of ordination, and deprivation. And whereas we the king's servants understand, according to the best understanding that God has given us that the apostle Paul, giving a rule of direction for the people of God how to worship God when they come together (1 Corinthians 14:26, 33), that "every one as he has a psalm or a doctrine or a tongue, may speak to edification and if any thing be revealed to another that sits by, the first is to hold his peace, for all that have gifts may prophecy one by one." In all this, God is not the God of confusion, but of order. Thus do we hold the disciples of Christ ought to come together to worship God and edify one another in the liberty of the Spirit, according to the gifts and graces that are given to every one (Romans 12:6) and that "every man as he has received the gift may administer the same to one another." (1 Peter 4:10) The lord bishops utterly deny the substance of all this understanding. And their spirit of understanding directs that when the congregation is come together, the priest or curate that is licensed by them only must perform the worship, and must begin their worship with their book, strictly tying them to such sentences, and then to that which is written after, then a confession, then an absolution, with versicles and answers, and psalms, and lessons, and Te Deum, and the litany, three days a week, and at other times when the ordinary shall command.

Thus may our lord the king see how his people's spirits are in bondage to the lord bishops' spirit in the understanding of the scriptures. And they must of force against their consciences understand them as they command or else go to prison.

And our lord the king may also see that whereas neither Christ nor his apostles ever commanded or practiced any set form of worship, whose spirit had been most fit to have ordained such an order, yet the lord bishops (in the perfect image of the first beast) have composed a proportion, and framed an order of prayers and readings for the worship of God, commanding absolutely the observation thereof, forcing the spirits of the king's people to be subject to their limitations herein, and so deliver God's people their "bread by weight" and their "water by measure,"[19] not suffering the hungry to be satisfied with the bread of life, nor the thirsty to be quenched from the rivers of waters, but forcing the unwilling to "drink stolen waters" out of their cisterns and eat "hidden bread" out of their storehouses. But the simple that eat and drink thereof "know not that the dead are there, and that their guests are in the depths of hell." (Proverbs 9:17-18) Let not our lord the king be displeased, seeing his servants speak but the words of sobriety. And if the king shall think we misapply them, that is the thing which we so humbly and earnestly beseech the king may come to trial by the king's free consent, and that the king's hand of power may not be against the just and due trial thereof.

Now when we the king's servants do sue for a trial, we desire our lord the king not to conceive that his servants mean a day of dispute, and so to handle the cause of the lord as men that contend for prizes, who submit their cause to private censure. For that it is private and concerns but themselves. But our humble and most equal suit to our lord the king is that seeing this hierarchy of archbishops and lord bishops challenges such power and prerogative over our consciences, that all who cannot of conscience yield it unto them may walk according to their consciences and publish their defense against them, that those that bear the names of spiritual lords may by spiritual power only convince their gainsayers, and not pretend to be spiritual bishops and use only the king's temporal sword to rule and convince men with, that our lord the king would suffer us his servants to demand of them that take upon them to be lord bishops of whom they have learned to rule by such power and who has taught them to put the contrary minded in prison, and how they will be able to answer Him (that will bring the greatest of them to answer) who taught all his disciples to "instruct the contrary minded with meekness, proving if at any time God will give them repentance," and has taught them "to be gentle suffering the evil. " (2 Timothy 2:24-25) And let our lord the king give us his servants leave to ask

[19]Ezekiel 4:16.

their lord bishops whether they think that God has forgotten this his commandment? Or that he will quite forget to put it in their account, because they have altogether forgotten to keep it?

Oh, that our lord the king would but take his sword out of these lord bishops' hands, to whose office it does in no sort appertain if they were Christ's bishops, and that the king would let them use only that sword which is sharper than any two-edged sword,[20] which belongs only to Christ's bishops in their office. Let the king turn them out. And let them if there be any manner of uprightness in them come forth with that sword and armor only which the Holy Ghost has appointed them, if they be Christ's disciples. (Ephesians 6:11,17) And we will come to them through God's grace in the fruit of love and meekness. But when they smite us with the king's sword of justice and maintain their authority only by that power, and yet will be spiritual lords, how can we with faithfulness to the cause of God but shoot them through with the arrows of the Almighty, and filling them the double, (Revelation 18:6) discover by the word of truth the height of their iniquity? For it may please our lord the king to consider there is no other way to try and discover them whether they be spiritual or no but to apply the Word of God to them, to examine and compare them by it, as the church of Ephesus did them "which said they were apostles but were not and found them liars." (Revelation 2:2) And if this hierarchy of archbishops and lord bishops will not nor may not be tried by the Word of God but will still cause (by all the means they can) as many as will not worship it should be killed, so that none may speak or write against it but they shall be by death, by imprisonment, or by banishment destroyed, then our lord the king that knows the practice of the first beast in all these things, that where the first beast has full power, none may write nor speak nor look amiss, but they die, the king can judge whether this hierarchy of archbishops and lord bishops is not the second beast who has thus caused to be made the image of the first beast. And if the king's people may not thus say and write and by the Word of God prove this hierarchy so to be, but must without gainsaying believe the scriptures and worship God as they command, then are they lords over our faith. And the people of God have no power from God to understand the scripture, but all power is given to them. And then must we believe that they cannot err.

---

[20]Hebrews 4:12.

And we beseech our lord the king (that is a man of wisdom) to give righteous judgment herein, whether the lord bishops do not challenge[21] only to themselves all power to understand the scriptures and not to err when they will by force and violence of imprisonment, banishment, or death, compel the king's people to yield obedience to their understanding only. For if the king's people must not believe that they only have the power of the Spirit and cannot err, how comes it that the king's people must be compelled only to obey them in all their understandings and practices, except the king's people must obey them though they do err? And if our lord the king will not altogether turn his ear from the deep complaints of his servants, then let the king hear his servants in this point, which is so hateful to the king, and is of all estates (that have any understanding in the mystery of godliness) so much detested, yea, the lord bishops themselves do in words profess great detestation thereof, and that is that presumptuous sin of blasphemy of that Romish beast who holds he cannot err and therefore "thinks that he may change times and laws," as is prophesied of him. (Daniel 7:25) And this he does, as our lord the king well knows, appointing or commanding laws, days and times, and forcing obedience, and saying he cannot err, so that whatsoever he does must be obeyed as holy and good. Oh, that our lord the king and all his people would see that the hierarchy of archbishops and lord bishops do no less, although in word they deny it. Yet in deeds they practice and hold the same thing, that they cannot err. And this can never be denied, neither shall they ever be able to open their mouths to deny it, if they might but be brought to answer. For shall they ever be able to answer it, that they should expound the scriptures and make spiritual laws, canons and decrees, and command absolute obedience and in divers of their canons, decreeing excommunication ipso facto, but that they shall be forced to show by their deeds that they cannot err. And men must obey them on that ground, because they cannot err, or else on this ground, that they must be obeyed although they do err. For they must be obeyed, upon which last ground thousands do obey them. But we beseech our lord the king that it may be lawful, without offense to the king, to try the hierarchy on the first ground, which is, that as the hierarchy of Rome says in words they cannot err, that so in their deeds this hierarchy do

---

[21]To claim as due or as one's right.

absolutely profess they cannot err. We with our best ability make it plain to our lord the king and to every eye and ear thus.

The hierarchy of Rome expounds the scriptures, makes laws, canons, and decrees, and binds all men's consciences to obey, forcing them thereunto by excommunication, imprisonment, banishment, death, and none may examine the power, authority or warrant thereof by the scriptures, but all must be received for holy and good, because the hierarchy of Rome say in words they cannot err. We beseech our lord the king to see that the hierarchy of archbishops and lord bishops do all the same things. They expound the scriptures, make laws, canons, and decrees, and bind all men's consciences to the obedience thereof, forcing the king's true and obedient subjects thereunto by excommunication, imprisonment, banishment (the king in mercy and justice refraining them of blood), and none may examine the power and authority of any of their decrees by the scriptures, but all must be received for holy and good. Does not the king in the wisdom of his heart see, and may not all the king's people see, that this hierarchy of archbishops and lord bishops in all their deeds do show they challenge to have the same power not to err which the hierarchy of Rome do say in words they have? And thus do they absolutely in deeds profess they cannot err. Herein the hierarchy of archbishops and lord bishops are the more deceitful deceiveableness of unrighteousness.

And now we beseech the Creator of hearts to give our lord the king a new heart to consider all the exalted abomination of desolation executed and practiced by this hierarchy of archbishops and lord bishops. And let our lord the king know that it concerns the king highly on to consider it, in that it is set up and supported, and all the cruelty thereof executed by the king's power, whereby they make our lord the king guilty of all the imprisonment, banishment, and persecution which by the king's power they impose on all the faithful subjects of the king who withstand their abominations. But above all, let our . . .[22] the king (for the glory of God and for the salvation of the king's own soul) suffer us the king's servants thus far to prevail with the king that our lord the king would but search the scriptures (whereby the king knows he must be directed if he will be saved), and let the king see with his own eye what show of warrant can be found that the king should take unto himself power to elect bishops. Oh, we beseech the king that the successive

---

[22]"Lord" omitted in text.

possession and the goodly appearance of this power may nothing sway with our lord the king herein. But let the king set before his eyes the worthy recorded remembrance (by the Spirit of God) of Cyrus king of Persia, who "brought forth the vessels of the house of David which Nebuchadnezzar had taken out of Jerusalem, and had put them in the house of God," (Ezra 1:7,11) not regarding the monuments of his predecessor's great conquests, nor the despoiling of his gods of such beautiful ornaments, nor the departing with treasure of so great value. All these respects could not hinder this king for restoring the vessels of the house of the Lord. Let our lord the king be no less minded to the house and church of God. But let our lord the king freely restore at once to the church and house of God the whole glorious power of Christ the only king thereof, and particularly that most beautiful ornament of election and ordination of bishops and deacons thereof, who ought to be elected and ordained according to the rule of the Holy Ghost (Acts 14:23; 6:3), and who ought to be qualified with all and every one of those gifts and graces set down by the apostle (1 Timothy 3; Titus 1). Yea, and their wives and children also, or else it is grievous iniquity to choose them. And who must only by their office bear those names and titles which the Holy Ghost has given them, and lead or rule by that power which Christ has appointed and by those laws and ordinances, and live by those maintenances, if they stand need. And will our lord the king change all these and many more laws, statutes, and ordinances which Christ Jesus the Mediator and King of the New Testament has appointed and ordained in his church? Will the king take this power to himself to elect in such manner and such men as the king thinks good, and give names, titles, and power such as best pleases the king? Has Jesus Christ with his blood purchased to himself this honor to be the head of his church? (Ephesians 5) And has he showed himself a faithful mediator? And has he been accounted worthy of more glory than Moses? And has he built his own house himself? (Hebrews 3) And shall he be despoiled of all his honor? And will our lord the king be enticed by evil men to enter upon the inheritance of the Son of God in appointing and by the king's power suffering to be appointed lords and laws in and over the house of God which are not according to the pattern? Which lords, because Christ is not their buckler, nor faith their shield, nor the sword of the Spirit the weapon of their warfare,[23] they have deceitfully

---

[23]Ephesians 6:16-17.

seduced our lord the king bringing themselves under his protection for their defense, and getting the king's sword into their hands to destroy all that speak or write against them, preferring their own kingdom before either Christ's kingdom or the kingdom and state of our lord the king, as we have already showed the king in that they with such loving patience suffer and permit so many thousands of Romists, who by their profession, and the practices of some of them are dangerously opposite to the kingdom of Christ and to the king and state. But these lord bishops cannot in any wise endure ones that do faithfully seek for reformation, because such are only adversaries to their kingdom. We still pray our lord the king that we may be free from suspect, for having any thoughts of provoking evil against them of the Romish religion, in regard of their profession, if they are true and faithful subjects to the king. For we do freely profess that our lord the king has no more power over their consciences than over ours, and that is none at all. For our lord the king is but an earthly king, and he has no authority as a king but in earthly causes. And if the king's people be obedient and true subjects, obeying all human laws made by the king, our lord the king can require no more. For men's religion to God is between God and themselves. The king shall not answer for it. Neither may the king be judge between God and man. Let them be heretics, Turks, Jews, or whatsoever, it appertains not to the earthly power to punish them in the least measure. This is made evident to our lord the king by the scriptures. When Paul was brought before Gallio, deputy of Achaia, and accused by the Jews for persuading men to worship God contrary to the law, Gallio said to the Jews, "If it were a matter of wrong or evil deed, O you Jews, I would according to right maintain you. And he drove them from the judgment hall," (Acts 18:12,17) showing them that matters of wrong and evil deeds, which were between man and man appertained only to the judgment seat, and not questions of religion. The like is showed by the town clerk of Ephesus in Acts 19:38-39. And further Paul, being in like case accused of many things (Acts 24), in the twenty-fifth chapter appealed to Caesar's judgement seat where he said he ought to be judged, approving and justifying thereby that Caesar's power and judgement seat was the holy ordinance of God. And our Savior Christ is himself obedient thereunto and commands and teaches his disciples obedience. But this judgement seat and power which was of God had nothing to do with the causes of the religion of God, as our lord the king may see. For if it had, then could not our Savior Christ have commanded obedience thereunto. But he must have utterly overthrown his own kingdom and power. Neither could the apostle Paul have said he ought to be judged at Caesar's judgement seat if Caesar had, or might have judged in causes of religion to God. For then had he utterly overthrown the office of his apostleship. And then had he submitted his apostleship wholly to the judgment of Caesar, and so had the power and authority of it been altogether be destroyed and made of no effect, which might in no wise be.

Now let our lord the king (whose honor it is wisely to judge in things that differ) judge whether there be in these days any other earthly power or any other spiritual power but the same that was in Christ and his apostles' times, in which times all earthly power was in the hands of earthly kings and princes and them that were in authority under them. And Christ and his apostles diminished not kings and princes of the least title thereof. And all spiritual power was in the hands of Christ and his apostles that were in authority under him, of which spiritual power and authority Christ nor his apostles would suffer no earthly king to diminish them of the least title thereof, but rather gave them their lives. If then our lord the king do discern that earthly kings and princes had the same power that kings and princes have now, and that kings and princes had no power then over men's religion, which was spiritual and belonged unto Christ, men were then to give to God that which was God's and unto Caesar and so unto all earthly princes only that which appertained to them, then let our lord the king judge by what warrant of God's Word the king can now take to himself a spiritual power and set up a hierarchy of archbishops and lord bishops, and give authority to them to make laws and canons of religion, and to give them power to compel men unto the obedience thereof, by such severe courses as they have done. Let our lord the king consider (and the Lord give the king wisdom therein) that if no king nor prince could have set up such a hierarchy with such power and titles then, but they had utterly trodden under foot all the dignity and power of Christ and his apostles (for Christ and his apostles must have been subjects thereunto), neither may any king set up such a hierarchy now, because it does utterly tread under foot all the dignity and power of Christ and his apostles, as well now as it did then. For we have now Christ and his apostles in all their power and dignity as well as they had in those days, according to that saying of our Savior Christ in the parable: "They have Moses and the prophets."[24]

And we humble beseech our lord the king a little to suffer the foolishness of his servants, although we may seem as fools unto the king herein. If there had been such a strange hierarchy set up in Christ's and the apostles' days, would the hierarchy have suffered us (that are thousands of the king of Great Britain's subjects) to have gone to Christ and his apostles to have asked them whether we should have obeyed them or no in all their canons and ordinances, and whether we should have given them those titles of superiority and all that ruling power which they challenge over us the king's subjects? **Surely**, they will say, they would not have denied us that liberty to have gone in so weighty a cause and being so many to have asked counsel of Christ and his apostles what we should have done. Twenty thousand being ignorant and ten thousand being doubtful whether any such power might be submitted to or no, and thousands being out of doubt that it might not be submitted to, they will say they would not have denied us. But we know what their canons would have made of it. And we may suspect justly that they would have informed the king that it was very dangerous to suffer so many to go to Christ and his apostles for counsel, and that it was not fit to suffer such giddy heads to have that liberty, for making rents and divisions, and that it was much more **(uncertain)** for the king to suffer them to make all whole by their power, and to subdue such busy refractory spirits. Let the king with favor suffer his servants thus to speak by the way, lest peradventure any such things come in the way. And we the king's servants now taking it for granted that archbishops and lord bishops (that profess such great holiness) would not have denied us to have gone to Jesus Christ and his apostles to be directed. And if Christ and his apostles had (in the hearing of all our own ears, being so **many** witnesses) commanded us absolutely not to yield the archbishops and lord bishops any such power or names, could we yield it them, although the archbishops and lord bishops should (with twenty thousand witnesses) affirm that Christ and his apostles speak otherwise to their hearing? Would our lord the king think it equal that we should be forced to believe their hearing, because they are lord bishops, contrary to our own ears, and being so many witnesses of one nation and tongue besides hundreds thousands of witnesses of other nations

---

[24]Luke 16:29.

and tongues? We know our lord the king would think it no more equal (if the case were so) that we should be forced to believe the lord bishops hearing than that they should be forced to believe our hearing.

Then judge, O king, for the case is all one and the same. For we have Christ and his apostles in their writings, and they do absolutely speak to our understanding, that in no wise there ought to be any such hierarchy of archbishops and lord bishops in Christ's church. And the lord bishops say that Christ and his apostles speak to their understandings, that their power and names are not contrary to Christ's words. Can our lord the king (who is accounted a most wise and just prince in his judgment) judge that we are all bound to cast away our own understandings of Christ's speaking and are to be compelled to believe and understand Christ to speak as the lord bishops understand Christ's speaking? Oh, let our lord the king with compassion consider whether ever since the heavens and earth were created there was a more unequal extreme cruelty than this, that the king's people should be compelled (in a cause that concerns the everlasting condemnation of their souls and bodies to hell) of force to submit their souls and bodies to the understanding of the lord bishops who are not able to direct themselves from the ways of death, but are perished every man that ever bore that office with those names and power, if they repented not thereof, although they had no other sin. And they also that now bear that office with those titles and power shall likewise perish to everlasting destruction, if they do not repent thereof and cast it away. The Spirit of the Lord has spoken it: "The beast was taken, and with him that false prophet that wrought miracles before him, whereby he deceived them that received the beast's mark, and them that worshipped his image, these both were cast alive into a lake of fire, burning with brimstone," (Revelation 19:20) and thus manifesting to our lord the king that Jesus Christ is only King of Israel, that sits upon David's throne, and therefore only has the power of the king of Israel, and none may partake with him in that kingdom and power, who had the Spirit without measure. And yet neither he nor his apostles that had the Spirit without error to deliver the counsels of God did ever by example, practice, or by rule command nor give power that any should be compelled by any bodily punishment to obey their laws and ordinances, which were infallibly true, holy, and good. How much less ought our lord the king to command or give power to archbishops and lord bishops (men full of the spirit of error) to make laws and canons with authority from the king to compel by imprisonment and sharp persecutions the king's true subjects and people of God unto the obedience thereof, who for their religion to God (although they be contrary minded to the king therein) ought not (seeing they discern not) to be punished either with death or bonds. And this is confirmed to the king by the testimony of King Agrippa and noble Festus the governor, who adjudged Paul to have done nothing "worthy of death or bonds,"[25] but that he might have been loosed if he had not appealed to Caesar. And yet Paul was contrary minded to Caesar and to the Jews in his religion to God. But they judged him by the law of nations, by the power of which law the kings of the nations are to rule and judge, according to their own several laws, and against which law Paul had not transgressed, for his cause was concerning the faith of Jesus Christ which could not be judged by that law.

And let our lord the king give his servants leave to commend this to the king's best observation, which is worthy to be obeyed, that wheresoever in the New Testament throughout the professors of the faith of Jesus were adjudged by earthly rulers and governors for any thing that they did or held of conscience to God and of faith to Jesus Christ, if earthly rulers and governors took the cause in hand by their power, the judgment was always wicked and abominable. And if our lord the king will but begin his observation at the forerunner of Christ, John Baptist, whom Herod put in prison and beheaded. And then let the king come to Jesus Christ, whom they judged and crucified, "finding no evil he had done."[26] And so if it please the king to look throughout the whole book of the Acts, there the king knows how the disciples of Christ, were imprisoned, threatened, beaten, stoned. Then "made Saul havoc" with his letters of commission, "and entered into every house and drew out both men and women and put them in prison."[27] Then "Herod stretched forth his hand and vexed certain of the church, and killed James the brother of John with the sword" and "caught Peter and put him in prison."[28] Then were Paul and Silas taken at Philippi by the governors and people and were sore beaten and cast into prison, and the jailer commanded to keep them **(uncertain)**, being charged to preach ordinances which were not lawful for the Romans to receive nor observe.[29] Here may

---

[25]Acts 26:32.
[26]John 18:38.
[27]Acts 8:3.
[28]Acts 12:1-4.
[29]Acts 16:21-24.

our lord the king see a true pattern, how the people of God are persecuted when the civil power does judge their cause of their faith and profession in their religion to God. Thus have worldly governors dealt with the church of Christ when the disciples fell under their censure for their faith to God. And all these sentences of death, bonds, and persecutions the king can judge to be unjust and unlawful in that their rulers and governors had no lawful power nor authority to judge Christ nor his disciples for matters of faith, they being in all other things obedient to their laws. But men will say all this is answered in one word. They were heathen rulers. Now, if our lord the king will challenge a prerogative or power because he professes Christ, then let it be lawful for the king's servants to tell the king that if he will profess to be a disciple of Christ, that gives the king no power to do any of all these things to imprison, to banish, to put to death, that belongs only to his earthly kingdom. For Christ and apostles had no such power to take upon them, neither taught they the disciples to take upon them any such power and to execute it upon the contrary minded, but taught them the contrary to instruct with meekness, and by preaching the Word, seek their conversion, with all longsuffering, and not to destroy them by severe punishments. Yea, the disciples of Christ must wait and labor for the "grafting in again of the Jews," according to the prophecies of the scriptures. (Romans 11:24-27) And therefore the king knows they may not be destroyed, although they be the greatest enemies of Christ that are upon the earth, and have, and yet do cast the greatest reproach and contempt upon Christ with such words as are most fearful to utter. Yet must the disciples of Christ wait for their conversion, and not work their destruction. And let our lord the king call to mind how the apostle Paul teaches all the disciples of Christ to be minded toward all infidels, where he says, "I am debtor both to the Grecian and to the barbarian, both to the wise and to the unwise." (Romans 1:14-15) And the same apostle, says, "To the Jews I become as a Jew; to them that are under the law, as though I were under the law. To them that are without the law, as though I were without the law. To the weak I become as weak, that I may win the weak. I am made," says the apostle, "all things to all men, that I might by all means save some." (1 Corinthians 9:20-22) All these instructions and directions are for our lord the king, to direct the king how he should go in and out with holiness and all meekness before his people to win them to Christ, and not to set up a cruel hierarchy to make havoc of the king's people (as Saul did), pulling them out of their homes, both men and women, casting them into prisons, forcing them to flee the land, and persecuting them with all cruelty. May the king suffer all this to be done by his power upon this ground of being a Christian king? The king's servants show the king yet once again in all humility that Christ the King did not so himself. He never appointed to be punished any one man for disobeying his gospel, with the least bodily punishment. And therefore we instantly exhort our lord the king that the king would be no longer seduced by those most dangerous deceivers that have gotten the king's power to punish those that Christ, the King of Israel, would not punish, and that persuade the king that the king has the same power in the kingdom and over the house and people of Christ that the kings of Israel had in that kingdom, and over the house and people of God as it was the church of God.

We (according to our great weakness) have showed to our lord the king before that the king cannot challenge that power, meaning only in respect of religion. And we will by the king's favor, repeat the substance of the whole ground in few words. And we beseech the king that we may the rather do it, in that the whole cause depends thereon. And we repeat it to the king in these few words, which shall never be disannulled or made void while the heavens and earth endure, not because they are our words, God forbid any such arrogance should possess our hearts, but they shall never be made void, neither shall any ever be able to gainsay them with any show of truth, because they are the words of the everlasting God of truth, whereby we show to the king that the king cannot have that power in respect of religion to God in the kingdom and over the house and Israel or people of Christ now that the kings of Israel had in the Old Testament or in the time of the law. The ground we repeat to the king is this: that the kingdom of Israel was an earthly or worldly kingdom, an earthly or worldly temple, tabernacle or house, an earthly or worldly people, and the king an earthly king, who in and over all that kingdom, temple, and people could require only earthly obedience. But the kingdom of Christ now is a heavenly kingdom, not of this world; his temple, tabernacle, or house, an heavenly temple, tabernacle or house; his people, a heavenly or spiritual people, not of this world; and the King Christ Jesus, a heavenly spiritual king, requiring spiritual obedience.

Therefore, our lord the king cannot as a king have any power over this kingdom, temple, tabernacle, house, and people of God in respect of the religion to God, because our lord the king's kingdom is an earthly kingdom. And to our lord the king belongs only all earthly obedience, service and duty, which ought to suffice any earthly man. And the God of all grace give our lord the king a gracious heart fully to be satisfied and contented with that great honor, power, and dignity that belongs to the king, and to give glory and honor to God for it, that it may go well with the king and his posterity forever. And the God of heaven deliver the king from all such enchanters of Egypt as shall persuade the king to take upon him the power of the kings of Israel over the church of Christ only for the setting up and supporting of their high priesthood with urim and thummim, with pomp and power, and the Levitical revenues of Israel, which they challenge and hold as appertaining thereunto forcing the king's people by cruelty to obey them, as though with them only remained the oracles of God.

And now if they will show any manner of uprightness unto God or faithfulness to the king or any regard to God's people, let them not maintain their kingdom which they have obtained of the king by deceit and flatteries, as is prophesied in Daniel 11:21. Let them not maintain it by the king's sword and power, but let them come forth with that sword and power whereof they glory so much and use so little and maintain their names, power, and cruelty with it. And we profess before God, and the whole host of heaven, and before our lord the king and all his people, that if they can prove evidently to our consciences by the holy Word of God that we may obey them in all their canons and decrees, and give them those names and titles without the everlasting destruction of our souls and bodies in hell; yea, if they can but prove that we ought to rest or depend upon their judgments and understandings in the exposition of any one part of God's Word, or that they have power to ordain and appoint any one ordinance, or the manner of administering any one ordinance in the worship of God and church of Christ, we profess unto our lord the king we will yield them all the obedience they require. But if they will prove these things only by convocation canons, how can our lord the king require that the king's servants should dishonor God by casting his holy truth away and with it the salvation of our souls and depend upon their canons, and yield them to obedience and perish, both in souls and bodies? We have rather chosen thus to lay down our lives at the feet of our lord the king in presenting the cause into the king's presence, saying with Esther, "If we perish, we perish,"[30] for coming thus boldly uncalled into the king's presence. But we will wait with hope and **expectation**, that through the gracious work of the Lord the king

---

[30]Esther 4:16.

will hold forth his golden rod that we may live. And not so only, but also that by the king's means comfort and deliverance shall appear unto Israel, and that our lord the king will say, as that great king of Persia said, "The Lord God of heaven has given me many kingdoms of the earth, and has commanded me to build him an house in Jerusalem. Who is he amongst you of all his people with whom his God is, let him go to Jerusalem and build the house of the Lord God of Israel." (Ezra 1:2) And as King Darius said, "Suffer the work of the house of God, that the Israelites may build this house of God in his place, that they may offer sweet odors unto the God of heaven, and pray for the king's life and for his sons." And as Artaxerxes, king of Persia, said, "Whatsoever is by the commandment of the God of heaven, let it be done speedily for the house of the God of heaven. For why should he be wroth against the realm of the king and his children?" (Ezra 7:23)

Thus beseeching the director of all hearts to direct the king's heart in these things, we continue praying for the king and his son, and the king's realms and children, that the king and his seed, to God's glory, may sit upon the throne of Great Britain while the earth endures, possessing from God wisdom, and riches, and honor befitting the dignity of their high renown, and that they may walk in the ways of God that God, according to his promise, may prolong their days. And the Lord give all the king's people faithful, upright, and honest hearts, that they may all with one heart as one man, fear God and honor and obey the king, with all the honor and obedience that has, or can be due to any earthly king or prince, which is, all earthly and worldly obedience with lands, goods, body and life.

And we most humbly supplicate our lord the king and all the honorable and worthy governors under the king that they will not suffer themselves to be misled in judgment in condemning us as movers of sedition, and our books for seditious books, because we differ from the received profession of religion in the land, but that they will, according to the great gravity and wisdom that is upon them, weigh what sedition is. And they will easily find that to profess and teach a differing judgment in religion to the state cannot be proved sedition. For then had our Savior Christ and all his apostles been found seditious persons, which never could be proved against them, neither could Tertullus with all his oratory prove Paul a mover of sedition to Felix the governor "who was willing to pleasure the Jews in this matter," (Acts 24) if he could have found any advantage against Paul. But under all that excellent and mighty government of Caesar, under whom there was so many wise kings and noble governors, difference in religion could never be proved sedition against the state. Neither could it ever be proved sedition in all or any of those that differed from the profession of religion established in Queen Mary's days, although they taught and professed the same as even the lord bishops themselves will confess.

And it is neither accounted nor found sedition in divers excellent well-governed nations round about to profess and teach a differing judgment in religion from the profession generally established, as our lord the king and all his worthy governors see and know. It is but the false surmise and accusation of the scribes and Pharisees who feared their own kingdom, and of Demetrius, the silversmith with the craftsmen, whose craft was in danger, whereby they got their goods. (Acts 19) They themselves raised tumults and moved sedition, and ever laid the blame upon the disciples. Even so is it now and ever will be, that such as fear their own kingdom and private gain, do, and will falsely accuse the disciples of Christ as movers of sedition against the state. And if the lord bishops will not be found false accusers herein, as their predecessors have been, then let them (if they can) forbear to accuse before they have cause.

But let them take heed lest when they shall see five in one house divided, three against two, and two against three, the father divided against the son, and the son against the father, etc., let them take heed they call not that sedition. If they do, they shall call Christ a sower of sedition, for what was his desire but that the fire of such sedition should be kindled. (Luke 12:49, 52, 53) And may it please our lord the king and all that are in authority in government under the king, with their wise judgment to consider that it will be a strange thing to condemn men for sedition who profess and teach that in all earthly things the king's power is to be submitted unto, and in heavenly or spiritual things, if the king or any in authority under him shall exercise their power against any, they are not to resist, by any way or means although it were in their power, but rather submit to give their lives, as Christ and his disciples did, and yet keep their consciences to God. And they that teach any other doctrine, let them be accursed.

Book III

We, being yet (through the help of our God) most desirous to awaken all of you of our own nation out of that dead **security** and spiritual slumber, wherein, as in the sea, you are all overwhelmed, and finding no better nor any so fit portion of God's Word to effect these our unfeigned desires as this prophecy of our Savior Christ (Matthew 24:15), which prophesies of days of so great tribulation, and it is repeated (in) Mark 13 and Luke 17 and Luke 21, all which places of the evangelists must be most carefully and diligently compared together, because the wise reader shall find (by good observation) that there are four prophecies of our Savior Christ, by the evangelists set down together, which are: first, the destruction of Jerusalem; secondly, the days of the exaltation of the man of sin, seen and discovered; thirdly, the days of the Son of Man in the brightness of his coming for the consuming and abolishing of the mystery of iniquity, the abomination of desolation, the man of sin; and lastly, the day of Christ's coming to judgment.

Every one of these prophecies must be diversely considered with their proper appertainings for the true and holy understanding thereof, and not confounded together. Two whereof, we have, and shall (by the grace of God) speak of, as God shall enable us—first, the exaltation seen and dis-covered, and the dangers of those days; second, of the days of the Son of Man in the brightness of his coming for the consuming of the man of sin—as being most fit scriptures to stir you up to the consideration of your spiritual estates and standings, and to direct you therein (the scriptures we mean, not we), if you will not harden your necks and perish in the ways of death and sin.

And as we have endeavored to provoke you to look up that you might see "the abomination of desolation set up in the holy place,"[1] and how the kingdom of the man of sin is even within you all that submit yourselves in

---

[1]Matthew 24:15.

any obedience to the power of the first or second beast, "bearing the beast's mark or the print of his name,"[2] so shall we also be willing, with the help of our God, to stir you up to consider of the great danger that our Savior Christ has foreshown shall be in these days, when men see the abomination of desolation set up, and according to our Savior's exhortation begin to flee, as all that have eyes may see, men now begin to do. The danger that Christ foretold so is that in those days (which are these days) "many shall come (who now are come) in Christ's name, and say, Lo, here is Christ. Lo, there is Christ. And many false Christs shall arise, and many false prophets, and shall show great signs and wonders so as if were possible, they should deceive the very elect."[3] Weigh then with yourselves whether you had not need to consider when the days are so dangerous and perilous, as "if it were possible the very elect should be deceived." Such is the danger of these days, by reason of the false professions of Christ, and false prophets that do arise. And seeing the false prophets are the teachers and maintainers of false professions, we shall endeavor to discover them both under one, and will only speak of such false prophets and professions as are among you, and known to you, not burdening you with the multitude of strange and foreign false prophets and false professions that are in the world, whereof we generally admonish you to beware of. But it is full time that you look to those false professions and false prophets that are among you, if you have any regard at all of God's glory, or the salvation of your own souls.

And seeing we cannot speak of the false Christ, or false professions of Christ that are among you, but we must name them, we pray it may not be offensive that we term them by such names and titles as men distinguish them.

The first whereof is that great and so much applauded profession of Puritanism, the which profession to prove it is a false profession, yea, and such a false profession as we know not the like upon the earth, we shall not need to produce any testimony but your own. For whereas in your so many books you cry out of the things that are amiss among you, and sue and supplicate, and yet still continue in your former ways, you testify hereby against yourselves that you are unreformed, and that there is a way of refor-

---

[2]Revelation 14:11 et al.
[3]Matthew 24:23.

mation, wherein you would be, if you might have leave or license to enter thereinto, which seeing you cannot obtain, you justify it lawful to walk in an unreformed profession of religion upon this ground because you may not have leave by act of Parliament to reform. What falser profession can be found on earth than this of yours, who profess that you know a way of much truth wherein you would walk, but you do not, because you cannot by superior power be permitted.

Let this suffice in this place to prove that you walk in a false profession of Christ by your own acknowledgement, calling daily for liberty that you might reform yourselves, but seeing it will not be granted, you go on in the false way you disapprove of. Your grounds and reasons we shall hereafter (by God's assistance) try. But in the meantime let God's people know that there will never warrant be found to give men liberty for any time to defer to eschew evil, or to refrain to do good, for fear of men, or in obedience to men, or under any pretense whatsoever. Most wicked and false is that profession. And most false prophets are all those that profess and teach such a doctrine that men are not bound without any delay, all respects laid aside, with all speed to eschew evil and do good, as the true prophet David did, and taught who says, "I made haste and delayed not, to keep thy commandments. " (Psalm 119:60) And so we proceed to show that all your Puritan prophets (so called) are false prophets, and such as our Savior Christ foretells of who say, "Lo, here is Christ," but commands, "Believe them not."

And although we might prove you all false prophets because you teach many false doctrines, yet we hold it the most easy and plain way for the understanding of all to show you to be false prophets, because you are not sent, nor called by God, and herein shall you have the least deceivable show for yourselves.

But before we speak of your not being called and sent by God (which must appear by your election and ordination to the office or work of a bishop or pastor, for other prophets we know none among you), we will set down the gifts and graces, wherewith they are to be qualified that are to be elected and ordained, and undertake that office, as also how their wives and children are to be qualified. And these are the words of him that said, "Let there be light, and there was light," and of him that said, "Thou shalt have no other gods before my face," and of the lawgiver, all whose laws are perfect laws.

These are his words, and this is his law. "Let a bishop or pastor be the husband of one wife; watching, temperate, modest, harborous, apt to teach, and able to exhort with wholesome doctrine, and to convince them that say against it, not given to wine, no striker, not given to filthy lucre, but gentle, no fighter, not covetous, one that can rule his own house honestly, having children under obedience with all reverence. Let him not be a young disciple, or newly planted in. Let him be well reported of, even of them that are without. Let his wife be honest, no evil speaker, sober, faithful in all things." I Timothy 3; Titus 1) This is the law of God. According to this law, in every particular must a bishop or pastor, and his wife and children, be qualified. For it is the law of the lawgiver. And you shall have no other bishop or pastor before his face. This we set down to put you and the people of God in mind to look first that you, their bishops, or pastors be thus qualified. For all that are not so, both in themselves and their wives and children, are not sent of God to be pastors of his flock, but are false prophets in the first degree. For God sends none but those that are according to his own rule. And hereby may you see that every holy man and excellent preacher may not be a bishop and pastor over the house of God.

And now election and ordination, which is the door and way whereby the true bishops and pastors of the flock do enter. The Holy Ghost does teach (Acts 14:23) that election and ordination were performed in and by the church or congregation with fasting and prayer. This is the door and way, and all that have entered by any other way are thieves and robbers, as our Savior Christ testifies (John 10). Are you not all now at once convinced? And must you not all be forced to confess that you have no such election nor ordination? Is your purchased election of patrons, either particular men, or of dean and chapter, or of some college, or the private election of some friend, like to this holy order of election, which Christ has appointed to his church to be made with the gracious free and full consent of every heart and tongue in the whole congregation? How woeful and wretched is the estate of you all (if you repent not) that join in this great wickedness to deprive the church of Christ of such a blessed and comfortable ordinance of Christ. How blessed and comfortable a thing were it, for a holy people so to elect their pastor that should lead them, and feed them with the wholesome word of doctrine and exhortation, and watch over their souls in the Lord.

And what a blessed comfort were it for a holy man to be so elected of a holy people. So should a godly people have holy pastors over them, whom they would all love and reverence. And so should godly pastors have a holy people to follow them whom they would carefully feed and cherish. And this is the ordinance of God, and law of election. But to get an election for money, either of a man's own, or of his friends, or by private favor or friendship or beholdings to men, and so corruptly to become a pastor over a flock of people diversely affected, and many openly profane and wicked, here is an unholy election of an unholy pastor over a corrupt and unholy flock. This is not to enter in by the door but to come by another way, which seeing you all do, not any one of you entering by that holy election which Christ has appointed, Christ himself has adjudged you all, not to be shepherds of the sheep, but to be thieves and robbers.

And thus are you all false prophets. How shall you be able to stand before the Lord in this matter? Or how can you justify yourselves before men? Will you make the Word of the Lord of no effect, and bless yourselves in your own ways? If you shall do so, as you have long done, yet shall you not be blessed of the Lord, in that you do herein violate and utterly abolish that holy law of election, which Christ has ordained in his church for the choosing of the true shepherds of his sheep, and for the keeping of thieves and robbers out of his sheepfold.

Next in order to be spoken of is ordination, a holy ordinance of God commanded by the Holy Ghost (Titus 1:5), and the example of the administration thereof, given us by the apostles in the church of Christ (Acts 6:6), and practiced by the disciples (Acts 13:1,3), and taught us to be a doctrine of the beginnings of Christ, and of the foundation (Hebrews 6:1,2), being called the doctrine of laying on of hands. And this ordinance was performed and done in the presence of the church or congregation by fasting and prayer and laying on of hands, ordaining, and appointing and separating thereby those that were elected and chosen to office (Acts 6:6; 13:2,3; 14:23). And all this was performed and done by and in that congregation whereof they were chosen officers, the church or congregation being in this holy manner assembled together to perform this ordinance, all fasting and praying to the Lord with one heart and soul to give a blessing unto that his own ordinance.

Is your ordination like unto this, which the best of you all are fain[4] to get by suit and service, by riding and running, by attending and waiting, by

---

[4]Happy, pleased, willing.

capping and curtseying, and at last by prostrating yourselves on your knees at the feet of an archbishop or lord bishop, receiving your ordination from him who herein exalts himself above God, exercising the power of the beast, despoiling Christ and his church of this holy ordinance, taking it wholly into their own power, and disposing of it only to such as promise faithful obedience to the hierarchy of archbishop and lord bishop, which is the second beast, and which yourselves say, both in words and writings, is an antichristian hierarchy? The Lord give you eyes to see how you have broken the covenant of the Lord in polluting and abolishing this his holy ordinance, and be ashamed to remember the covenant you have made with this hierarchy, by which covenant of obedience you have gotten your ordination, and so are the prophets of the beast. For "to whomsoever you give yourselves to obey, his servant you are to whom you obey," (Romans 6:6) although you deny him in words as you do. Have you gotten an office of the hierarchy, and under the hierarchy, and will you in words and writings protest against the hierarchy, and yet retain your office, which you have gotten by promising obedience thereunto? And think you to serve Christ with this your stolen office? Halt not so between Christ and the man of sin. But if you will deny your lords that have preferred you to office, deny your office also. In both which you shall do well. But if you will retain your office, retain your lords also that have preferred you. In both which you shall do well. What conscionable answer will you make to these things? Dare any affirm that Christ has appointed such an ordination, either in the manner of administration or in the means of coming by it? Has Christ appointed you to sue, and make means to a prelate, and ride many miles with letters of recommendations, and pay all fees that are due (we speak within our compass) to get ordination? Did the apostles ever ordain pastor but before or in the presence of the flock? Did any ever go and sue or seek to the apostles to be ordained? And when any were ordained, did they kneel down at the apostles' feet? And did the apostles bid them receive the Holy Ghost? Is this the manner and means set down in the scriptures of coming by ordination? And if it be not, how dare you seek and submit yourself to it. Will you say that Christ has appointed no certain due order and means of ordination? Then do you blaspheme in saying the rules and examples of the New Testament are uncertain rules of direction, and so make you Christ not so faithful as Moses. Is the holy ordinance of laying on of hands one of the doctrines of the foundation (Hebrews 6:1,2), and may it be come by any means, or from any persons, yea, even from the pope? And you approve of it as you do, seeing you have no ministry but from Rome. It is the root from whence all your ministry is sprung, and the wild olive wherein you are all by your ordination engrafted. And therefore as the root is, such are the branches. And the root you all confess is most unholy. And so does the Lord judge you. You evil servants, out of your own mouths you are all most unholy, and false prophets, prophets of the beast, and not of Christ in that you are not elected and ordained by the rules of Christ and have not the Word of God nor testimony of your flocks for your entrance.

What can you now have to say for this your ordination thus unjustly come by, except you will plead possession (howsoever unjustly it be come by) for a good title, and so justify Ahab's possession of Naboth's vineyard, when Jezebel had slain the right owner thereof. As the Lord lives, no less but much more is the wickedness of your possession, in that the beast has trodden under foot and "crucified the Son of God" (Revelation 11:8) and "sits as God in the temple of God," and has appointed you his priests to serve at the altar. And thus have you consented together in evil, and trample under foot the testament which Christ has purchased with his blood, and have broken into the sheepfold of the Lord like thieves and robbers, and do nothing but steal, kill, and destroy. For you destroy all the people that submit to your ministry in that you bring them therein under the power of the beast, you having fallen down on your knees and worshipped the beast, receiving your spirit and office from the beast. And the people are partakers of this sin in that they admit of you in your office, and thereby yield that power which Christ has reserved in his own body (which is his church) to the beast. So are you all despisers of the law of God, and have given away his holy ordinance of election and ordination, which he has by his own Word and Spirit appointed in his church. You have given Christ's honor herein to the beast. And so are all, both priests and people, worshippers of the beast and his image, and have received his mark, and therefore shall you all drink of the mere wine of the wrath of God, if you repent not. (Revelation 14:9,10)

And thus much to the ministry of the Puritan profession, to prove them all false prophets, as those that run and God has not sent them, their election and ordination to their office, and their possession of their office being most unholy and unjust, not being according to the exact rule of the law of Christ Jesus distinctly and most perfectly set down in the New Testament forever, unto which whosoever adds or takes away either in word or action, by doctrine or example, the Lord will "add unto them, all his judgments, and take away his mercies." (Revelation 22:18,19)

You being thus by the word of truth all declared and proved to be false prophets, not having entered into the sheepfold by the door, it must needs follow according to the words of the Lord that all the great signs and wonders that you show in this your false ministry are lying signs and wonders.

Let it not be grievous to you to hear of these things whereby to provoke you to wrath, but let it be grievous to you that you thus sin, and so be provoked to indignation against yourselves that you may come to repentance.

Here is all your zeal of wonder, and signs of so great fervency, wherein you work on the blind consciences and ignorant affections of the simple deceived souls, proved to be false and deceivable. All your fire wherewith you kindle the hearts of men and seduce simple women, making them believe you have brought it from heaven, all this is but the false enlightening and heat of a false spirit, even of that spirit which your spiritual lord breathed on you when you knelt on your knees before him, and he laid his hands on you, and most blasphemously, even in the high dishonor of the Spirit of grace, had you receive the Holy Ghost. By and in the power of this spirit do you preach and pray, and do all your great wonders. And other spirit have you none, for this is the spirit to which you have submitted, and by this spirit only are you sent. And therefore are you all false prophets, and you have not the Spirit of God abiding in you. "You are gone out of the way. You have caused many to fall. You have broken the covenant of Levi,"[5] in that you are admitted to the order of the priesthood by the man of sin, who is an adversary of God, to whose blasphemous consecrating of priests directly contrary and opposite to the holy established ordinance of Jesus Christ in the Gospel the Spirit of God can give no approbation. . . .[6] neither admit of such to be the prophets of God (that have not entered by Christ the true door and way, but have entered by him that sits as God in the temple of God) but adjudges you all to be false prophets.

Leave off therefore your great days of humiliation by fasting and prayer, wherein **sometimes** you make the people to cover the altar with tears, and whereby some of you have taken upon you to cast out many devils, going

---

[5]Malachi 2:8.
[6]A word has been marked through in the fascimile copy.

on to the height in showing signs and lying wonders, to deceive if it were possible the very elect according to the prophecy of Christ which is thus fulfilled in you. "Kindle fire upon the altar of the Lord no more in vain. The Lord has no pleasure in you, neither will accept an offering at your hand, but will curse you as deceivers who vow a holy offering but bring a corrupt sacrifice unto the Lord." (Malachi 1:14) And all this you do, and shall do, so long as you serve in your office and ministry, received by the power and authority of the man of sin, contrary to the holy ordinance of election and ordination appointed by Christ in the New Testament.

And now all these things we dare not but think you have done, and do through ignorance. Amend your lives therefore and turn, that these your great and grievous sins may be put away, when the times of refreshing shall come from the presence of the Lord. And take heed, both you and all the people that do with such admiration run after you, as we ourselves have done (we speak it to our own shame). Take heed lest that now your ignorant zeal and fiery spirits of error wherewith you have inflamed the hearts of the simple, being discovered, take heed lest you "boil in great heat, and gnaw your tongues for sorrow, and blaspheme the God of heaven for your pains, and for your sores, and repent not of your works, as is prophesied men shall do," (Revelation 16:9-11) from which highest measure of sin the Lord for his Christ's sake deliver you. And through God's grace we will hope better things of you, which the Lord grant we may find in you, for the Lord knows our unfeigned heart's desire is that you might also be saved. And we exhort the people of God no longer to "hearken to the voice of strangers," but that they flee from them, according to the counsel of our Savior Jesus Christ. (John 10:5) And let the people see with their own eyes how you have all shown yourselves to be hirelings, which are not the shepherds, neither the sheep are your own, in that seeing the wolf coming, you have fled, and left the sheep. Nay, many of you even of those that are accounted most faithful and holy, have, and do go yourselves and lead your flocks to hear the voice of strangers that are set up, and stand by in that office and public place, which you challenge for your own, and are glad yourselves to preach in corners. Others of you make a secret composition with the hierarchy (which you profess to abhor), and then hire some wretched man under you to surplice and cross, and sin for you. Oh, how hateful and abominable are the works of darkness of this kind, which are done of you in the light. And all this under a great seeming show of holiness, but is mere hypocrisy and dissimulation, because you are hirelings and not good shepherds, who would lay down their lives for their sheep rather than lead them into the hand of the destroyer. And if you deny them to be thieves and robbers that come into your places and are made pastors over your flocks against your wills, and against the mind of the flock, then must you needs acknowledge them true shepherds over the flock, and that have come in by the door, and acknowledge yourselves justly thrust out, seeing you in your judgments hold but one pastor over a flock.

We will not follow you in these particulars, except further occasion be offered. But remember how you compare your fellow priests to **(uncertain)** or friars, going up and down with the bishop's bulls like beggars to see where they can get entertainment, and see not all this while yourselves, yea, some of your chief spirits for working lying wonders stand in the market-place to be **(uncertain)** from the east to the west, and to be transported from north to south, wheresoever you can get a good town pulpit, or a privileged chapel, a great chamber or dining parlor to administer in. Howsoever profane the town or household be, you will not **(uncertain)** to make them all partakers of the holy things at first, before you know your sheep, or your sheep know you, contrary to Christ's own word. (John 10:14) And all the power you have to administer is by the authority of the bishop's bull, which you have in so great contempt. And yet it is all the seal of your admittance to your ministry, and warrant for your administration therein, a most fit warrant for such administrations. Oh, that you could see these things. If you have any, the least love of God in you, cast off all these abominations and become the disciples of Christ, and preach Christ in his own ordinance as his disciples did. (Acts 11:19) Which if you will not do, but run on in the heat of your blind zeal in this your false ministry, then shall you be found to be those false prophets that come in sheep's clothing, of whom our Savior Christ has foretold (Matthew 7:22), that shall say, "Lord, Lord, have we not by thy name prophesied, and by thy name cast out devils, and by thy name done many great works?" To whom he will answer, "I never knew you. Depart from me, you that work iniquity." Let this suffice to have proved by God's Word that your election and ordination to the office of your ministries is not of God, and that you have not "entered in by the door, but have climbed up another way," and therefore are "thieves and robbers, false prophets, hirelings, strangers," whose voice Christ's sheep know not, but they flee from you and will not follow you. (John 10:5) And this is all the comfort that God's Word does afford any of you in your flocks that follow you: they are not Christ's sheep. And this is all the comfort that the people can have of you: you are not Christ's shepherds. So are you like people, like priest; like shepherds, like sheep. And you shall perish every man for teaching and drawing them after you, because you are false prophets and are not sent of God. And the people shall perish every one of them, for hearing and following you, because you are strangers and hirelings, if you and they repent not. (Luke 13:3) This is the Word of the Lord, the which you shall neither all nor any one of you be able to gainsay, for you shall never be able while heaven and earth endure to make any show from God's Word for your entrance into your office of ministry, and then are you utterly confounded in all your ways, and all the people that follow you.

We have spoken sharply unto you, as it may be **thought**, and if we have not, we had need, seeing you have been so often spoken unto of this your false ministry, and that with excellent words, and yet you have not regarded, which might discomfort us in you and discourage us in our own simple plans. But the love of God's glory which (through his grace) we hold most precious, and the longing desire of our souls after your salvation, and the salvation of this whole land which is so dear unto us, and we so much wish and pray for, and the hope and assurance we have of God's mercy and power to prevail by weak means, these causes have stirred us up, driven us on, and encouraged us to speak thus unto you. And we pray you by the name of Jesus, that as there is any purpose of heart in you to fear God and walk in his ways, or any love in you to this people, whom you are bound so much to regard with all faithful carefulness, make haste to reform your own ways, and to inform this people in the way to life, and salvation, according to the strict rule of God's Word, and do not lead them on in the way to death and condemnation, according to the new inventions of your own hearts, and old traditions of other men.

We will now return to speak a few words of your ground, and reasons (or rather excuses) that cause you to undergo these things whereof you cry out so much for reformation. One is because it is under a Christian king. We demand of you, how, if the king should bid you truly inform him whether it were more lawful for a Christian king to restrain the church of some of the ordinances which Christ has appointed than for a heathen king, it cannot be that you would tell the king that a Christian king might more lawfully do such evil than a heathen king. If you would, you would make Christianity a liberty to sin, which may not be. Why then, if a Christian king may not more lawfully do such evil (evil sure you hold it to be, else why cry out so much for reformation), neither may you more lawfully obey him in such than a heathen king. Leave off such deceitful pretenses and vain imaginations, for the which if you should be required warrant out of God's Word, you would easily see that it is but an excuse of a false show. The disciples of Christ, who were most obedient subjects, and taught you and us all obedience unto our king, yet they would not be restrained in the causes of God, but chose rather to obey God than men, and rather to suffer imprisonment and beating, than to be restrained either of preaching or practicing any of the ways of God, although they were commanded, imprisoned, and beaten up by the high priest, the council, and all the elders of Israel that were no heathen governors, (Acts 5) those were faithful disciples and were content to obey in all sufferings. And such obedience should you have submitted unto, if your hearts had been upright to God and the king herein. But you have all been found deceitful upon the weights and lighter than vanity itself in these things when you came to trial, and have daubed with untempered mortar. And no marvel though you fell, because the Lord was not your strength, in that you sought not the right way, but would have established a presbytery, hierarchy, and a decreeing synod, which would have been no more pleasing to God than an hierarchy of archbishops and lord bishops, and a canonical convocation house. For they have both one mind with the beast, and give the right hand of fellowship one to another, seeking and exercising one power, which is, to rule over men's consciences by their own laws and decrees. Therefore, strive no more for that your way. The Lord will ever be against you in it. For if a ruling presbytery by their synodal decrees and ordinances be lawful, and then why not a ruling prelacy by convocation canons lawful? And then why not a ruling pope? These are all one condition in their degrees, and not any one of them more pleasing to God than another. Although they be every one more sinful in their degrees than other, yet they all abolish Christ's ruling power. But if they repent not, Christ will "crush them with a scepter of iron, and break them in pieces like a potter's wheel,"[7] and will rule his people with his scepter of righteousness.

Your next ground and cause of undergoing these things you so much dislike is because you are loath to break the peace of the church. Where you have learned to undergo sin for peace sake we know not, but sure we

---

[7] Psalm 2:9.

are of God you have not learned it. Paul and Barnabas had not learned your lesson therein, for if they had, they would not have made such great dissension in the church at Antioch as they did about the doctrine of circumcision. If Paul had been of your peaceable minds, he would (seeing he had suffered Timothy to be circumcised for peace sake) also have suffered a little the doctrine of crucifixion, but he would not. Furthermore, the apostle commands the church (Romans 16:17) to avoid, or to have no fellowship with those that cause division and offenses contrary to the doctrine which they had learned. And the same apostle warns the Thessalonians (2 Thessalonians 3:6) in the name of the Lord Jesus Christ that they withdraw themselves from every brother that walks inordinantly and not after the instruction which they had received. Now, if there be in you any conscience of the religion of God, see how corruptly you walk in these things, making a show of godliness but denying the power thereof. Do not your brethren, the archbishops and lord bishops with archdeacons, chancellors, and the rest, cause divisions and offenses contrary to the doctrine which you have learned? And do they not walk inordinantly and work, too, and not after the instructions that both you and they have received of the apostles? How then is it that you will not (according to the apostles' commandment, exhortation, and so straight warning) avoid them, and have no fellowship with them, and withdraw yourselves from them? Is this your peace a godly peace, which is so contrary to the whole Word of God? Besides this we must tell you (bear it patiently) that it is but ignorant dissimulation in you to say you undergo all these things because you would not break the peace of the church. For if you did so much tender[8] the peace of the church as you pretend, and that you would not have your beloved stirred up, nor wakened before she please, why then have you written so many books of open contempt? Why have you fought so much, and made challenge for disputations? Why do you make so many loud outcries and daily complaints and tedious Parliament suits? How can you possibly devise more unpeaceable courses? Except you should raise tumults contrary to the law of God and of the king (which we know is not in your thoughts), you can no way devise to be more unpeaceable. Had it not been a much more peaceable course quietly to have separated with love and humility than to have stirred up so much bitter strife in the bosom of the

---

[8]To regard or treat with tenderness.

church whose peace you pretend so much to regard? Oh, that you could see that it is your own peace that you respect in all this. For what breach of peace had it been in the church if you all had peaceably withdrawn yourselves, and lovingly admonished the church, holding it a true church, as you do? Had it not been much more peace, and much less trouble for the church if you had so done? There is no question it had. But whether your peace and profit would have followed is the question. And take heed that be not the cause of your (for peace as you call it) undergoing of these things. We could speak largely of this point, but we spare you, only wishing you not to persuade yourselves, nor to make the people think that you have suffered great things, while you eat the fat of the land. But know this, all you that eat any bread from whosoever hands, by, or in respect of your office of ministry, that you feed off the portion of his meat whom you **seek** to destroy, fulfilling the prophecy of Daniel 11:26, where he prophesies of the destruction of the man of sin, saying, "They that feed off the portion of his meat shall destroy him." And may not the simple understand that you getting your bread by that office, which office (as is proved) you have and execute by the power and under the authority of the man of sin, you feed off the portion of his meat, serving at his altar, and so eat you of the things that appertain to that altar, you **gaining** them by that office. And let all the people know of all estates and degrees whatsoever that give you any maintenance or entertainment in respect of that office, entertaining you as prophets, they shall never receive a prophet's reward, but sin against God in maintaining and entertaining false prophets, although they be as full of good **meanings** as the papists are in entertaining their priests. We have not least intent herein of dissuading any from doing good unto you, but that they should not receive you, nor give you a cup of cold water in the name of prophets. For all their liberality bestowed upon you in that regard shall never receive recompense of reward at God's hands, seeing you are all false prophets, and so adjudged by Christ himself in that you have not entered by Christ into the sheepfold. And if you shall any of you open your mouths to defend yourselves herein, the Word of the Lord shall convince you, and stop your mouths, that you shall not be able to speak with any understanding. And now we advise you to be ashamed to plead that you do undergo these things for the peace of the church, except you will hold your peace. For you are wise enough to know that there is no other way to break the inward peace of the church, which peace you must needs mean, for it is not in your powers nor hearts to break the outward peace of the church. And there is no other way to break the inward peace of the church, but by words and writings of opposition and contention, and making division, all which you have practiced to the uttermost of your own powers. And when for fear of your own peace you **durst** go no further, then have you set out your books of unknown authors (which therein are no better than libels), wherein you have no regard what troubles and dissensions you make in the church, so you can preserve your own peace. And thus do you maintain by all force and violence of contention a most troublesome civil war, which of all is most dangerous in church and commonwealth. And yet you profess you **suffer** and undergo all these evils you complain of, because you tender the peace of the church. And so through ignorance you fall into great dissimulation and hypocrisy, it being (if you could see) only your own peace you seek. And therefore it is you undergo these things that you disapprove of. For would you not, if you might (without danger or loss), reform yourselves and as many as you could, according to that reformation you sue for? Your own consciences can tell you you would, if the king at first had made a law that all should have been in subjection to the bishop's power and government in the church, but he would have no man punished by imprisonment nor put out of their livings that should refuse, would you not all that make any conscience of your ways have reformed? If you would not, then the reformation you plead for is not useful, except the king will approve of it. And so have you striven all this while about needless things, if the king's commandment may disannul the necessity of them. Then are they needful, if the king will permit. If not, your reformation may be spared, and so ought you not to have gainsaid it, as you have done.

And in this does your iniquity generally abound in that you make so small a matter of those things wherein you in judgment differ from the lord bishops, seeing the difference is no less than for the whole government of Christ in his church. And the Lord give you and all his people grace duly to consider of it, how greatly you dishonor Christ, and make a mock of him, when you profess him to be your king, and yet say his government is not of absolute necessity. So do you hold it of absolute necessity to give him the name of a king, but not to give him the power of a king. What great impiety of high contempt is this? What earthly king would endure this at his subjects' hands? If you should do so by our lord the king of Great Britain, acknowledge him to be your lord and king, and call him by that name and title, and bend and bow to him with words and all reverence, but wholly submit yourselves to be governed by the laws and officers of a foreign power, and that by rebellious **subjects** who ought to be obedient unto the king, and yet are **set** up as kings and take the king's power from him, were you not all worthy to be accounted **traitors** and rebels? And would not the king cast you all out of his kingdom, or destroy you all in it? Would the king be satisfied with all your words of flattery that you could use in acknowledging him, and calling him by the name of your king, when he should see he had no power to govern you by his laws and officers but that you did submit to be ruled by the laws and officers of his rebellious subjects and enemies? Would our lord the king endure this? Having power in his hand to avenge himself of you, would he not, after his often proclamations made and his many messengers sent unto you to command you to come from under those governors, and that government, lest you be destroyed with them, and you submit yourselves to him, and he will be your king and your defense, if for all this you would not hearken and obey, would not the king come with his power according to his word, and destroy you all together that would not suffer him to rule over you? Certainly, the king would do it in justice, and for his own honor, and having protested it with his word. Even so, be you sure, will Christ Jesus your king do by you all, if you stand still in rebellion against him, submitting yourselves to that rebellious hierarchy of archbishops and lord bishops who ought to be his subjects, but are his enemies, and exalt themselves above him, governing you by foreign power and government, and not by Christ's power and government. And the king's proclamations are come unto you, commanding you to "come out from among them, and separate yourselves, and be his children and people. And he will receive you, and be your God and Father." (2 Corinthians 6) And, "Go out of her, my people, that you be not partakers of her sins, and that you receive not of her plagues." (Revelation 18) Thus does Christ Jesus your king call unto you. And if you will not yet hearken to his voice, but flatter with your tongues, and say you acknowledge him to be your king, but submit not to be governed by his power, he will certainly in his justice for his honor, having protested it by the word of his mouth, come against you all, and give you the "cup of the wine of the fierceness of his wrath." (Revelation 16:19) Oh, people destitute of understanding. Oh, nation not worthy to be loved. Can you think in your minds that God has given all earthly kings power to make good laws, to rule and govern their people by, and commanded their subjects to be obedient thereunto, and has he not given Christ Jesus his beloved Son (whom he has set upon David's throne forever, and made king over his people Israel) power to make true laws and good ordinances to govern and rule his people by? And has he not commanded all his subjects to be obedient thereunto? Will no king of power suffer his subjects to submit themselves to be governed by the government of any other, and to be deprived of that government which God has given them over their subjects? And can you be so unwise to think that Christ Jesus, who is a king of greater power, will suffer it in his subjects? Can you not see that a king is no king if his government over his people be taken away? And can you think that Christ may be a king without his government? What vanity does possess your minds while you make so small a matter of Christ's government, saying you differ with the bishops in no fundamental point, but only in matter of government. See (if there be any fight in you) if the lord bishops' power of government were taken away, where were their kingdoms? Their names and titles would not support their kingdom. And this they see, and you find by their Canon 7 Anno. 1603, which they have made for the firm establishing of their government, knowing it to be fundamental, without the which their kingdom would presently come to naught even in one hour. Even so have they brought Christ's kingdom to naught among you by taking his government from him. Who has bewitched you thus to say and teach, and seduce the simple as though government were no fundamental point? Know you not what government is? Can you divide Christ's government (as he is a king) from his power, or his power from his government? Will you make him a king without government? Wherein then is he a king otherwise than in name? If the lord bishops should compel you to deny Christ of the name of a king in or over his church, would you not then say they overthrow a fundamental point of faith? And have you not understanding to discern that the power or government of a king is of far greater authority than the name of a king? And were it a much less matter for a king to be deprived of the name and title of a king than of the power and government of a king? Let the simple judge whether is greater, a king of great power and government, or a king of great name and title. Let them contend, and see who shall get the victory. All this we set down to show how greatly you do err through ignorance that cannot discern that power and government in earthly kings is much greater than name and title and therefore you err in common judgment. But you do err much more in spiritual judgment in that you cannot discern Christ's name, and power of government to be of equal **estimation**. For if you do not hold all things in Christ, and all things of Christ to be equal, and of like condition or proportion, you overthrow the nature and property of God. As thus: all the graces of Christ in himself are equal alike, and all his works are equal alike. It was all one with God to make behemoth spoken of (in) Job 40, and the pismire (Proverbs 30)[9] and God esteemed them both alike. So all the Word of God is alike and of like power and authority, as Christ himself showed when an expounder of the law asked him, "Which is the first and great commandment?" Jesus answered, "Thou shalt love the Lord thy God with all thy heart, soul and mind. This is the first and great commandment. And the second is like to this. Thou shalt love thy neighbor as thyself."[10] And the apostle James makes it most plain that the commandments of God are all of like power and authority, and all of like necessity to be obeyed. And the Holy Ghost does show an evident reason wherefore every commandment is alike to be obeyed, and why the breaking of one is the breaking of all, because (says the Holy Ghost by the apostle) he that commanded one commanded all. (James 2:10,11) From which ground of truth we thus speak unto you in the words of the Holy Ghost. He that has commanded in the church the true preaching of the Word, true baptism, and true administration of the Lord's Supper, the same God has commanded also true government in the church. Therefore although you should **have** the Word of God truly preached, and baptism and the supper of the Lord truly administered, yet if you have a false government, you are transgressors of the whole law of God, and guilty of all.

Thus does the Word of God disapprove and bitterly condemn that blasphemous doctrine of yours whereby you fearfully deceive yourselves and the people of God, which you hold and teach that Christ's government in his church is not fundamental. And besides the Word of God we have endeavored to show you that in all **(uncertain)** sense and understanding, a king that has not the power of government over his subjects, but they submit to the government of strange lords, they are disobedient and rebellious, and give their king only the name of king. And such subjects are you, giving Christ only the name of a king, but give his power of government to strange lords, your lord archbishops and bishops, who enlarge you by their spirit, and you are enlarged; and who restrains you by their power, and you are restrained; who set you by for shepherds, when you please them, and put you down like hirelings when you offend them; who if they destroy your

---

[9]Ant. Proverbs 30:25.
[10]Matthew 22:35-39.

flock before your faces, and you stand by you dare not aid them, but give counsel for peace, to submit to their cruelty, although they should condemn your most innocent, and justify the most guilty. And all this evil and much more you justly bring upon yourselves and the people in teaching and professing that you differ not from the lord bishops on any fundamental point, making and accounting thereby the government which Christ has appointed in his church not to be fundamental, wherein you sin against God with a high hand, making Christ Jesus a vain lawgiver, while by your practice and profession, both in deeds and words, you declare that the ordinances of Christ, which he has appointed for the whole government of his church, are not of absolute necessity, and fundamental. If the Jews had so said and practiced against the ordinances which they received for the government of the temple and tabernacle, and appointing the officers by the mouth of Moses, it had made an utter confusion of all, and they must have died. And behold a greater than Moses is here, giving ordinances to the government of his temple and tabernacle, and for the ordaining of officers, against which if **you resist** and admit of any other you must die, except you repent. (Hebrews 10:28,29 and 12:25) For you make an utter confusion of all. Oh, that you would but look with your eyes and see what a confusion it would have brought into the temple and tabernacle, if any other officers, and any other government had been brought in than Moses appointed. Had not all their sacrifices and services been polluted and most abominable to the Lord? Would Moses ever have endured it, and would Aaron have consented thereunto? They would not. And if all the people had, they all had been destroyed with Korah, Dathan, and Abiram,[11] who would have overthrown the government and officers of the temple, for the Lord would have been as just in his judgment upon all as upon **some**. Oh, that you would consider this, "and forget not God, lest he tear you in pieces, and there be none that can deliver you."[12] Are the laws and ordinances given by Jesus Christ for the government of his temple and tabernacle, and appointing of his officers, not so perfect as those that were given by Moses? And will not the bringing in of any other officers and government unto the church of Christ than he has appointed cause as great a confusion as it would have done in the temple? And shall not all the sacrifices and services be polluted, and most abomi-

---

[11]Numbers 16.
[12]Psalm 50:22.

nable, as theirs would have been? Will Christ Jesus the Mediator and High Priest endure it, or consent unto it any more than Moses and Aaron would have done? If you say he would, then you make Christ less faithful than Moses, and make his church less holy than the temple was, and his laws and ordinances not so perfect as those that were given by Moses, and so shall the transgression against them deserve less punishment. But all the prophets and apostles, and Christ Jesus himself testifies the contrary to this, as you know right well. And most especially the author to the Hebrews handles these things at large, showing that the temple, tabernacle, and all the officers, and offices, and ordinances of administration for government and service given by Moses, were but a pattern, shadow, and similitude of the heavenly temple and ordinances established and given by Christ, who is "the mediator of a better testament, established upon better promises," and is "the high priest of a more perfect tabernacle," and has purified all the ordinances with a better blood. And he is faithful as Moses, and is worthy of more glory and honor (Hebrews 8:5,6 and 9:11, 23 and 3:2,3), and he will punish with much sorer punishment those that despise his law than Moses could. (Hebrews 10:28,29) Therefore, take heed to yourselves for you have brought an utter confusion upon the house of God by submitting unto another government and other officers than Christ has appointed in his church. And so are all your sacrifices and services polluted, as theirs would have been in the temple, if they had permitted any such thing. And if the government of the temple was fundamental, how much more the government of the church of Christ? Be wise in spiritual wisdom, and then you will yield that true government is of as absolute necessity in the church of Christ under the Gospel as it was in the temple under the law. And if you will be of understanding according to all the understanding of men, you will confess that a king's own government, by his own laws and ordinances, is fundamental and of absolute necessity in his own kingdom, and over his own subjects, or else he is a king but only in name and not in power. Then must you needs confess that Christ's government is of absolute necessity and fundamental in his kingdom, or else you make him but a king in name. And how can you in all true judgment but acknowledge that it is much better to have the power and government of a king without the name of king, than to have the name of a king and not the power and government of a king? And therefore you might as well submit to the lord bishops to take away Christ's name of a king as submit to take away from him the power and government of a king. But therein lies the depth of the mystery of iniquity in the man of sin, in taking wholly from him his power, and yet professing his name. And hereby are all the nations of the earth deceived, and this it is that blinds you all, because you have the profession of Christ's name among you, saying he is your king. This makes you rest satisfied, although you yield unto him no one thing **(uncertain)** that appertains to his kingly office, but only the name and title of a king. That we may make this plain unto you (for you see it not) that you give Christ only the name of a king in your church, we show it unto you thus: all that can be given to a king of his subjects is to give unto him all the titles of honor due unto his name, and to submit in obedience unto his power. This is all that God requires to himself in first, second, third, and fourth commandments. And this must every king have, their name and power, and especially Christ our king. Now, the name of a king you give unto Christ, but no power of a king. The which that it may appear evidently unto the simple we pray you to consider that all the power of a king consists in punishing the evildoers and rewarding the well doers, as is proved (in) Romans 13:1-4, where the apostle shows that all the power that are, they are of God. And they are to this end only, to punish the evil and reward the good. Speak now uprightly before God and men, has Christ this power in your Church? And are his officers and people permitted to execute it? Are the good by Christ's kingly power cherished, comforted, and rewarded, and are the evil by the power of Christ corrected and punished? Has Christ power by his own ordinances, laws, and officers to receive and keep in the good, and to cast out, and keep the bad out of the church? If you should say, Christ has his power in your church, you all (called Puritans) are condemned at once, for the most evildoers in the whole church, because you above all are most evil spoken of, mocked, condemned, hated, cited, silenced, excommunicated, and imprisoned. Is all this done by the holy kingly power of Christ? Then are you the most evildoers, and then are all the proud boasters, cursed speakers, malicious, covetous, and flatterers, that have peace and preferment in the church, well doers. Is this the power of Christ? If it be not, as we know you will all confess it is not, then must you needs confess that Christ has not the power of a king in the church. For if he has no power to punish evildoers, and reward the well doers then has he no manner of power by his kingly office among you, and then do you give him but only the name of a king. And so do you give him no more than Pilate gave him, when he wrote a title and put it on the cross, "This is the king of the Jews."[13] But in all this you think to excuse yourselves in that you are innocent in these things, and protest and seek much to have it otherwise. Even so was Pilate. He washed his hands, and would be innocent from the blood of that just man. He protested he saw no evil in him. And he sought to loose him, but when he saw he availed not, he delivered him to the high priests and elders to be crucified. And thus do you, the best of you all, that when you cannot prevail that Christ might have his power set up, (as you pretend) you deliver it into their hands that destroy it, and submit yourselves unto them also. Will you yet say Christ is your king, when it is thus evident that he has no power to rule over you? Will Christ be such a king? Be not deceived, God is not mocked.[14] He will command you, his enemies, which would not that he should reign over you to be slain before him if you repent not. No pretense of excuse shall be admitted for committing of evil, neither excuse of fear, nor of ignorance. The Lord does "teach all men everywhere to repent, and they that believe and obey shall be saved. And they that do not believe shall be damned,"[15] which you shall all be, every one of you that submit to any other government than that most holy and blessed government which Christ has established in his church, whereof he is the head and king. And therefore the church of Christ is "in subjection in every thing." (Ephesians 5:24) And our Savior Christ will no more be the head nor savior of such a church that submits itself unto the power of a stranger, his enemy, than any godly wise husband will be the head of a wife that submits her body unto the power of another man, although she make never so many fair pretenses of excuses. And for this end and to show all other love and duties has the Holy Ghost aptly here by the apostle compared Christ and his church and a husband and a wife together, to teach thereby all the love and duties of husband and wife one to another, and to declare all Christ's love to his church, and the duties of his church to him again. How can the Holy Ghost by more fit and plain comparisons to the capacity of man show and declare the power and love of Christ, over and to his church, and the subjection that the church is to yield to him in everything, which subjection seeing your church will not yield to Christ, but denies him the whole power of govern-

---

[13]John 19:19.
[14]Galatians 6:7.
[15]Mark 16:16?

ment over it. Christ cannot be head of such a church, neither can your church be his body, for every body is guided and governed by (its) own head, and none of all you that are members of that body are members of the body of Christ. But the spiritual lord archbishop and lord bishop are head of your church, in that it is in subjection to them in every thing, as you well know. And therefore is it their body, for every head has its own body. And you are all members of their body, whereof Christ is not the Savior. "But he is the Savior of his own body, which is the church, whereof he is head." (Ephesians 5:23) The God of grace give you grace to consider your fearful estate and standings therein and deliver you from that dangerous, delightful security wherewith your hearts are so (uncertain), all your senses and affection being bewitched and ravished by that "ware of gold and silver, and all excellent metals of pearls, and all precious stones, of silk, and scarlet, and all costly vestures of vessels of ivory, and of all most precious wood, and of cinnamon, and odors, and ointments, and frankincense, and wine, and oil, and fine flour, and wheat, and beasts, and sheep, and horses, and chariots, and servants, and souls of men, and apples that your souls lust after." All these things has the Holy Ghost set down most largely (Revelation 18) to discover the deceivableness of unrighteousness, in all the precious delightful sweet and pleasant spiritual baits and snares that are in that your glorious profession of Puritanism, whereby your souls are bewitched and ravished, as also in all other professions among those people that "are the waters, whereupon the woman arrayed in purple and scarlet does sit." (Revelation 17) Of which people you are, in that you are in subjection unto the power of the beast and his image, and therefore are all your sacrifices, oblations, and incense in vain, your prophesyings or preachings, your prayers and prayings of God are an abomination unto the Lord. "Your silver is become dross. Your wine is mixed with water."[16] The Lord has "covered you with a spirit of slumber,"[17] and has shut up your eyes. Your prophets and your chief seers has he covered, because you "come near unto him with your mouth, and honor him with your lips,"[18] in calling Christ your king, but you have taken "government from his shoulder, who is called wonderful, counsellor, the mighty God, the everlasting Father, the Prince of

---

[16]Isaiah 1:22.

[17]Isaiah 29:10; Romans 11:8.

[18]Isaiah 29:13; Matthew 15:8.

Peace, the increase of whose government and peace shall have no end."
(Isaiah 9:6,7) But all this power you give unto your strange lords, and you
cry and say that Christ is your king. Thus do you flatter "with your lips and
dissemble with your tongues,"[19] and your ways are not upright before the
Lord.

What might we say to provoke you, to set your hearts to seek the Lord,
and to turn your feet to walk in his paths, and your ears to hearken to his
voice, which seeing you will all with earnestness profess to do, do it with
faithfulness, and cast away all ignorant hypocrisy? And now that the
abomination of desolation is set up before your eyes, hear this voice of the
Lord: "Flee into the mountains. And come out of her my people, and turn
not back to that which is left behind. Remember Lot's wife." (Matthew
24:15,16; Revelation 18:4; Luke 17:31,32) We will use no more reasons
to prove you are not come out of Babylon, but your own confession shall
witness against you, in that you daily complain of your bondage. Therefore
you may see you are in the house of bondage. But there is no bondage in
the house of God, where the children of the free woman stand fast in
liberty, wherewith Christ has made them free. (Galatians 4:31 and 5:1) Why
are you then still in bondage under all those ceremonial traditions (which
you say your souls abhor), if you be of those that Christ has made free?
Shall we entreat you with godly advisedness to consider what the bondage
is, and see how you look to be delivered? Is not your bondage you complain
of a spiritual bondage, in that you are restrained of spiritual liberty in holy
things, having ceremonies and ecclesiastical laws and canons pressed upon
you, which of conscience you cannot obey? So is it plain your bondage is
spiritual. And how would you be delivered from your spiritual bondage, and
who should be your deliverer? Can you be delivered but by a spiritual
power? And can you have any deliverer but a spiritual Lord? If you seek to
and depend upon any other lord to be delivered from spiritual bondage, you
take unto yourselves another God, and set up a spiritual power against the
power of God. And whereas you should "put on the whole armor of God,"
and "wrestle against principalities and powers, and spiritual wickedness
which are in high places and stand fast,"[20] you have **shrunk** in the day of
battle and have not faithfully "contended for the maintenance of the faith

---

[19]Isaiah 59:3?
[20]Ephesians 6:11-12.

given to the saints,"[21] but have, and do yield to the spiritual wickedness, which are under the power of those spiritual lords, the archbishops and lord bishops, and have cast off the armor and sword of the Spirit wherewith you should resist and overcome, and wherein those spiritual wickednesses shall be consumed and abolished. And you have taken unto yourselves a direction after the device of your own hearts, **seeking** and **sueing**, by petitions not to God, but to men, that you might have leave (as you pretend) to set up Christ for your king and governor. And if you could get leave, you make show as though you would reform matters that are greatly amiss. But seeing you cannot, you are content to let them alone, and groan under them (for so you speak) and not to be too busy, least you should make matters worse. Of this same condition were the people of Israel, when Moses was sent to bring them out of Egypt. For when they saw that leave would not be granted, but that more work was laid upon them, and that there was danger and trouble, they would have made their peace, and have groaned still under their burdens as they had done, and so have continued in that their bondage, as you do in your spiritual bondage. But the Lord was merciful unto them according to his own promise, and brought them out by a mighty hand, and with great signs and wonders. And even so has the Lord promised to bring his elect (which are those that hearken to the voice of his call) out of this spiritual bondage of Babylon, Egypt, and Sodom (wherein you are), by great and marvelous signs and wonders, as the Spirit of God has declared (Revelation 15 and 16) by the seven angels, which pour out the seven vials of the wrath of God upon the earth. But you must know that this is a spiritual prophecy, and all these are spiritual signs and wonders, which the Lord has graciously promised to show upon Babylon, Egypt, and Sodom (spiritually so called), to the destruction and everlasting overthrow of the scarlet colored beast, and the woman that sits upon him, which woman is that great city Babylon, and upon all the people that came not forth at the call of his voice. (Revelation 17:18) But take heed you be not deceived by looking for these things with carnal eyes as the Jews did, who looked for an earthly king to deliver them, so that when their spiritual king came they knew him not, but hated him, despised him, persecuted him, killed him, and cast him out, and so remain in transgression and under condemnation unto this day, by the just judgment of God. Take heed lest you do so in sueing

---

[21]Jude 3.

after and seeking by earthly means to be delivered out of your spiritual bondage, and when the spiritual means and way is showed you, you condemn it, despise it, hate it, persecute it, speak all manner of evil against it, oppose it, reject it, and condemn it, and so remain still in your transgression, and under the condemnation of the just judgment of God, which the Lord has pronounced against all those that come not forth of Babylon, partaking thereby with her in her sins, and so shall be made partakers of her plagues, which plagues you cannot escape if you come not forth, but believe those false prophets that prophesy lies unto you. Be not deceived by your good intents and meanings, and good desires whereof you are full. Nor by your great affections of zeal wherewith you abound above all people that we know or have heard of, that have any knowledge of the Gospel. We speak not of the ignorant, zealous papists that go before you and all the earth (that know the name of Jesus) in these things, which makes them think their estates most happy. Take you heed lest you be also still hereby deceived. We confess these are excellent things, if knowledge and faith go with them. Furthermore, your obedience unto the second and great commandment, which is, "Love thy neighbor as thyself,"[22] and all the particular duties thereof, as "Honor parents, do not commit adultery, kill, steal, bear false witness, covet nothing that is thy neighbors," in these excellent duties very many of you greatly abound, and we cannot but with great affections look upon you, and love you for them, yet know that many papists are nothing behind you in these things. Therefore, let not these things deceive you as though you had all things, because you have these. You see it testified by our Savior Christ that a man may have, or do all these things, and yet not follow Christ, as is showed in the example of that excellent ruler whom Christ "looked upon and loved" for those excellent things in him. (Mark 10:21) And therefore please not yourselves so much in those things, although we acknowledge they are worthy of great commendations in you, and our souls are much affected to you for them. But if you follow not Christ in the regeneration, that is, if you be not "born again of water and of the Spirit, and so enter into the kingdom of heaven,"[23] all is nothing, as you see by the example of this ruler. And Cornelius (Acts 10), if he had not been baptized with the Holy Ghost and

---

[22]Matthew 22:39.
[23]John 3:5.

with water, for all his prayers and alms he had not, nor could not have entered into the kingdom of heaven.

Thus entered all the people of God of whose entrance the scriptures give testimony, either by rule or by example, and thereof if there be any other entrance found out, it is not, nor cannot be of God. This only is the door which Jesus Christ has set open for all to enter in at, that enter into his kingdom. (John 3:5) And the Lord sanctify all your hearts with grace that you may enter therein. For no other way of salvation has Christ appointed but that men first believe and be baptized. (Mark 16:16)

Thus have we freely spoken the truth unto you from our hearts. Suspect us not of the least contempt or despite,[24] if we seem sharp. There are multitudes of you of that Puritan profession (so called) that know our love is most true and unfeigned to you all, and that we cannot but love and reverence you, and therefore we cannot the more seek your reformation, wish it, and pray for it. And we will not give the Lord rest until he hear us, that we may see your salvation accomplished.

---

[24]Spite.

Book IV

The next false profession of Christ, and false prophets among you, that we will (by God's assistance) speak of is that false profession and those false prophets which are usually called Brownists.[1] You are they that say you are Jews, but you are none, and have made yourselves a name to be the Separation, and are falsely so called, but are not, as through the help of God we shall make it plain by the Word of the Lord, both to your own consciences (if you will not always resist the truth) and also to the consciences of all others. And this we will do by those grounds of truth which you acknowledge, which you must be forced either to forsake, or else be convinced by them.

And the first ground is this, in your book called *The Apology*, the first part of your third position stands thus set down: "A true visible church is a company of people called and separated from the world by the Word of God, and joined together by a voluntary profession of the faith of Christ in the fellowship of God."[2] And by this means, that is, by the Word of God, and by this doing, that is, separating themselves from the world and joining together, (say you) they are become a true visible church. Now, to come to a full discovery of your false profession of Christ. Let it be observed that

---

[1] The early Separatist movement came to be identified with Robert Browne (ca. 1553–1633) who, along with Robert Harrison, friend from his days at Cambridge, moved beyond Puritanism to a repudiation of the established church. His views were set out in a series of books in 1582: *A Treatise of Reformation without tarrying for anie*, *A Treatise upon the 23 of Matthew*, and *A Book which sheweth the life and manner of all true Christians*. For Browne the church was constituted by believers who had willingly entered into a covenant with God. Though officers of the church receive their authority from God, they are called "by due consent and agreement of the church." After being imprisoned twice, Browne took his congregation into exile in the Netherlands.

[2] *An apologie or defence of such true Christians as are commonly called Brownists* (Amsterdam, 1604).

you confess you were of the world before you separated, which when you were, then were you enemies unto Christ, for Christ testifies the world hates him. (John 7:7) Then were you none of Christ's, for those that are Christ's, or of Christ, "are not of this world." (John 17:14) And now to become Christ's you say you are called and separated from the world by the Word of God, and joined together by voluntary profession of the faith of Christ in the fellowship of the Gospel. This is your constitution, wherein you have erred, as may plainly appear. For when you were called, and (as you say) separated, you should have joined to Christ, and have entered into his kingdom, which seeing you have not done, you are not separated from the world, nor have no fellowship in the Gospel. We confess the Lord has called unto you, and you have joined yourselves together in a voluntary profession, but you have not joined yourselves to Christ. And therefore is your profession a false profession, and you have a false Christ that is no Christ, as shall be hereafter plainly proved. And to show you that you are not joined to Christ, you being of the world before you constituted or set up your church by your own confessions, the Word of the Lord does evidently declare that there is no way for them that are of the world, who are not in Christ, but enemies to Christ, as all that are of the world are, there is no way to join and come to Christ, but only to "amend their lives, and be baptized." (Acts 2:38) And "all ye that are baptized into Christ have put on Christ." (Galatians 3:27) Let us now entreat you on God's behalf that you will no longer be fighters against God in contending against his truth, from the which we trust through the mercy of God, you shall not be able any longer to hide yourselves. For if all men that know God and his Son will not confess that infidels and unbelievers have no other way to come, and be joined to Christ, but only by believing and being baptized, then you that confess that you were of the world before you set up your church, must needs confess also that you were infidels and unbelievers. For you shall be ashamed to say that there are any believers of the world, seeing our Savior Christ says, "The world cannot receive the Spirit of truth." (John 14:17) And John 16:8-9, "The Comforter shall reprove the world of sin, because they believed not in me." And John 17:25, "O righteous Father, the world has not known thee." And John in his first Epistle, chapter 5:18-19, speaks thus, "We know that we are of God, and this whole world lies in wicked-ness." And this being the condition of them that are of the world: 1. They cannot receive the Spirit of truth. 2. That they believe not in Christ. 3. That they know not God. 4. That they lie in wickedness. You confessing yourselves to be of the world before you joined yourselves together in your voluntary profession, by a covenant of your own divisings (you being of the world), your condition was the same. Then were you without the Spirit of truth, unbelievers, not knowing God, lying all in wickedness. And so are you all infidels, and there was, nor is, no way for you to join unto Christ, but to "amend your lives and be baptized," and by baptism "to put on Christ," which seeing you have not done, you are still of the world. The Spirit of truth is not in you, you are infidels and unbelievers, you know not God, and you remain in your wickedness. And so is your profession a false profession of Christ, and you have not the true Christ, but a false Christ. And so is your baptism a worldly baptism brought out of the world, an ordinance of the world, and not the baptism and ordinance of Christ, whose baptism is not of the world, as he is not of the world.

Shall we need to lay down any other ground to convince you, and stop all your mouths? Is not this easy, plain and evident enough? What can be more plain? You confess (yourselves) you were of the world before you made your separation from England. And our Savior Christ says that they which are of the world believe not in him. And who will not grant that they that believe not in Christ are infidels or unbelievers? Then you, being of the world, were infidels or unbelievers, and the Holy Ghost teaches that infidels or unbelievers must amend their lives and be baptized and by baptism put on Christ. And our Savior Christ, giving a general direction to his disciples to preach the Gospel to all, gives likewise a general direction what all unbelievers must do if they will be saved. "They must believe and be baptized." (Mark 16:16) This straight are you now driven unto, either to confess that before your separation you were infidels or unbelievers, and then you must believe and be baptized, or else that you were believers and faithful, and have you separated from a faithful and believing people, and not from the world. And you must return to your vomit with that false prophet, your first and chief shepherd, that has misled you upon these false grounds, who not being able (through his infidelity) to keep his face towards Jerusalem and the land of Canaan, has fainted in the way, and rebelled in the wilderness, and is returned to his so much formerly detested Babylon and Egypt.[3]

---

[3]Ironically, the man whose name became synonomous with Separatism, Robert Browne, became disillusioned with his experience in the Separatist community in

And next let us show to you that your prophets are all false prophets. And although it be a full sufficient proof that they are false prophets because they are elected and ordained to their office by a congregation of infidels or unbelievers that are not joined to Christ, and have not put on Christ by baptism, yet we will further show them to be false prophets, because they prophesy lies, and by their lying wonders would if it were possible to deceive the very elect. These are deceitful workers, and transform themselves into the prophets of Christ, as though they were the ministers of righteousness, whose end (says the apostle) shall be according to their works. (2 Corinthians 11:13, 15) Yet they doing it ignorantly through unbelief, if they repent, may be received to mercy. (1 Timothy 1:13) But they must repent as Paul did, who left off being a persecutor, a blasphemer, and an oppressor, else he could never have been saved. So must they leave off being false prophets, seducers, and deceivers, or else they shall all be damned. (Revelation 19:20)

And first to show how your false prophets do transform themselves, whereby they are most dangerous deceivers and tempters. They in the forefront of their cry come with a main ground of truth, and this they utter with a loud voice, "It is fallen, it is fallen, Babylon that great city. Go out of her, my people," etc., and separate yourselves and come out. This is all their cry to bring the people from the assemblies of England. And then they run upon England and prove it Babel, and Babylon, we confess, with proof enough which, when they have done, working a just **distaste** in the hearts of some people of the spiritual abominations in those assemblies, so far as they themselves dislike. But being loath to cast Babylon clean on the ground, and utterly to make her naked and desolate, and to lay all her honor in the dust, and not being willing, through hardness of heart, and want of true zeal, and holiness to run the race to the end, and to separate themselves from all uncleanness, they teach you still to retain your first and chief badge or mark of Babylon, which is your baptism, wherein you receive

---

the Netherlands and returned to England in 1584. He made submission to the established church in 1585 and was appointed master of St. Olave's School the following year. Five years later he became rector of the village of Achurch, a position he held for twenty-five years. He was excommunicated in 1631, and in 1633 died in Northampton gaol, to which he had been committed for striking a constable. Michael R. Watts, *The Dissenters* (Oxford: Clarendon Press, Oxford, 1978) 33.

the seal of the covenant of grace, as they say, and teach you. And this you may not part with all upon any condition. Is there any false prophets like these prophets that will teach you to separate and, "Come out from Babylon, and to touch no unclean thing," and when they have done, teach you to retain the baptism received there, which they teach, and you profess to be the seal of the covenant of grace? So are you sealed into the covenant of grace by Babylon. So are you made Christians and members of Christ by Babylon, for without this baptism you are no Christians. Oh, how you cry out against the sweetness of the stolen waters of Babylon, and yet yourselves cannot beware thereof, but are bewitched therewith, the which you retain with as little understanding as when you received it, and were washed or baptized therewith. But your false prophets, to make good the retaining of your Babylonish baptism, like deep deceivers with turning of devices, plead that your baptism must be retained, and is not to be repeated, no more than Israel's circumcision, when they came to the Passover in Hezekiah's time. Oh, that all men would see your deceivableness of unrighteousness herein, that to draw simple people after you, and to build yourselves up a kingdom, you cry against the assemblies of England, "They are Babylon, Egypt, and Sodom. Separate yourselves. Be not unequally yoked with infidels. What fellowship has light with darkness? What concord has Christ with Belial? etc. Therefore, a . . .[4] must be cast away. No communion is to be kept." But when you are urged or called on for the retaining of our baptism you received in Babylon, then Israel's circumcision is your hold. So make you England Israel, and yourselves Judah, pretending hereby as though you came out of Israel. What deceitful deceiving is this? What turning of devices to cry, "Come out of Babylon, and touch no unclean thing," and to show and declare in all words and writings, that if any man worship the beast and his image, and receive his mark in his forehead or in his hand, he shall drink of the cup of God's wrath, applying this particularly to England, and when you have done, come forth sealed in the forehead with the seal of baptism (as you call it) having no other seal for your whole Christianity. For we hope you will not say that there may be a church of unbaptized Christians. And all this you prove good, because Israel's circumcision was good under Jeroboam. So make you a show in this particular as though you came out of Israel. But if your first cry had been,

---

[4]Word missing in text.

"Come out of Israel, and separate yourselves from Israel," you might have cried long enough before any that had feared God, or had any understanding of his truth, would have followed you to have built new churches, and set up a hierarchy of ruling elders, as they and you (brethren in evil therein also) have done. To draw to an end in this point: if you be come from Israel, then were you true Israelites before. Then all that you have left behind you are true Israelites, as well as you. For all the ten tribes under Jeroboam were true Israelites. And you and the assemblies of England from whence you came were all in one estate and condition of profession before you separated. And they still remain as you left them, and as you daily leave them. They are not Samaritans, if they were none before. If you like therefore to stand upon this ground, that you have brought your baptism from rebellious Israel, then you, Judah, must needs acknowledge Israel to be your sister. For the Lord testifies that Israel was Judah's sister. Neither did Judah ever deny Israel to be her sister. Therefore, may not you utterly cast off England that is your sister Israel.

And whereas you acknowledge in your book called, *The Apology* (page 113), through ignorant dissimulation and flattery, that you never doubted but "there are thousands in the Romish apostasy in England which receive not the beast's mark in their forehead or hand, but be careful to keep the commandments of God and faith of Jesus," must you not acknowledge, except you be destitute of all understanding, that these thousands that are baptized with the same baptism that you are, and that receive not the mark of the beast, and be careful to keep the commandments of God, and faith of Jesus, must you not acknowledge that these thousands are true church, or true churches as well as you? Dare you say more of yourselves? Whereby to challenge any preeminence, are you any more (if you were so much) than truly baptized, free from the mark of the beast, careful to keep the commandments of God and faith of Jesus? What dark blindness is this, and palpable words of flattery, to confess in words there are thousands in England's apostasy in as holy and blessed estate as any people of God can be, and when you have so done, both by practice, writing and teaching, deny all spiritual communion with any one of them, and not to suffer any one of them to have communion with you, except they make and submit to a new covenant with you, which covenant you have made according to the devisings of your own heart? What Zion have you built that will not open her gates to men (as you confess) truly baptized, having no mark of the beast, keeping the commandments of God and faith of Jesus? How woefully are you overtaken in these things. How can we think less of this, than that it is ignorant dissimulation and flattery, with such fair words to stop the mouths, and blind the eyes of Mr. Bilson[5] and the Oxford doctors? And when you had walled up that breach, and daubed it with mortar of deceitful temper, then to profess and practice the contrary. Thus do you when it will serve your turn, make England Israel, and when you please, it is Babylon, Sodom, and Egypt. And hereby have you a long time, and still do, like most subtle charmers, charm the simple and ignorant, so that they receive not the love of the truth, that they might be saved, building and holding up hereby your kingdom and throne. And if any incline to return from you to England again, then is England Sodom, Egypt, Babylon, and worse if worse could be. And if any make question of casting away that baptism or washing received there, then England is but rebellious Israel, and let her take away her fornications out of her sight, and her adulteries from between her breasts, and she may still be a wife. What can be said to this your deceitful double dealing? We must be forced to leave a simple double answer thus. If you were Babylonians, and have Babylon's baptism upon you, then have you no rule nor example that the Babylonian's circumcision could be accepted and admitted to the Passover. And if you were true Israelites before you separated, and have Israel's baptism upon you, and so become to Judah, then must you acknowledge Israel, from whence you are come (which is England), your sister. And so may you again go follow the voice of that old deceiver, that has so long bewitched you, who lies in wait for you, knowing that you cannot stand upon these grounds, but you must be forced either to cast away your baptism, or else return from whence you had it, except you will be the most willful blind people upon the whole earth that have any knowledge of Christ, of the which you give just cause of jealousy. Therefore, in God's fear, take heed, and perish not in your stiffnecked perverseness.

------

[5]Thomas Bilson, a respected academic and church leader, who after a distinguished scholarly career became bishop of Worcester and, later, bishop of Winchester. He was one of two bishops present at the Hampton Court Conference (1604). Along with Miles Smith, Bilson was one of the final editors of the Authorized Version of the Bible. A rigid episcopalian, Bilson wrote *A Compendium Discourse Proving Episcopcacy to Be of Divine Institution* (1593). He also wrote *The Perpetual Governement of Christes Church* (1593), and *The True Difference betweene Christian Subiection and unchristian rebellion* (1585).

To show yet further that you are false prophets, and prophecy lies, we produce out of your book subscribed with general subscription, your *Apology* (page 110), where you gainsay[6] Mr. Bilson for saying you affirm by consequence their sacraments no sacraments, and church no church. To clear yourselves of this imputation, you teach that "we must be careful in all such causes always to discern and distinguish between a true church, a false church, and no church, between true sacraments, false sacraments, and no sacraments." Your proof and example is: "Judah, a true church; the ten tribes of Israel, a false church; the Philistines and other the like, no church. And so at this day, the Turks and pagans may be reputed no churches, the Romish synagogue and all her daughters false churches, the Christians which be set in the true faith and order true churches." Thus you say the difference may be put. But you are all false prophets herein and teach lies. These are but the devices of your own hearts. These are your school distinctions whereby you pervert the holy word of truth. And we exhort all the people of God to take heed of you when you distinguish, and when you bring your matters about with "in a respect and in a double respect," not but that we hold it lawful to use distinctions, and to show respects, but because you usually deceive thereby. There is no truth of God so evident, but with your distinctions and respects, and twofold, you will pervert it. And when you are not able with evidence of truth to maintain your false wares, then your distinctions and respects must make it good, whereby you ensnare the simple, and compass them about as with a thick mist, wherein they cannot see which way to go, but are fain through hardness of heart and infidelity (which are causes of their ignorance and blindness) to give their hearts to you to be led. And you like deceitful blind guides lead them into the pit, as in this particular in hand, wherein if you be overthrown and discovered, your whole cause is thus far destroyed, as you are all yet once again proved infidels and unbelievers. And we doubt not but by the gracious aid and help of our God, we shall be able by his Word to convince you all herein, without whose great help and aid, we in humility confess, we are not able to withstand such strange and wise adversaries of his truth as you are, who do exercise your fellows to deceive. Our own experiences and knowledge of you causes us thus to speak. We hope you do it ignorantly, or else there were no hope of your repentance and salvation.

---

[6]To deny or dispute.

To the point in hand we say and prove by the Word of God that you can in no ordinance of God distinguish or put difference by the warrant of God's Word between false and none, and your vain distinction will hold only in worldly things, and you are carnal herein and sold under sin. Blame us not, though we reprove you sharply for this, because you have deceived yourselves and the whole world hereby, so far as your voices have sounded, and you have and do daily destroy the faith of many.

We proceed to prove that you cannot by God's Word distinguish nor put difference between false and none in God's ordinances. And this the eternal Word of truth does show (Revelation 2:2) where the Holy Ghost speaking of false apostles commends the church of Ephesus, for "examining them which said they were apostles, but were none and were found liars." And (v.9) "know the blasphemy of them which say they are Jews but are none, but are the synagogue of Satan." And (in) Revelation 3:9 the same words are uttered by the Holy Ghost. Thus does the Spirit of God teach us that a false church is no church, but a synagogue of Satan, and false apostles are no apostles, so then are false sacraments no sacraments. And so false and none in God's ordinances are all one, and you cannot distinguish nor put difference between them. And for further manifestation of the truth hereof, let us refer the things that are of God to God, and so shall it appear to all but those that will not see that there is no difference nor distinction to be made in God's ordinances between false and none. As thus: a true church of Christ; a false church; and no church. If now a false church be not no church of Christ, then it is a false church of Christ. So is there two sorts or kinds of churches of Christ, and so should Christ have two bodies, a true body, and a false body. What a blasphemy is this, when the apostle says, "There is but one body." So likewise if you say, there is a true faith of Christ, a false faith, and no faith of Christ, if a false faith and no faith be not all one, then there are two faiths of Christ, a true faith, and a false faith of Christ. But apostle says, "There is but one faith." In like manner, if you will say, as you do, that there is a true baptism, a false baptism, and no baptism, if a false baptism and no baptism be not all one, then is there two baptisms. But the apostle says, "There is but one baptism." And of all these there is but one, as "there is but one God and Father of all, which is above all, and through all," (Ephesians 4:4,5,6) who if he were in you all, you would submit to this his truth, and never open your mouths more against it. Cast away these your logical distinctions, which are fit to distinguish between a false hour glass and no hour glass, and a false looking glass and no looking glass, and not fit to distinguish between a false baptism and no baptism, a false church and no church, between which your Holy Ghost admits of no distinction nor difference. We conclude therefore with the word of truth against all these your deceitful distinctions and lying prophecies, that a false church is no church of Christ at all, for Christ has no false church. Therefore, you holding England a false church, it is no church of Christ, and so your false baptism is no baptism of Christ. And so you are infidels, unbelievers, and false Christians, that is, no Christians, and you are they that say, "You are Jews and are not, but are the synagogue of Satan."[7] And let this suffice for the overthrow of your most false and deceitful distinction.

And whereas you bring for your proof of a true church, a false church, and no church, and say, Judah was a true church, Israel, a false church, and the Philistines no church, these are but your own sayings and devisings without proof, whereby you have and do mightily deceive, although your words be without understanding. For Israel was a true church as Judah was. For the Israelites were the true seed of Abraham, separated from the world under the covenant of God, which was the covenant of circumcision (Genesis 17:7-15), as well as Judah in Hezekiah's time, when they came to the Passover. And if they had been false Israelites, then had their circumcision been false, and they had been a false church. So had they been no seed of Abraham, no Israelites, their circumcision no circumcision, and so no church. For a **full** conclusion and a certain rule of direction from the Word of God, whereby the people of God may try all your deceitful distinctions of this kind, when you put difference between true, false, and none, in or of any ordinance of God, let all observe, and would to God you yourselves would be informed, that God and his laws and ordinances are one, (John 14:6) of equal power, authority, and truth, and therefore you can no more say, a true church, a false church, and no church, a true baptism, a false baptism, and no baptism, which are holy ordinances of God, than you can say a true God, a false God, and no God. And your distinction will hold no more between a false church, and no church, a false baptism and no baptism, than between a false God and no God. And if a false God be no God, then a false church is no church of God, and a false baptism is no baptism of Christ. Your false church then, being as is showed and proved

---

[7]Revelation 3:9.

no church of God, then it is the synagogue of Satan, and your false baptism being no baptism of Christ, then it is the baptism of Satan. The Lord give you to consider of your estates and standings herein, that although your contempt of us is, and has been great, yet you may not still **(uncertain)** Christ and his truth the means of your salvation, though witnessed by us, that are so much despised in your eyes.

Having thus showed you by evidence of truth that you bringing your false baptism out of a false church (both which yourselves confess), your baptism is no baptism, and that false church is no church, this being made plain, as the indifferent may judge, we will try Mr. Robinson's ground for this retained baptism, who will be found to make haste to deceive with as many windings and turnings as any, and be not altogether trusting to bring his baptism from Israel, he strives with all deceitful skill to prove that their baptism is true in one respect, though brought from Babylon. And this matter he undertakes after this manner, in his book of justification of separation (pp. 184-85)[8] He commends to the reader a distinction of a two-fold respect. "Baptism," says Mr. Robinson, "is to be considered first nakedly, and in the essential causes: the matter, water; the form, washing with water into the name of the Father, etc." These are the essential causes of Mr. Robinson. Naked baptism in this respect, he confesses true baptism both in England and Rome. Mr. Robinson, shall we speak angrily to you, and mourn for the hardness of your heart, and great blindness and ignorance? Have you lost the beginnings of knowledge in the mystery of godliness? Is all light shut from your eyes, and all truth debarred from your understanding, that you should write thus, that water, and washing, and words are the essential causes or matter of baptism? If you had known Christ, of whose baptism you pretend to speak, you would never have written thus. Do you know that Christ's kingdom is a spiritual kingdom, his ordinances spiritual ordinances? And will you confess this with your tongue, and with your tongue and deeds deny it? Which that it may appear plainly you do, consider with yourself, and let all that seek the Lord in spirit and truth consider with what understanding you can say that naked water, washing, and words are the essential causes of a spiritual baptism. Thus do you spoil men through philosophy and vain deceit, in which iniquity you

---

[8]John Robinson, *The Works of John Robinson*, vol. 2, ed. R. Ashton (London, 1851).

abound. Away with your naked respect, and be counseled to buy "white raiment that you may be clothed, that your vile nakedness do not appear."[9] Know you not that "all they that are baptized into Christ have put on Christ"? And do you come with your philosophy to teach simple souls a naked baptism, and make it good with respects? The Lord give you grace to see your greatest evil herein. And the Lord deliver his poor people from these your deceitful ways. And the Lord give them to learn to know from the Word of God that there is but one baptism of Christ, (Ephesians 4:5) and that whosoever is baptized into Christ has put on Christ, or is clothed with Christ. (Galatians 3:27) And therefore whosoever shall walk with your naked baptism shall be found naked at the day of Christ's appearing, though you piece it and patch it with green leaves. And for your essential causes, lay down plainly what baptism you speak of, and you shall be convinced in yourself. As thus: if you say of Christ's baptism, which is spiritual, that the essential matter thereof is earthly water, would not your ignorance easily appear? The like of your form, if you should say that the form of spiritual baptism is bodily washing only with bare words, your own understanding would reprove you. It were to be wished. And you have often been required to lay away your school terms in the causes of God, whereby you do for the most part but hide the truth, and blind the eyes of the simple. Now do you think the simple should understand you in the essential causes, and matter, and form of baptism? Do the scriptures show that any of the holy men of God did ever thus distinguish? If your art had been good or profitable, could not our Savior Christ have used it for the manifestation of his truth? And would he not have endued his apostles with that gift? Yes, the Lord endued them with the most excellent gifts for the evident declaration of his truth, whereof logic and philosophy was none, which vain sciences if you had not used you could never have forged so many deceits as you have in your book. And now we desire you to know that the scriptures teach not any baptism that is in one respect true, and in the other respect false. There is no such thing in the whole Word of God. These are but your own devices, wherein you divide Christ, to serve your own turns to deceive, persuading men that they are in one respect truly baptized, and in another respect falsely baptized, and if they will come and walk in your way, and join to your societies, you can make that part which was false, true. What popery

---

[9]Revelation 3:18.

is this to take upon you to dispense with the false administrations in the ordinances of Christ? Thus do you run into dark places while you forsake the lantern that should light your paths, which light of truth teaches you, and all men, that the baptism of Christ is "the baptism of amendment of life, for the remission of sins." (Mark 1:4) And our Savior Christ says, "Except a man be born of water and of the Spirit, he cannot enter into the kingdom of God." (John 3) And Hebrews 10:22, "Let us draw near with a true heart in assurance of faith, our hearts being pure from evil confidence, and washed in our bodies with pure water."

Here is the true baptism set down, which is the baptism of amendment of life for the remission of sins. And here is the true matter where men must be washed, which is water and the Holy Ghost, that is pure from a evil conscience, and washed with water. Therefore can you not divide the water and the Spirit in this baptism. Christ has joined them together, and he that denies washing, or is not washed with the Spirit is not baptized, and he that denies washing, or is not washed with water, is not baptized, because we see the baptism of Christ is to be washed with water and the Holy Ghost. And to take away a subtle exception, if a man be in prison, or any place, and be converted to the Lord, and would be baptized with water but cannot, he is accepted with God, "who accepts the will for the deed" (2 Corinthians 8:12), and herein is the Lord's mercy equal with his justice. For if a man's heart consent to evil, he is guilty, although he do it not. (Matthew 5:27-28)

Thus much to discover the great deceitfulness of your way in the first respect of your false distinction, wherein you would prove only the essential matter, water, and washing with water, and words, the essential form. We pass by your form of words, because we think you will not stand upon it, in that you see there is no certain form of words held. (Acts 10:48 and 19:5) And take this with you to consider of, that if there were any truth in your distinction and respect, then were any washing with water, with those words, the true matter and form of Christ's baptism. And so if any child baptized another with water and those words, it is true baptism in that respect. And let the child come and join to you, and you can make it good in all respects. Pass not these things over as you have done, for you are not able to answer them with any true understanding from God's Word. And so we come to your second respect.

Secondly, you say, "Baptism is to be considered clothed with such appurtenances as wherewith the Lord has appointed it to be administered, as, for example, a lawful person by whom, a right subject upon which, a true communion wherein it is to be administered and dispensed," in which regard you say you do not "approve it to be true baptism either in Rome or England." If darkest error did not possess your heart, you could never have written such things. But that we know your stiffness in your false ways we should pity to point out your palpable ignorance in these things. Did ever man of any understanding in religion write thus? You are lighter than vanity herein. Will any man that has any knowledge of God be so blind as not to see how the spirit of error does lead you to justify that a baptism where there is neither the Spirit of God, lawful minister, right subject, nor true communion is the true baptism and ordinance of Christ in the essential parts thereof?

Has the like ignorance appeared in these days, especially among men that will cry out for proof by scripture in all things? If this your ground were true, then a Turk baptizing a Turk with water and those words in any assembly whatsoever is the true baptism of Christ in the essential parts thereof. See what rocks you run upon while you forsake the way of truth? It may now appear no **marvel**, though you would have baptism to be nakedly considered, you have made a most naked baptism and ordinance of Christ of it. First, where there is no Spirit of God, no lawful minister, no right party to be baptized, no true communion, it may well be called a naked baptism, and you a naked man of all grace and godly understanding to maintain it for a true baptism and ordinance of Christ, in any respect. If all this will not serve to convince you, we will yet smite you with the rod of iron, and break you like the potter's vessel in this point. You profess and acknowledge that baptism comes in the head of circumcision. Then let all men judge whether if circumcision being administered by an unlawful person, upon no right subject, and in no true communion, could ever have been approved for the true ordinance of God in the essential causes thereof, and whether one so circumcised could upon any conditions have been admitted to the Passover. You will (we hope) be destitute of all devices to answer this. All those that are any way indifferent between you and us will see your great error herein, that if a Babylonian had circumcised a Babylonian in their Babylonish assemblies, that circumcision had not been in any respect the ordinance of God, and such a one could upon no condition have been admitted to the Passover by that circumcision. Now to show that you hold England Babylon in your book, throughout it appears, but we especially hold you to these (pp. 277 and 338) where you affirm "that Rome and England were never within the covenant of God, as Judah was." So have you debarred yourself from bringing your circumcision, and so your baptism from apostate Israel. And therefore you must hold yourself to this, to prove circumcision administered in Babylon by an unlawful person, upon a wrong subject, and in no true communion, you must prove such a circumcision the ordinance of God in any respect, and that one so circumcised might be admitted to the Passover. Prove this, and we will confess that your skill is above all men's herein, and Ezra and Nehemiah shall be reproved by you for causing the people to put away the children that were born of the strange wives in Babylon, (Ezra 10:3 and Nehemiah 13:23, 24, 25) of whom, if you make question whether they were circumcised, you **cavil**[10] without color. For then had the Israelites been guilty of the breach of the Lord's covenant, whereby they were commanded to circumcise all their males in their household. But we will leave you to prove your Babylonian circumcision to be in any respect the ordinance of God, and prove it by scripture, and by sound reasoning from the ground of scripture, and not by logic and natural philosophy, showing things in nature to be true, which will not in spirit be proved true. And thus do you deceive natural men, and yourself, as in this point in hand, because with your carnal eyes and ears you see and hear water, and washing, with such words to be used in the administration of the Lord's baptism, therefore you, according to your natural understanding, judge these things to be the essential causes of spiritual baptism, and teach simple souls that these things being once truly done, they are not to be repeated or done again, when they are wholly natural actions, and profanely done, as you confess, and therefore can in no resect be said to be the baptism of Christ, which is wholly a spiritual action, and ought holily to be performed and done. Thus do you make the ignorant believe that you can put the spirit of grace into natural actions formerly profanely done, and make the same actions spiritual and acceptable to God.

Thus do you make midwives' baptism good and the holy ordinance of God in the essential causes. So can you make all the profane waters and sermons in plays (which are usual) holy, and good actions, and the ordinances of God. This then is your rule (deny it if you can), every washing with water into the name of the Father, etc., is the true baptism and ordinance of Christ, in the essential causes thereof, by whomsoever administered, and upon whatsoever person or thing. This may be good in

---

[10]To raise trivial or frivolous objection.

logic and philosophy, but this is blasphemous, cursed doctrine in divinity. And woe are we for you that ever such abominations should be uttered by you. We are ashamed to follow you in the particular application of these things, which if they should be urged to the full, it would make every heart that had any grace, and knows you, tremble, and grieve for you. This has your logic and philosophy brought you to, whereby you have confounded many a simple heart, and weak understanding, and whereby (you think) you have a privilege to understand the meaning of God in the scriptures before them that are ignorant of these arts. But now has the Lord confounded you in them. Glory be his name. And the Lord give you a heart to acknowledge it, and to repent, and deny yourself, and give glory to God. We will omit to speak of your improper speech, saying that baptism must be "clothed with a right person upon whom it must be administered." Thus to make your matters to agree, you speak preposterous things, for the party must put on and be clothed with baptism, and not baptism be clothed with the party.

The next thing that (by the help of our God) we will endeavor to discover you to be a false prophet, and a deceiver, in a strong ground you have, whereupon you much rely and often repeat it in your book, and that is this. You say, "Baptism is the vessel of the Lord, and as when the house of the Lord was destroyed, and the vessels thereof, together with the people were carried into Babylon, they remained still the vessels of the Lord's house in nature, and right, though profaned by Belshazzar and made quaffing bowls, and being brought again out of Babylon to the house of the Lord were not to be new cast, but (being purified) might again be used to holy use. So this holy vessel baptism though profaned in Babylon being brought again to the house of the Lord, remains still the holy vessel of the Lord." (9) This is a strong doctrine from example both with you and all the rest of the false prophets of your profession. And no marvel though you deceive greatly herein, because the doctrine and example is good, but most deceitfully misapplied of you. For you pretend hereby as though your baptism were brought from the house of the Lord, as the holy vessels were. Will you, if there be any uprightness in you, show how, and from what house of the Lord your holy vessel of baptism was brought? You show us plainly from whence you have brought it again out of Babylon, that is England. But out of what house of God came it, before it came into Babylon (that is, England), that is not showed. How deceitfully do you feign these things. These are the imaginations of your own vain hearts. For have any of you brought your baptism from the house of the Lord into England?

Have you any other root or foundation for your baptism than England? Do not all men know that your vessel of Babylon was composed, formed, framed, and made there? How shall any man be able to open his mouth to deny this? Why then, your holy vessel (falsely so called) was made in Babylon. Thus are you found false dissemblers to say and feign that your baptism is a vessel brought out of the house of the Lord into Babylon, as the vessels of the temple were, when it is more evident that it was molded and made in the Church of England, which you confess is Babylon. Mr. Robinson, had not you and all your congregation the true matter (as you call it) and true form of your baptism in England? And was it not administered upon you all in the assemblies of England? Then was your vessel of baptism made there. See your deceit herein, if there be any grace or understanding in you, and how has Satan seduced you, and your own heart deceived you. Now the Lord Jesus give you a heart to repent, and in the name of the Lord, we beseech you repent, for you have been and are a malicious adversary of God's truth, and you lead many souls in the way of destruction. The Lord for his Christ's sake deliver you out of these and all the snares of Satan. And the Lord deliver his people out of the net wherein you have like a cunning fowler taken them and overcome them. And we pray you that you will with patience suffer us to show you how you are all deceived in this point, in saying baptism is the vessel of the Lord's house, and brought from thence, and so apply it to your own baptism, which you may see, if you do not both wink and cover your eyes, never came out of the house of the Lord, except you will say, the Church of England is the house of the Lord, which we hope the Lord's Word has convinced to all your consciences that it is not. Therefore your baptism cannot be the vessel of the Lord's house, but it is the true doctrine or ordinance of baptism that may be said or called by way of comparison the vessel of the Lord's house. And this we and all must needs confess is the vessel of the Lord's house, whethersoever it is carried either to Rome or England, and though it is polluted and profaned there, as both it and many other doctrines and ordinances of the Lord are. Yet being purged from those errors and abuses, wherewith both they and you have and do pollute them, they may, and ought to be brought into the house of the Lord again, and remain holy vessels unto the Lord forever. But the corrupt pollutions and administrations in this holy vessel or ordinance of baptism, wherewith it has been defiled and profaned, these may no more be brought into the house of God than Balshazzar's quaffings, or any other profane administrations wherewith he did abuse and pollute those holy vessels. Yea, although he had used them to the same uses the which they had been used in the house of the Lord, as if he had set shew bread upon the vessels, and had kindled and made the same lights for the candlesticks, all must be cast away as abominable, with all the uses that he has used them unto, and the vessels must be purified and brought again into the house of the Lord only as they were carried forth. Therefore, even so must this holy vessel, the true doctrine or ordinance of baptism, be brought again into the house of the Lord only as it was carried forth, and all the corrupt uses and abuses whereunto it has been used, and all the profane administrations in this holy ordinance must be cast away as being all abominable before the Lord. And none of those uses, and profane and false administrations may be admitted into the house of the Lord. This now is the sum of all that we have spoken of this ground: the vessels of the Lord's house are carried into Babylon, and Belshazzar and his princes, his wives and concubines drink in them and profane them. The vessels of the Lord are brought again to the house of the Lord, and are sanctified, but Belshazzar's drinkings in them and profaning of them is cast away as abominable. So the like may be said, following your own example of comparison: the vessel of the Lord's house, the holy ordinance of baptism, is carried into Babylon, and the Babylonians, they wash or baptize in this ordinance, and profane it. This vessel of the Lord, the holy ordinance of baptism, is brought again to the house of the Lord, but the Babylonians washing, or baptizing, and profaning it must be cast away as abominable. And thus must your baptizing be cast away and may not be permitted in the house of the Lord, you confessing England to be Babylon where you received it, except you will also admit Belshazzar's drinkings and quaffings. Do not still deceive yourself and delude others in saying baptism is the vessel of the Lord, making a deceitful show, as though therefore your baptism were the vessel of the Lord, and by an example of the vessels of the Lord that were brought forth of the house of the Lord, and carried into Babylon and polluted there in use only, and being sanctified from that polluted use, were brought again into the house of the Lord, by this example to bring in an imagination, as though your baptism were brought out of the house of the Lord, when it is brought forth of the assemblies of England, with whom you justify God never made covenant and that they were never his people, nor God their God. (page 338) You err not knowing the scriptures, or else will fully misapply them for your purpose (which God forbid). For it is the ordinance of baptism that is the vessel of the Lord's house which has been, and is carried into Babylon, and has been polluted in use in baptizing of you and all of your profession, which vessel or ordinance of the Lord is to be brought again into the house of the Lord, and to be sanctified from that polluted use of your baptizing, which it cannot be if it bring that polluted use which is your baptizing into the house of the Lord with it, no more than the vessels of the Lord could have been sanctified if Belshazzar's quaffings had been brought into the house of the Lord with them. And this is a due proportion according to your own example of comparison.

We will pass by many things in your book wherein there is great falsehood and deceit, because it were an endless work to follow you. You are so intricate, tedious, and full of turnings and windings, losing yourself and losing such simple readers as we are. And that is one hope we have of your book, that the simple will not read it, because they are not capable of understanding you. And among them that are as full of art as yourself we think it will do small hurt. We cannot deny but there are many worthy truths in it, but mixed with so much falsehood as the reader had need to be wise-hearted. And in that you and all the false prophets of your profession do mix your falsehood with divers truths, all God's people had need to beware of you. For that is your sheep's clothing, by the fair show whereof you ensnare, and work your lying wonders, as when you smite men's hearts to the ground with laying out the deformities of Babylon, and **ravish** their affections with the description of your Zion (falsely so-called), declaring the beauty and supposed comely order thereof, and setting forth the communion of saints, as with the tongue of an angel of light. Thus, do you deck your bed with ornaments, carpets, and laces and perfume it with myrrh, aloes, and cinnamon, and so with your great craft to cause men to yield, and with flattering lips you entice many, straight following you as an ox that goes to the slaughter, and as a fool to the stocks for correction. And they are stricken thorough as a bird that hastens to the snare, not knowing he is in danger. Of such has the wise man by the wisdom of the Spirit forewarned us. (Proverbs 7)[11]

We have endeavored to show you your halting between Babylon and Israel. We exhort you to tread straight steps before the Lord. And that men may see your paths to be straight, show us the writing of your genealogy, that we may see certainly from which you are come. If you be come from

---

[11]Proverbs 7:16-17, 21-23.

Israel, and be Judah, then war not against England as against Babylonians, but remember they are the ten tribes, your brethren, (1 Kings 12:24) which ten tribes were not false Israelites, but the true seed of Abraham and so true Israelites. For the two calves set up at Dan and Bethel did no more make them false Israelites than the calf which they made in Horeb. And this wickedness of Jeroboam did no more make Israel a false church than Solomon his wickedness made Judah a false church when he followed Ashtaroth, the god of the Zidonians, and Milcom the abomination of the Amorites, and builded high places for Chemosh, the abomination of Moab, and to Molech, the abomination of Ammon, in the mountain over against Jerusalem. And who knows not that reads the scriptures that Judah abounded in abominations, in so much as the Lord by the prophet Ezekiel (chapter 16) says of Judah, "Samaria has not committed half their sins, but thou hast exceeded them in all their abominations." And (in) verse 15 the Lord by the prophet called Judah an harlot because of the greatness of her fornications. And yet all this made not Judah a false church. If therefore you hold or account England as Israel, then must you hold and account England a true church. For it is but your devisings to say Israel was a false church. And if England be as Israel a true church, then are all your sins exceeding great, who have made such a separation as you have. And if you be come from Babylon, then look the whole book of God throughout, and you shall find that no Babylonian circumcision could be admitted to the house of the Lord. And let all behold in the book of the Revelation what the estate and condition of Babylon is, and of all them that are in her, and how the voice of the Lord is, "Come out of her, my people." And, "if any shall worship the beast and his image, and receive his mark in his forehead, or in his hand or receive the print of his name, he shall drink of the wine of the wrath of God."[12] Therefore there may nothing be retained that is brought from Babylon, no mark, nor print of the name. And will you bring the print, seal, and name of your Christianity from thence? What veil of darkness overspreads your hearts therein? You are deceived through the vain imaginations of your own hearts, supposing that although you come out of Babylon yet you were not Babylonians. But it you hold the assemblies of England Babylon (as you declare you do), then except you can show your genealogy that you, with your vessel of baptism (which is your baptizing),

---

[12]Revelation 14:9.

were brought from Jerusalem, and out of the house of the Lord (which were double folly to go about), then must you be content to know yourselves that you were Babylonians, and yet are **(uncertain)** that your seal of Christianity is the seal of Babylon. And so are you but Babylonian Christians, and servants of the beast, bearing the beasts' mark, title, and name in your foreheads. And whereas you and all the rest of the false prophets of your profession do in flattery and dissimulation, not knowing the mystery of godliness, affirm and acknowledge of the assemblies in England that there are thousands among them that truly fear God, alluding to the seven thousand in Israel, you make them believe thereby that they stand in the state of grace and salvation. So do you prophecy peace and salvation where the Lord prophecies destruction. For the Lord prophecies that all that come not forth of Babylon shall be partakers of her plagues and that whosoever yields in obedience or bears mark of the beast "shall be tormented with fire and brimstone." (Revelation 14) But you prophecy that there are thousands in England (which you acknowledge to be Babylon) who receive not the beast's mark and that are careful to keep the commandments of God and faith of Jesus, and that truly fear God. If such be not in the estate of salvation then no flesh is or can be. But this cannot be the estate of anyone in Babylon, which (if you understood the mystery of godliness) you might **easily** see. For the bondage of Babylon is spiritual bondage, and all that are in Babylon are in spiritual bondage, and none that are in spiritual bondage can be in the estate of grace and salvation. For all that are in the estate of grace and salvation must "stand fast in the liberty wherewith Christ has made them free," and may not "be in entangled with the yoke of bondage." (Galatians 5:1) "And where the spirit of the Lord is there is liberty." (2 Corinthians 3:17) Add unto this that which is formerly showed, that all that come not forth of Babylon must perish with Babylon. Deceive not yourselves therefore, and flatter not them of England. For there is no one person either of them or you (we speak of persons of understanding) that are in the estate of grace or salvation, or shall ever be saved, if you come not forth of Babylon, and cast away the mark of the beast, wherewith you all are marked. (Revelation 19:20-21) We exhort you all therefore that by grace in Christ you work out your own salvation with fear and trembling, or else you perish from the highest to the lowest. The King of Kings, the Lord of Lords has said it, that Babylon shall be destroyed with all that are found in her. (Jeremiah 51:6; Revelation 18:4)

We will now conclude with you, putting in your remembrance, that seeing no distinction nor difference can be made between a false and no church, but they are both one, for a false church are they that say and make show they are a true church but are not, as false apostles are they that say and make show they are apostles and are not (2 Corinthians 11:13), and false Jews are they that say and make show they are Jews and are not. (Revelation 2) This your distinction being utterly overthrown so as you shall never be able to open your mouths to maintain it, but the simplest soul among you shall be able to discover your deceit, your whole false building is at once fallen to the ground. For a false church being no church, then England being by you all judged to be a false church is no church. So is your baptism brought out of no church, and your false baptism is no baptism. And thus shall the simplest among you be able to say to you, is our baptism that we had in England a false baptism? Then it is no baptism. Then are we not baptized. And to this you shall never to answer them, although you should set your souls to **(uncertain)** God's truth and their souls. So likewise if you tell them that England is a false church, they shall say unto you, then is it no church. And you shall not know which way to contradict them, in that the scriptures do teach that a false church is no church, as a false God is no God, a false Christ, no Christ, a false apostle, no apostle, so is a false ordinance no ordinance of Christ, a false baptism no baptism of Christ. Thus we doubt not but (through the grace of God) we shall see by the **brightness** of Christ's coming that your dark deceitful ways will be discovered to the simplest, and you shall be ashamed to speak of a false baptism, and to **say**, it is **partly** the true baptism of Christ, and partly the baptism of the devil, and so join Christ and Beelzebub together, and make them partners in one baptism. We hope the fear of God will teach you better wisdom than thus still to be blaspheme for the supporting of your kingdom of darkness. And if you were not a stiff-necked people, and of uncircumcised and hearts and **ears**, you would not thus long with contempt and violence have resisted the truth of God, as you have done and do, persecuting it with bitter envyings and railings, **for** the which the Lord may justly give you up to hardness of heart. But the Lord in great mercy shall show mercy upon you all that do it ignorantly. We having from the Word of God showed you all the evidence of truth that we are for the present able to do, that your distinction between the false church and no church is vain and feigned, and that the Word of God admits of no such distinction in the Lord's ordinances, but that which is a false ordinance of God is no ordinance of God. For God has no false ordinances. You must therefore be forced to hold and say of the assemblies of England that they are either true churches of Christ or no churches of Christ. And if you hold them no churches of Christ, then can you not with any manner of show of **(uncertain)** say that you may retain your baptism which you have received in no church of Christ, but in a church or congregation of infidels and unbelievers, which you must needs account them if they be no church of Christ. For now all people in the world are either of the world, or chosen out of the world, and those are Christ's disciples. (John 15:19) And all people are either with Christ or against Christ. "He that is not with me is against me," says Christ. (Matthew 12:30). It is now high time to leave off halting between opinions and **(uncertain)** one another in their sins. It is time now to leave off talking of separation, and to separate indeed, and to tell the people of God their sins, and show them their transgressions, and not to account them Christians that by the hearing of the Word do become almost Christians as King Agrippa did, but to show them that if they do not become altogether Christians they must be content to be accounted infidels as Agrippa was. For all the world are either believers or infidels. If there be any knowledge of God in men they will grant thus. And who will not grant that all that believe in Christ Jesus are holy and elect, and shall be saved, if they continue to the end? Concerning England therefore, you must "either make the tree good and the fruit good or the tree evil and the fruit evil."[13] If the faith of the Church of England is a true faith, then is the Church of England a true church. And if the faith be a false faith, then it is a false church, that is, no faith of Christ and no church of Christ. And if their faith be no faith of Christ, then are they all infidels and unbelievers, of whom, although you have so accounted by your working toward them, yet by your words you declare to be otherwise when you are urged to speak plainly, though in your writings you show them to be infidels when you affirm that God never made covenant with them. But you have too long walked deceitfully in this point. Therefore, we press you to it, if you profess uprightness either to God or men, to manifest in all plainness whether you hold the assemblies of England believers in Christ. Let us have no respects, no double respects, nor no putting of differences of persons. For all the church of England are one body, "seeing they all drink of one cup," (1

---

[13]Matthew 12:33.

Corinthians 12) and if you hold them believers in Christ, and truly baptized into his name, then are they your brethren. And you may not "account them as enemies but admonish them as brethren." (2 Thessalonians 3:14-15) Then is your separation most wicked, and your building of new churches contrary to all rule of scripture, and you have falsely applied the voice of the angel, crying against England, "Babylon is fallen, she has fallen. Come out of her." If they be believers in Christ Jesus, the voice of this angel cannot applied unto them. You must walk toward them by another rule, even by that rule which Christ has appointed, that all should walk by toward their brethren if they sin, (Matt:18) and not separate from them and build churches upon new foundations. If in this our writing concerning you called Brownists we be judged to convince sharply, we hold it lawfully done, because you are a forward generation, and great deceivers of minds, making a glorious vain show to come out of Babylon, but do not. And not withstanding that we have written in some things sharply, we could desire to be freed from forward suspects, which you **might** free us from, the rather because there are divers of you both near and dear unto us whom we require in love (as we do all) to apply the sharpest reproofs to themselves, for they had need.

And touching you, Mr. Robinson, remember that you have a letter of most loving respect in your hands concerning these things, to which you have not made answer, whereby to prevent the publishing of this that specially concern you.

Now, as we have said unto you called Brownists in this point, so say we to England, and to the presbytery. If the pope and they of that profession be believers in Christ Jesus, and be truly believers into his name, then have you of England and all the nations of the earth sinned greatly to separate from Rome in that you were all of one body, and members of one another. And being believers in Christ Jesus, they are your brethren. And you ought to walk toward them as brethren, and ought not to separate from Rome as you have done, and do, and build new churches every one upon several foundations. If you of England, and the presbytery, and you called Brownists, did make any conscience to walk by the rules of Christ herein, you would not walk toward Rome as you do. If you hold them believers in Christ Jesus, and truly baptized into his name, which if they be then are all the scriptures that are applied against Rome to prove her Babylon, and that great whore that sits upon many waters, and upon the scarlet colored beast, and Antichrist, all these scriptures are misapplied to Rome, these cannot be applied to any persons or people that are believers in Christ Jesus, and have put on Christ by baptism. And there is no voice of the Lord that calls to come out from believers in Christ Jesus. The scriptures teach no such thing. Therefore, Brownists must return to the Church of England, and the Church of England and the presbytery must return to Rome, and be all sheep of one sheepfold, and repent of your unjust separation from the body whereof you were, and are all members. We say, are all members because by one Spirit you are all baptized into one body, and though you say you are not of the body with the church of Rome, are you not of the body? (1 Corinthians 12:13-15) You have and do all by one baptism put on Christ, and you all have brought that your baptism from Rome. And so are you all Christians and believers by succession from Rome. And you all account Rome believers in Christ. Therefore, though you say you are not of one body with Rome, yet you are all members of one body with Rome.

Furthermore, if Rome be believers in Christ Jesus, then are these prophecies of scripture nowhere to be found fulfilled upon the whole earth. First, the prophecy of Christ (Matthew 24) "of the abomination of desolation set in the holy place," is not to be seen. The "days of such great tribulation as was not from the beginning of the world, in which days no flesh shall be saved, and except they should be shortened, all flesh should be condemned," these days are not yet heard of. And the prophecy of Daniel the prophet (9:2:7; 12:11), who prophesied that "the sacrifices and the oblations shall cease, and the daily sacrifices shall be taken away." This prophecy cannot yet be come to pass, if Rome be believers in Christ, and that their sacrifices and oblations be the true sacrifices and oblations. For Rome's sacrifices and oblations have never ceased. And the prophesy of the apostle (2 Thessalonians 2) who prophesies that there shall come a departing, this prophecy is in no part fulfilled, if Rome be believers, except it be fulfilled in them that have departed from Rome. And then the Church of England, and all the presbytery had need to look to it who first departed. But if Rome and England and the presbytery, and the Brownists be all believers, and of the faith of England, then has there been no departing from the faith, but a great increasing far beyond the primitive times, in that the scriptures nowhere show of whole nations, kingdoms, and countries, to be of the faith of Jesus, as now there is, yea, a great whole part of the world, the like was never heard of, nor prophesied of, if all you be believers, as you either all are believers or infidels, for you are all of one faith and baptism. But if you be believers, there is no departing yet heard of, neither is the man of sin yet disclosed or revealed, nor exalted, nor sits or has sat as God in the temple of God, showing himself that he is God. There is no such prophesy yet come to pass. And if Rome be all believers in Christ, that prophecy (Revelation 11) where it is prophesied "that the people and kindreds, and tongues, and Gentiles, shall see the corpses of the two witnesses of the Lord, killed and lie in the streets of the great city which is spiritually called Sodom and Egypt, and that the inhabitants of the earth shall rejoice over them," this prophesy cannot yet be accomplished nor begun. And if Rome be believers, then that prophesy of the first beast to whom is given "a mouth to speak great things and blasphemies, and to make war with the saints, and to overcome them, and to whom power is give over every kindred and tongue and nation, so that all that dwell upon the earth shall worship him,"[14] and the prophesy of the whore that sits upon many waters, with whom have committed fornication with kings of the earth, and all the inhabitants of the earth are made drunk with the wine of her fornication," all these prophecies and many more cannot in any measure be fulfilled, or begun, if the church of Rome be believers and of the faith of Jesus.

And if these prophecies be not fulfilled, nor begun then have the mystery of iniquity that began to work in the apostles' days, to the exaltation of the man of sin, **given** ever working, which were contrary to the prophesy of scripture, and that may not be. Let Rome therefore and all that profession see and consider that all these prophesies of exaltations are fulfilled in that profession, and thus is their glory their shame. For they glory in nothing more than in their exaltation, and great power, authority, and magnificence of their church, and all that is true. And thereby is this also true, that all these prophesies are fulfilled in that their exaltation, the which you of the Church of England, and the whole presbytery confessing, and protesting against them for the same, you must needs hold them all infidels and unbelievers, except you will fall into great blasphemy and say that they are believers who execute the power of the man of sin, and cause the sacrifices and oblations to cease, and so be taken away from the altar of the Lord, so as there are no sacrifices to be offered unto him. Will any say that these are believers that take from the Lord's altar his daily sacrifices, causing

---

[14]Revelation 13:5, 7-8; 18:3.

that none shall be offered unto him? If these be believers that utterly over-throw the worship of the Lord, then can there be no infidels.

Further, you cannot say the church of Rome are believers, except you will say they are believers that depart away from the faith, and are ministers of the man of sin exalting a power above the power of God, and setting up his power (the ministers whereof they are) to sit as God in the temple of God, making show of that power that it is the power of God, when it is the effectual working of Satan, with all his power and signs and lying wonders. And they that are subject in this power are such as the Holy Ghost testifies, "receive not the love of truth, and which believe not the truth."[15] Can you of the Church of England, and you of the presbytery and you that are called Brownists that hold this prophesy is fulfilled in that exaltation of the Romish profession, can you hold these to be believers in Christ of whom the Lord says, "They receive not the truth, nor believe not the truth, but have pleasure in unrighteousness," and exalt a power against God, to be worshipped as God? What wickedness and blasphemy is this to say they are Christians and believers in Christ.

Moreover, you cannot say that the Romish professors are believers, except you will say they are believers that set up the first beast, and are the ministers of that power or beast, which beast or power has "seven heads and ten horns, and upon his horns ten crowns, and he is like a leopard, and his feet like a bear, and his mouth as the mouth of a lion, to whom the dragon give his power, throne, and authority."[16] All this do they of that pro-fession, and not this only, but "they also worship the dragon which gives power to the beast, and they worship the beast, saying, who is like the beast, who is able to fight with him?"[17] And they being ministers of this beast or power do in their ministration open their mouths to blaspheme against God, to blaspheme his name and his tabernacle, and them that dwell therein. And by this power they have made war with the saints and over-come them. Can you without great blasphemy against the Holy One of Israel, the most high God, say that these are believers in Christ Jesus and Christians that do these fearful things, seeking to destroy God, and the faith of Jesus, and all his saints that hold the truth of Jesus? If you cannot say

---

[15]2 Thessalonians 2:10, 12.
[16]Revelation 13:2-3.
[17]Revelation 13:4.

that they which do such things are believers and Christians, then cannot you say that they of the Romish profession are believers or Christians, but that they are infidels and unbelievers, seeing you confess this prophesy is fulfilled in the Romish profession. So are all these things done by them. And moreover, to these the prophesy (Revelation 17) of the woman, and the beast, and the ten kings that give their power and authority to the beast, these fight with the Lamb. Can you say that any of these are believers and Christians that fight against the Lamb? No, the Spirit of God testifies in this place that they which are called, and chosen, and faithful are on the Lamb's side. They then that fight against the Lamb are those that are not called, nor chosen, nor faithful. Therefore must they needs be infidels and unbelievers. All these prophesies being confessed of you to be already accomplish by and under that Roman profession, how shall you of the Church of England and the presbytery be able to say that they of the church of Rome are believers and Christians? And if they be not believers and Christians, then are they infidels and unbelievers, and so is your baptism and ministry of England, and the baptism of the presbytery, and all the ordinances that you have received from Rome to be cast away as the marks of the beast, and most abominable to the Lord.

But it shall not be amiss, seeing there arises so just an occasion to show (the Lord directing us) the ground and root of all this evil and sin against the majesty and holiness of God, against all which you of England and the presbytery sin in accounting Rome and all them of that profession Christians, although all these abominations which we have showed in all these prophesies (and might be showed in many more) be committed and to this day maintained by them to the highest dishonor of God, in exalting the man of sin to sit as God in the temple of God, and to utter polluting of all the holy ordinances of God, in abolishing the witness of the Lord, his Word and Spirit, and killing the saints, fighting against the Lamb, making all the nations of the earth to worship the beast, and to drink of the wine of her fornications that sits upon many waters, notwithstanding all this, these you account Christians, upon this ground and from this root because when they are infants, they are washed with water in the name of the Father, etc., and you approve that they are baptized when they are infants because they are the seed of Christians and of the faithful.

What words might we take to ourselves to make this madness, and the madness of all the world, hereunto appear, who pretend that all the seed of Christians and of the faithful are to be baptized only, and under this pretense baptize, and approve of the baptism of the seed of all the wicked and ungodly in these parts of the world, yea, those that have been wicked to the third and fourth generation, and to the tenth generation enemies of God, and blood persecutors of his truth, destroying the faith of Jesus, and advancing the man of sin? The seed of all these are baptized, and by reason of this baptism they are all held and accounted Christians by you, although they walk in the steps of their forefathers. Is there any knowledge of God in these things? Or do men think that now under the Gospel they may do and approve of what they will? Will men neither walk by the law of God nor by the law they propound unto themselves? Do you set down a law to yourselves that the infants of the faithful are to be baptized, and do you approve of the baptizing of the infants of the enemies of God, that fight against the Lamb, and the infants of Rome, also, that have not so much faith as the devils, who believe and tremble? In the word of unspeakable wisdom has the Holy Ghost said that the "nations shall be drunk with the wine of her fornications." Who may not see this prophesy fulfilled? For if men were not drunk so as they can neither see their way, nor tell what they say, they would not walk thus, and speak thus, like drunken men.

The Church of England and the presbytery do allow of the baptizing of all the infants of Rome, whose pope and cardinals and all their whole ministry that administer the baptism, and the parents of the infants that are baptized, and those infants being already come to be men of years, would destroy their kings, and princes, and countries, and all them, for professing Christ as they do. Are these the seed of the faithful? And is this to baptize and allow of the baptism of the seed of the faithful? Weigh with yourselves what truth there is in this? And the Brownists they approve of the baptism and baptizing of them whose parents persecute their own children for walking in their way. Are these the seed of the faithful? What blindness and inuprightness is this to profess a ground, and walk by no ground. You must agree (if you can) among yourselves, and make a new law. This (you see) will not serve your turn, for if you allow none to be baptized but the seed of the faithful, you will not have whole countries and nations all Christians, as you have. It is apparent therefore whatsoever you say, that you hold that all infants, whether their parents be faithful or unbelievers, shall be baptized. Your rule then is that both the seed of the faithful and unfaithful shall be baptized, and that is your practice. What warrant can be found for this? Or it is no matter whether there be warrant or not? You allege circumcision for your ground, that because infants were circumcised, therefore infants must be baptized. But yet you cannot find that the infants of any people were to be circumcised. And if any were circumcised but those that God command-ed, the Lord, nor his faithful servants never approved of it. And will you now approve of any baptism, and make it good, and yet make circumcision your example? The Lord persuade your hearts and the hearts of all men to begin while it is day to examine the ground of your practice herein, that you may stand before the Lord in the last day, and through Christ be able to approve that you have walked by the strict rule of God's Word, and not by the vain inventions of men, which God hates, and let all God's people hate. "But his law let them love, which is a perfect love, and converts the soul, and it is pure and gives light to the eyes." (Psalm 19) But by this your practice it is made a most imperfect law when you say that the infants of the faithful are to be baptized only, and when you have laid that down for your law, you both baptize and approve for good the baptism of the infants of the unfaithful and unbelievers, and enemies of God, and his truth. This is neither perfect nor pure law. Therefore, it is not the law of God. You then that wait for salvation by Christ Jesus may not walk by that imperfect and impure law, but must seek diligently with your whole hearts the law and statutes of the Lord that you may keep them, which **law** when you shall diligently and faithfully search into throughout, you shall nowhere find it once mentioned that any infants are to be baptized. And therefore it is but the mere vain invention and tradition of men, which whoso follows can never have favor nor acceptance with God, because they make the law of God of no authority. (Mark 7:13) In this great and weighty cause, we will not (through the grace of God) burden you with many grounds or argu-ments, but lay down before you some few things which all the plainness and evidence of truth wherewith God shall make us able.

And first, we pray all those whose hearts God has inclined to seek his truth, and who desire in uprightness to walk in the light, that they will duly consider what the covenant of the Gospel is, and with whom it is made. And thus has the Lord set it down: "This is the covenant, says the Lord, that I will make with the house of Israel. I will put my law in their inward parts, and write it in their hearts, and will be their God, and they shall be my people." (Jeremiah 31:33; Hebrews 8:10) And our Savior Christ declares this more fully (Mark 16:16), where he says, "Go ye into all the world and preach the Gospel to every creature. He that shall believe and be baptized shall be saved." Thus does the Lord by his Spirit in the preaching of the Gospel put and write this law in the hearts of men, according to the parable of the sower. (Matthew 13:23) And they shall believe in him and be baptized. Thus, they shall be his people. And he will save them, and so is he their God. Here is the new covenant set down by the Holy Ghost, both on God's behalf, and on their behalf with whom it is made, and here is it plainly declared and expounded by Christ himself. The Lord on his behalf does covenant that he will put and write his law in men's hearts by the power of his Spirit in the preaching of the Gospel, and he will be their God and save them. And the covenant on his people's behalf which they are to keep and perform is to believe the Gospel and be baptized. Let all men now that have any willingness of heart to be informed by the Word of God, and whose hearts are not willfully set to go on in their ignorant . . .[18] ways, without trying their ways whether they be of God or no, let them, we say, search, examine, and try by what show of truth it can possibly be conceived that under, or by this covenant of the new testament infants should be baptized, where the Lord requires no such things in this covenant of men to baptize their infants. And if you will but see and consider with wise and gracious hearts, how the Lord does set down the covenant which he made with Abraham (Genesis 17), you shall see with what evidence the Lord in mercy does set it down. Thus says the Lord to Abraham, "I will establish my covenant between you and me, and your seed after you in their generation for an everlasting covenant to be God unto you and your seed after you. And I will give to you and to your seed after you, all the land of Canaan for an everlasting covenant. And I will be their God."[19] This is on the Lord's behalf. And says the Lord, "This is the covenant that you and your seed after you shall keep. Let every man-child among you be circumcised. You shall circumcise the foreskin of your flesh, and every man-child at eight days old, as well as he that is born in the house as he that is bought with money."[20] This is the covenant on Abraham's behalf and his seed. Thus does the Lord declare in every particular his covenant with his people, as well what he will do for them as also what he requires them to do in obedience to him. And here we see God has commanded Abraham, and his seed to circumcise all the males in their house. And now this covenant is disannulled, and all the ordinances thereof, as is showed (in) Hebrews 7:18.

---

[18]Word(s) omitted in text.
[19]Genesis 17:7-8.
[20]Genesis 17:10-12.

And the Lord says he will make a new covenant with the house of Israel, not like the old, teaching us that we should not form and frame it according to the old, but that we should receive it, according to the new form and frame wherein he delivers it, under which covenant the Lord does not command or require of his people that they should baptize all their household, and infants, both born in their house and bought with money, according as under the old covenant he commanded that they should circumcise them. How dare you then thus contend against the Lord. And whereas he says he will make a new covenant not according to the old, you will say and have it according to the old. For you will have it that according as infants were circumcised under the old covenant, so you will have infants baptized under the new. Is not this to set yourselves against the Lord and to change his covenant, which he has sealed with his blood, and after your own wills in what you think good, to make it according to the old covenant, directly contrary to the Lord's own word and saying? And you have no way to maintain the baptizing of infants, but by saying the new covenant is according to the old. And this is to say directly contrary to the saying of the Lord, who is the covenant maker, and who says, in plain words, the new covenant which I will make with Israel shall not be according to the old. Here it is made evident to all that will not resist the **(uncertain)** that your baptizing of infants is contrary to the new covenant of the Lord. Thus do you, to make your own tradition good, make the new covenant like the old, which the Lord says is not like the old. How can you possibly oppose the Word of the Lord more directly? Furthermore, the Holy Ghost, by the author unto the Hebrews (chapter 9), endeavoring by all evidence to prove that the new covenant is not like the old, shows that the old testament or covenant had a worldly sanctuary, and that the service of that tabernacle only stood in "meats and drinks and divers washings, and carnal rites,"[21] which purified the flesh, but purged not the conscience. And the Holy Ghost shows there that the new testament or covenant has not a worldly sanctuary, and that the service of that tabernacle stands not in carnalities which purge not the conscience, but it is a perfect tabernacle, the sacrifice whereof does "purge the conscience from dead works to serve the living God."[22] Thus does the scripture show that the ordinances of the new are

---

[21]Hebrews 9:10.
[22]Hebrews 9:14.

not according to the ordinances of the old. And for this cause says the Holy Ghost, Christ is the mediator of the new testament. That is because the new testament or covenant, and tabernacle, and ordinances are not carnal but spiritual. But if you will have infants baptized, that is, washed with water and certain words, then you bring in a carnal rite, which purges not the conscience (for you do not hold that the infants' consciences are purged thereby), and so do you make the new covenant and ordinances carnal, like unto the old, which may not be, except you will directly oppose the evident Word of the Lord, as you have long herein done, to your utter destruction, except you repent. We desire moreover the people of God, whose whole hearts are set to seek his face, that they will search the scriptures to see what the baptism of the new testament is declared to be, which being faithfully searched into shall convince unto all the earth that it cannot appertain unto infants.

And, first, in the Gospel According to Mark (1:4), it is preached by John to be baptism of amendment of life for the remission of sins. And the apostle (in) Romans 6:4 says, "Baptism is a burying into the death of Christ, that we should walk in newness of life." And (in) Galatians 3:26-27 the apostle says, "Baptism is the putting on of Christ by faith." How should this baptism belong unto infants? Can there be amendment of life for the remission of sins in infants? And can infants be buried into the death of Christ to walk in newness of life? And can infants put on Christ by faith? If they can do none of these things, which is most plain they cannot, then may they not be baptized. What were sufficient to give satisfaction in this long conceived error of baptizing infants, you may see by the ordinance itself. They are not capable of it. And you may see that the Lord by the covenant does not command nor require any such thing at the hands of parents to baptize their infants and all their household. The covenant is that men should believe and be baptized, but there is no one word to command them to baptize their infants, and all their household. Oh, that you would be weary of this your great ignorance, to say that baptism is the seal of the covenant. And yet you will seal them that cannot receive the seal, and them that are not once mentioned in the covenant, bringing in under the covenant whom you will, without the will and mind of the Lord, and although the covenant shall still overthrow you, that there can none be under the covenant, but they which believe and are baptized. For the Lord will admit of no other than he has mentioned in his covenant, though you seal never so many with water and words. Although this might suffice, yet we will endeavor by the Lord's assistance to convince you by your own ground.

You cannot deny but that there is neither rule nor example in all the New Testament for the baptizing of infants, whereby you confess that the mediator of the new testament has not appointed it. Therefore, you are driven to prove it by consequence making yourselves and the simple believe that it must needs follow by a necessary consequence that as infants were circumcised, so must they be baptized. If you will have a necessary consequence of this, then must you make it of the whole matter and not of part, as you think good. As thus: he that will be a proselyte must be circumcised, and all the males in his household. So then if your consequence from this ground be necessary, he that will be a disciple of Christ must be baptized and all his household. It follows then upon your consequence that no man can be admitted a disciple except all his household will be baptized, for no man could be admitted a proselyte except all his males were circumcised. If then a Jew that has a wife and divers children and bondmen (as they have) come to the faith of Jesus, if his wife or any of his children or bondsmen will not be baptized, then cannot he be admitted to be a disciple of Christ, except you will allow him by his authority to cause them to be baptized whether they believe or no, as they did by their authority circumcise their household. Thus must your consequence stand if you will not be willing to deceive yourselves in the means of your salvation. Deal faithfully therefore with God and his truth and his people, you that take upon you to be guides, and lead not God's people to destruction by such deceits as this, that when you have neither rule nor example to prove that infants must be baptized, yea, and when the covenant of the Lord does evidently debar[23] them, and the ordinance of baptism considered in itself also, yet you will, to bring in and maintain the tradition of your elders, prove it by a consequence from the covenant of the Old Testament, and make the new like the old, when the Lord says it is not like nor shall be according to the old. And if the people of God would but with upright hearts read diligently the whole Epistle to the Hebrews, they should (through the grace of God) find to their full satisfaction the difference between the old covenant and the new, and the priesthood, and the tabernacle, and the ordinances, services, and sacrifices set down so plainly as it would make an end of this

---

[23]To bar from having or doing something.

controversy, and many more, to the advancement of God's truth, and the salvation of the souls of his people that shall follow him in the regeneration or new birth, which is to be born again of water and of the Spirit, in which regeneration or new birth whoso follows him not cannot enter into the kingdom of heaven. In that Epistle to the Hebrews they that read shall find (as we have formerly showed) that the old covenant was a carnal covenant and commandment. (Hebrews 7:16) And as the Lord speaks to Abraham (Genesis 17:3) speaking of the covenant of circumcision, says, "My covenant shall be in your flesh for an everlasting covenant." And as the covenant was, so was the priesthood, and the tabernacle, and the sacrifices, and service, all carnal and worldly, as is with all evidence and plainness in that epistle set down. But the new covenant is not a covenant in the flesh. But it is a covenant in the Spirit, a spiritual covenant written in the hearts and minds of God's people, established upon better promises than the first covenant. And all this is evident by the words of the covenant, which are, "They that believe and are baptized shall be saved." And as this covenant is spiritual, so is the priesthood, so is the tabernacle, and all the ordinances, sacrifices, and services thereof. And all this is most plainly set down in that Epistle to the Hebrews, which difference between the old and the new covenant, if it were carefully searched unto and found out, it would overthrow your deceitful consequence which you draw from covenants that are dislike, or not like in substance, contrary to all understanding. And it would make you cast away your carnal baptizing of infants and to baptize no infants, but such infants as were babes in Christ, such as are begotten by the immortal seed of the Word. And it would discover unto you your carnal ignorance and blindness in holding that Israelites beget Israelites **now**, as under the law, or that Christians beget Christians by generation, which has brought in such madness among men, as the Brownists hold and profess that no infants that die are under the covenant of grace and salvation, but such as they beget. Thus do they only beget infants that are heirs of salvation. And all this, and much more, evil comes upon making the new covenant like the old, and so make them both carnal, which you do herein, in holding that parents beget children to be under the spiritual covenant by carnal generation.

But because some through the weakness of their judgment and understanding cannot see the old covenant to be a carnal covenant, we will in **short** yet further endeavor to show how it is a carnal or worldly covenant. First, it was a carnal covenant in that all the promises that God made to

Abraham in that covenant of circumcision were of worldly things, as we may see (in) Genesis 17:5-7), where the Lord says, "I will make thee exceeding fruitful. I make nations of thee, yea, kings shall proceed of thee. And I will give thee and thy seed after thee all the land of Canaan for an everlasting possession." Here is this whole covenant of circumcision which God makes, wherein there is no promise but of worldly things. Secondly, in this covenant of circumcision the Lord requires a carnal obedience, that is, "Let every man-child be circumcised in the foreskin of the flesh." Thirdly, the judgment for the breach of this covenant is a worldly judgment. (verse 14) "The uncircumcised man-child in whose flesh the foreskin is not circumcised, that person shall be cut off from his people, because he has broken my covenant." Add moreover verse 13, where the Lord says, "This is my covenant in your flesh." Who will be so blind as not to see that this is a carnal covenant? **Will** men be so void of all understanding, as to say that God makes a spiritual covenant with a people in their flesh? Though men have been so ignorant, let them not be so ignorant still.

After the like manner as has been spoken of, the covenant may be spoken of, **the tabernacle**, priesthood, and all those services and carnal rites, in all which covenant and worldly ordinances, **(uncertain)** is no promise of salvation for the keeping of them, nor cannot be, because they make not holy concerning the conscience. (Hebrews 9:9) "Neither sanctify they the comers thereunto." (10:1) For there is no judgment of condemnation pronounced against any, although they should presumptuously break them, but bodily death. (Numbers 15:30; Hebrews 13:28, etc.)[24] Yet through repentance such might be saved. But now under the new covenant, which is spiritual, there is promise of salvation to them that keep it. For "he that believes and is baptized shall be saved." And there is condemnation pronounced against them that keep it not. "He that will not believe shall be damned." And he that **sins** presumptuously or willingly of knowledge against this covenant, or any of the ordinances thereof shall never be forgiven. (Hebrews 20:29)[25] Thus may all see that will not wink with their eyes that the new covenant is not like the old. But it is a covenant established upon better promises, and that the first covenant is established upon worldly or earthly promises. But the new covenant is established upon

---

[24]No such reference in Hebrews.
[25]No such reference in Hebrews.

spiritual or heavenly promises, even of life and salvation. The difference of these two covenants being with a spiritual eye discerned, it will easily overthrow that most false and improper consequence which is drawn **from** the old covenant to the new, for the baptism of infants, which consequence if it were rightly laid down, the darkness of it would easily appear. As thus: under the old covenant infants were circumcised in the flesh, so under the new covenant, infants must be baptized in the flesh. What ignorance is this? What wine of fornication that has made drunk all nations? There is no such baptism in the New Testament as baptism in the flesh. God forbid that men should remain still so ignorant as to think that Christ Jesus in his heavenly kingdom and new covenant has established any carnal rite, or ceremonial ordinance, the "handwriting whereof he has put out and abolished." (Colossians 2:14) And therefore the baptism of the New Testament must needs be a spiritual baptism of water and the Spirit (John 3:5) with which baptism infants cannot be baptized. So is it great wickedness and a profanation of the holy and divine ordinance of God to use such administration upon infants, making herein the ordinance of God of no effect, there being no benefit or advantage, end, or use of it. For you will all confess that all infants must be regenerate and born again, or else they cannot enter into the kingdom of heaven. And our Savior Christ, the Savior of us all, says that they that are born again must be born of water and the Spirit. To what end then is the baptizing of infants, they not being regenerate thereof?

Furthermore, you frame your consequence with these words: as infants were sealed with the seal of the covenant under the law, so they must be sealed with the seal of the covenant under the Gospel. We demand of you, is washing with water a seal? If it be a seal, it is a seal in the flesh. Where then is the print or impression thereof? It has none, therefore it can be no seal. Oh, how blindly are the wise men of the world carried away in these things, contrary to all understanding, to be brought to imagine that washing an infant with water is a seal. Are not these vain inventions, without ground of scripture, reason, or common sense? Can you walk thus and think to please God? Will God be pleased with you when you walk in those ways that best please your own minds? Be not deceived. God will not hold you guiltless for thus using his name and ordinance in vain. If you will examine the New Testament throughout, you shall find no seal, nor none sealed, but they that believe, "who are sealed with the Holy Spirit of promise," (Ephesians 1:13) by which Holy Spirit "we are all baptized into one body." (1 Corinthians 12:13) And there is but "one Spirit, one baptism, and one body," (Ephesians 4:4-5) which holy seal of the Spirit seeing infants cannot have, they cannot be baptized with that one baptism into that one body. So is your consequence for the baptizing of infants directly contrary to the covenant and ordinance of God. The covenant of the Lord being that "they which believe and are baptized shall be saved," and the ordinance being the "baptism of repentance for the remission of sins."

To conclude this point with a ground that all who have any knowledge of the Word of God will confess, which is this: the covenant of the New Testament is a covenant of life and salvation only to all that believe and are baptized. (Mark 16:16) The seal of the covenant must needs be answerable to that holy covenant, a seal of life and salvation only to them that believe and are baptized. (Ephesians 1:13-14; Revelation 2:17-18) The apostle here to the Ephesians does show that "after they believed they were sealed with the Holy Spirit of promise." Let all them confess with whom there is any uprightness that infants who cannot believe (for "faith comes by hearing, and hearing by the Word of God," Romans 10:17) cannot be sealed with the seal of this covenant. It is not in the power of parents to set this seal upon their infants, as it was in their power to set the sign of circumcision upon their flesh. Therefore, it is not required of them by the Lord. And it is altogether impiety and wickedness, and a profanation of the holy ordinance of God to take in hand to administer it upon infants. And the Lord will revenge himself for such wickedness, if it be not repented of. But against this ground of truth that the covenant of life and salvation is made only with them that believe and are baptized, it is objected that the covenant is made with them and their seed. And though many writers write thus, and most affirm it, yet Mr. Robinson, being next hand, we will produce his warrant for this ground, being as good as any others, and he as unadvisedly overseen in the setting it down. Thus speaks he in his book (page 282): "The scriptures everywhere teach that parents by their faith bring their children into the covenant of the church, and entitle them to the promises." Little does Mr. Robinson think how suddenly in his accustomed haste he has brought in a meritorious faith. It were to be wished that he and all men did see and feel that their faith is little enough to bring themselves under the covenant of God, if it were not for the gracious and most merciful acceptance of God in Christ. But God has not promised anywhere to accept to salvation of the parents' faith for their children, nor to condemn them for their parents' infidelity. This is but one among many of Mr. Robinson's doctrines of devils which he has heaped up in his tedious book. His proof for his doctrine is Genesis 17. And we prove this doctrine most false by Genesis 17, where Abraham, his faith, and earnest prayer to God could not bring Ishmael his child of thirteen years old under that covenant. (verses 18-21)

Thus is Mr. Robinson altogether overseen the scripture that he himself alleges. Add moreover to this, Genesis 25:23, where Isaac's faith could not bring Esau under the covenant. Thus may all see that Mr. Robinson does but quote scripture for his proof, and not show how it proves his ground. The next proof for this ground is Acts 2:39, where the apostle speaking to and of all the unbelieving Jews and Gentiles says, "The promise is made to you and to your children, even as many as the Lord your God shall call." How Mr. Robinson will apply this to his purpose we know not, but we confess that this promise ("They that believe and are baptized shall be saved") is made to all the unbelieving Jews and Gentiles, and their children to this day. But this does no way prove that the faith of the parents entitles children to the promises, nor that the promise of salvation is made to the unbelieving Jews and Gentiles, or to their children, except they and their children amend their lives and be baptized. And whereas Mr. Robinson, as it should seem, understands children in this place to be infants, we will first leave that to him to prove that the apostle speaks here concerning infants. And then we will require of him how he proves that the inheritance of the kingdom of heaven goes by succession of generation, as the land of Canaan did.

For the second part of his unjust and ungodly affirmation that God takes occasion by the sins of the parents to execute his justice to condemnation upon the children. Herein Mr. Robinson doubles his sin, in that as he has before made the parents' faith the cause of blessing to salvation, which (he says) is everywhere to be found in the scriptures but shows nowhere, so now he affirms that parents' infidelity is the cause of God's judgement to condemnation upon their children. Mr. Robinson propounds his doctrine and rule for a general rule and doctrine. To prove him a false prophet in this also we refer the godly reader to the I Kings 14 where it is shown that Abijah, the son of the most wicked Jeroboam, being but young, was not cursed for his father's sins. And Josiah being but eight years old when his father died, the Lord blessed him abundantly in his infancy, notwithstanding all the grievous transgressions of his father Ammon. (2 Chronicles 33-34) Neither did the Lord punish the people of Israel's children for that their great transgression (Numbers 14:27-39) when they murmured because of the spies, by which sin, although they so provoked the Lord's wrath as he caused all their carcasses to fall, to be wasted and consumed in the wilderness, not suffering anyone of them to go to the land of Canaan save Joshua and Caleb, yet even then in his anger he declared his mercy to all their children, promising to bring them into the land. Now we confess with Mr. Robinson that we are all by nature the children of wrath, conceived and born in sin. But we desire to know of Mr. Robinson whether he hold not that all children are alike the children of wrath and alike the begotten in sin? Or that some parents confer grace by generation more than others, and if they do not (as we assure ourselves you will confess), but that all infants are alike in themselves the children of wrath, then let us see, not after a sort, but directly, by what evidence of scripture it can be proved (their sins being all alike in themselves) that God should execute his justice to condemnation upon some children for the sins of their parents, and show mercy to salvation upon others for the faith of their parents, seeing the just God has said that everyone shall receive salvation or condemnation according to that which he has done in the flesh and not according to that which his parents have done. And let all see Mr. Robinson's great iniquity in this his affirmation, in that he blasphemously charges the most holy and just God to punish infants to condemnation for the actual sins of their parents when they themselves have not sinned after the same manner of transgression. (Romans 5:13) And we pray Mr. Robinson and all men to consider the words of the Lord (Exodus 20),[26] who says he will "visit the sins of the fathers upon the children of them that hate him," which hatred is showed by the breach of his commandments. But do infants hate God and break his commandments? You all confess with the prophet (in) Ezekiel 18:14-17 (not withstanding these words in Exodus 20) that "if a wicked man begat a son that sees all his father's sins which he has done, and fears, neither does such like, he shall surely live." Then must you grant that the enfants of wicked parents that do not such like sin as their parents do, shall not die. Thus much to stop Mr. Robinson for the present in his speedy courses who runs his race as though he were strong and none could stay him. But the Lord and his Word will overthrow him in these his ways if he repent not, whose repentance we much desire to God's glory, and for his own good.

And now let the covenant of the Lord stand firm and good against the adversaries thereof, which covenant is "they which believe and are baptized

---

[26]Exodus 20:5.

shall be saved." The words whereof being spoken by him that made it do with authority convince to the consciences of all that will hear them that this covenant is made only with them that believe and are baptized, which is with them that (are) of the faith of Abraham, (Romans 4:12-16) and not they that are of the flesh of Abraham. "There are," says the apostle, "children of the flesh and children of the promise. But the children of the promise are counted for the seed." (Romans 9:8) How ignorant and obstinate are men become, whom no word of God can persuade. But they will have the children of the flesh to be the children of the promise, and the seed. For they will have the seed of the faithful, that is, all the children begotten of their bodies, to be the children of the promise, and the seed with whom the covenant is made, saying, "The covenant is made with the faithful and their seed," meaning all the children begotten of the flesh. Yet the apostle says the children of the flesh are not the seed. But the apostle's testimony will not serve the turn. The pope says it is not so. And the bishops and presbytery (having learned it of the pope) say it is not so. And the Brownists (having learned it of the bishop) say it not so. Here are many witnesses, and they have long and ancient custom, and the fruit is fair to look upon and pleasant to the eye and mind, that infants are begotten and born Christians. The most wicked and profane parents that are, like this well, that they may be accounted to begat Christians, and that their children may be made members of the body of Christ when they are newborn. The best men like this well. And the worst like it well. This pleases all flesh in these parts of the world. There was never any one doctrine of Christ nor of the apostles that ever were so acceptable to all men. It must needs be acceptable because so good a thing is so easily come by. What a grievous thing would it be if one might not be a Christian and member of Christ's body before they had learned Christ, and to believe in him. This would trouble children if they should be forced to know Christ before they could be admitted to be his disciples and to be baptized. And this would be a great trouble to parents that their children should not be baptized before they had carefully brought them up in the instruction and information of the Lord. And this would be a great burden to bishops and priests, if they should have none admitted members of their church until by their diligent and faithful preaching of the Gospel they were brought to knowledge, faith, and repentance, and to amend their lives and be baptized. If these old doctrines of Christ and his apostles should not be put into practice it would trouble and offend all the world, being so contrary to all custom, and counsels, and affections of men. Oh, crooked and foolish generation how long shall the Lord bear with you? How long shall he suffer you? Will you make the way broad and wide which he has made straight and narrow? Will you still walk in the traditions of men after the lust of your own hearts, and tread his statutes under your feet? Shall the long evil custom and false testimony of men, agreeable to your own affections, overthrow the divine and true witness of our Lord Christ and his apostles? Does our Savior Christ say that those with whom he has made the new covenant are they in whose minds and hearts he has written, whom he declares those that believe and be baptized? And will you add to the covenant of the Lord, and say it was made with the faithful and their seed before they can believe? And does the apostle say that the seed to whom the promise is made are they which are of the faith of Abraham, and not they that are of the flesh of Abraham? And will you say that they that are of the flesh of the faithful are the seed with whom the covenant is made? Can you devise in your hearts more directly to oppose the Lord and falsify his truth than you do herein? Will you thus contend against the Lord and despite[27] the Spirit of grace, and trample under foot the blood the new testament? And think that you shall escape much more punishment than they that despise Moses' law? Deceive not yourselves. And do not think that God cares not for these things, and that he regards not the breach of his holy ordinances, because he seems to hold his peace, in that he strikes you not with bodily judgments. But except you repent he will reprove you, and set all these things in order before you, and tear you in pieces, when there shall be none that can deliver you. Oh, consider this and forget not God. What shall it profit you to have your infants washed with water and a few words, whereby the name of the Lord is blasphemed, and you perish for so profaning his ordinance? The infant is never the better. It shall not be saved thereby. And there is no such ordinance required at your hands. Let the Word of the Lord be your guide in these things, and not the word of man nor long custom, although it be in a thing that is most pleasing to your carnal minds.

Thus leaving to your remembrance that Abraham's faith could not bring his children under the covenant, in that it did not bring Ishmael nor any of his six sons that he had by Ketourah, his wife, under the covenant (Genesis 25), and therefore that is a most deceitful and false ground to say that they

---

[27]Spite.

were circumcised because they were under the covenant, and that they are under the covenant by Abraham's faith, for then had all Abraham's bondmen and household under the covenant, and Ishmael whom the Lord deigns to be under the covenant, and yet he and they all were commanded to be circumcised.

This then is the ground of truth which cannot be gainsaid, that all the males, free and bond, that were born in Abraham's house or bought with his money, which were not of his seed, were all to be circumcised, because it was the covenant that God commanded Abraham to keep, to circumcise all his males, and not because they were all under the covenant of circumcision by Abraham's faith. This is but a vain invention of the man of sin, and a mystery of iniquity to deceive them that have pleasure in unrighteousness, having no show,[28] nor warrant of scripture to say they were circumcised because they were the covenant by Abraham's faith. All evidence of scripture is against it, in that the Lord does plainly declare in his Word that they were to be circumcised that were not under the covenant, even all Abraham's household, whereof there was no one under the covenant but himself when the commandment was given. Now then, you having no color,[29] show nor warrant from the scriptures for the baptizing of infants, but a deceitful consequence from the example of circumcision, we beseech all who hope for salvation by Jesus Christ to see the deceit of your consequence. Thus you say, and this is all your hold, that as the seed of the faithful were circumcised, so the seed of the faithful must be baptized. Proof for this your ground you have none, but your strong persuasions and long custom, wherein no one of you has faith. But to show yet again the deceit of your consequence.

First, it is not drawn by due proportion, which is a most deceitful way to deceive the simple. For thus ought your consequence to be drawn: as Abraham believing was circumcised and all the males of his household, both men and children of eight days, bond and free, so now any man believing must be baptized with all his household, both men and children of eight days old, bond and free. Secondly, the deceit of your consequence is because it is not a necessary consequence. For you must prove nothing by consequence but that which must of necessity follow. But this does not of

---

[28]Outward appearance; pretense.
[29]Appearance of authenticity; pretext.

necessity follow, neither can it follow, that because infants were circumcised with circumcision in the flesh under the law, therefore infants must of necessity be baptized with the baptism of the repentance for the remission of sins under the Gospel, with which baptism they cannot be baptized, as all of any understanding must needs confess. And there is but one baptism. And therefore most blindly, ignorantly, and deceitfully is this consequence drawn, being neither drawn by due proportion; neither can the rule possibly by true consequence; neither shall you be able to tell what to say when you shall be required to prove it a necessary consequence. If therefore you will not willfully go on in the ways of everlasting destruction, forsake this root of error which overthrows the covenant of the Gospel of Jesus Christ in the first foundation thereof, bringing in the seed of the flesh of the faithful by carnal generation for the seed of the promise, instead of the seed of the faith of Abraham by spiritual regeneration, making the infants that are begotten of the faithful after the flesh members of the body of Christ and heirs of the covenant of the new testament (which is the covenant of faith and repentance) through the faith of their parents. And by this means you have and do daily bring all the wicked and ungodly in these parts of the world to be members of Christ's body and heirs of the covenant, by natural birth, which our Savior Christ says (John 3) can no way be but by new birth, that is, by being born again by water and the spirit, which is, by believing and being baptized. Thus do you utterly destroy the holy covenant of the Lord, the holy baptism, and the body of Christ, making them common to all, young and old, wicked and profane, blasphemers, persecutors, murderers, adulterers, and witches, and all their children. But let all know this, such as the members are, such is the body, and such is the baptism, and such is their covenant, the covenant of death and condemnation unto all that are under it, and not the covenant of life and salvation, which is only made with them that believe and are baptized. And the Lord persuade every honest heart to ground their faith upon this rock, that as under the law none were circumcised but those that were expressly commanded by rule or example, so under the Gospel none may be baptized, but those that are expressly commanded by rule or example. And keeping to this true ground no simple soul shall be deceived. And so we leave this point with godly care to be considered of, beseeching the Lord to give you understanding hearts.

Thus have we with our most willing (though most feeble) endeavors, manifest unto you, these two false professions of Christ, and the false prophets that maintain them among you, with divers particular errors and strong delusions whereby they deceive you, transforming themselves as though they were prophets of God. But they are all deep deceivers, and prophecy lies, as we have proved, wherein they shall never be able to justify themselves, neither before God nor his people. And we much rather desire their repentance than that they should go about to approve themselves in their evil, whereby they shall heap sin upon their own heads, and bring shame to their own faces, seeing the time is come that the Lord will reprove the foolishness of such false prophets who make show of godliness, but deny the power thereof, who lead captive simple women, which are ever learning and never able to come to the knowledge of the truth. These are they that the apostle foretold of, (2 Timothy 3) who, like Jannes and Jambres, resist the truth, who are proud boasters and exalting themselves and challenging to others special power to know and understand the counsels of God, when they are men of corrupt knowledge and minds, and to be reproved concerning the faith. But (says the apostle) they shall "prevail no longer, for their madness shall be evident to all men." And we exhort you with the words of the apostle, "turn away therefore from such."[30]

It follows that we speak some few words of the second prophecy, which is of the days of the son of man in the brightness of his coming for the consuming of the man of sin, spoken of (in) 2 Thessalonians, the which days our Savior says, "shall be as the lightning that comes out of the east and is seen into the west," (Matthew 24) wherein is set forth unto us that the Lord shall make his truth to appear with unspeakable evidence of light, so as his people shall plainly see the way and light thereof, according as the Lord by the prophet Isaiah speaks (42:16), "I will bring the blind a way they know not, and lead them by paths they have not known. I will make darkness light before them, and crooked things straight." And the Lord will not speak in secret, neither in a place of darkness in the earth. And Isaiah 30:26, "The light of the moon shall be as the light of the sun, and the light of the sun shall be sevenfold and like the light of seven days, in the day that the Lord will bind up the breach of his people and heal the **stroke** of their wound." And Isaiah 33:19, "Thou shalt not see a fierce people, a people of dark speech, that thou cannot perceive, and of a strange tongue, that thou cannot understand." All this teaches the people of God to look for plain paths to walk in, which do shine with brightness, as also that the witnesses

---

[30]2 Timothy 3:6-9.

of the Lord shall be a people that shall speak plainly to the understanding of the simple. Therefore, the Lord's people must not walk in blind and secret ways, nor desert paths which are not light and plain, nor be seduced by false prophets and deceitful people that speak in their fierce heat darkness and obscure things, who are full of deceitful distinctions, blind consequences, and all turning of devices to deceive the simple, saying, "Lo, here is Christ, lo, there is Christ." Of such, our Savior forewarns his people that they believe them not, although they shall show great signs and wonders, but that they shall set their hearts and turn their eyes unto the clear light of truth which is the everlasting Gospel that the "angel fleeing through the midst of heaven preached unto them that dwell on the earth, and to every nation, and kindred, and tongue, and people." (Revelation 14:6) This is the Spirit of the Lord's mouth, wherewith he will consume the man of sin and abolish him by the brightness of his coming, (2 Thessalonians 2) by the ministry of the seventh angel, who when he has poured out his vial, "there shall be sounds, and lightnings, and thunders, and a great earthquake such as never was. And the great city shall be rent in three parts. And the cities of the nations shall fall. And that great Babylon shall come in remembrance before God, and he shall give unto her the cup of the wine of the fierceness of his wrath." (Revelation 16) Thus by the glory of the light of the Gospel shall the mystery of iniquity be abolished.

And whereas our Savior Christ says that this his coming shall be as the lightning comes out of the east and seen into the west, this makes it manifest unto us that the glorious overspreading of the Gospel again shall be as at the first, general over all, and that men shall seek after and resort unto the light of the truth of God, as eagles do their prey, according to the prophecy of Isaiah 60:4, "Lift up thine eyes round about and behold all these are gathered and come to thee. Thy sons shall come from far." And Isaiah 66:18, "The Lord says it will come that I shall gather all nations and tongues, and they shall come and see my glory." And the Lord by the prophet Amos (9:11-12) says, "In that day will I raise up the tabernacle of David that has fallen down and close up the breaches thereof, and will raise up his ruins, and I will build it as in the days of old." And Isaiah 11:11-12, "In the same day shall the Lord stretch out his hand again the second time to possess the remnant of his people. And he shall assemble the dispersed of Israel, and gather the scattered of Judah from the four corners of the world." And hereunto agrees the prophecy (in) Revelation 19:17, where "the angel that stands in the sun cries with a loud voice to all the souls that fly through the midst of heaven, Come and gather yourselves together to the supper of the great God." And Revelation 21, the Holy Spirit, speaking of the glorious exaltation of the holy city after the destruction of Babylon, says, "The kings of earth shall bring their glory and honor unto it, and the glory and honor of the Gentiles shall be brought to it. And this is yet the hope and comfort of the saints of God, that it shall come to pass that which now come against Jerusalem shall go up from year to year to worship the King, the Lord of Hosts, and to keep the feast of tabernacles." (Zachariah 14:16) Therefore, says the voice out of the throne, "Praise our God, all you his servants and you that fear him both small and great. For the Lord, that Almighty God, does now reign. Let us be glad and rejoice, and give glory to him. For the marriage of the Lamb is come, and his wife has prepared herself." (Revelation 19:5-7) These words are faithful and true, which must shortly be fulfilled, "Blessed is he that observes the words of the prophecy of the book," (Revelation 22:6) but woe, woe, woe, then be unto all that do not mark and observe them, and faithfully and carefully keep the words of the prophesy of this book.

But we demand in all these days of tribulation, which are such as never were nor ever shall be, where shall the ignorant appear? If in the days of so great danger when there shall be (as their now is) so many false prophets showing such signs and wonders, so as if it were possible they would deceive the very elect, if in these days the ignorant be seduced through their ignorance, shall they drink of the cup of the wine of God's wrath? The Word of the Lord is perfect and plain they shall perish that are ignorant and are deceived, because "they receive not the love of the truth, therefore God shall send them strong delusions, that they should believe and be damned." (2 Thessalonians 2) And it is just with the Lord, their ignorance being declared to be for want of the love of the truth. Thus then is this ground of truth most evident and plain. They that through grace in Christ receive the love of the truth, they are the elect of God, and shall not be deceived, but shall be saved. But they that through the effectual working of Satan, with all his signs and lying wonders, receive not the love of truth, they shall be deceived, and believe and be damned. Moreover, our Savior Christ says, "If the ignorant lead the ignorant, they shall both fall into the pit." (Matthew 15:14) Let all therefore take heed, and learn to know the truth of God, and to love it, and to understand his Word themselves, seeing the Lord has commanded them not to follow such as say, "Lo, here is Christ, lo, there is Christ," but to look into the shining light of truth, whereof, if they be not

able to judge and discern of themselves (by the direction of God's Spirit)
they can never have faith nor assurance in the way they walk, so shall they
run blindfold to destruction, not knowing whether they are led. False prophets or true prophets are all alike to them, they being ignorant of scriptures,
whereby they should examine them and find them out, and try their doctrine. Such must needs be carried away with every blast of vain doctrine,
when they are not able to try the spirits whether they be of God. These are
the fruits of ignorance, not to know the voice of Christ from the voice of
false prophets. And yet such would have their ignorance excuse them,
although their ignorance be only for want of their love of the truth. And if
they that through ignorance are led into false ways shall be saved, then they
that through ignorance lead men into false ways shall also be saved, and so
shall (almost) all flesh shall be saved. For who can plead ignorance for all
their transgressions, in all false worship, and all their false ways? But they
that are ignorant, let them be ignorant. And let all disciples of Christ "covet
spiritual gifts that they may prophecy, and pray with understanding, and sing
with understanding, and speak with understanding, that they may instruct
others, and in understanding be of a ripe age." (1 Corinthians 14) This
knowledge of salvation is required of all the disciples of Christ alike, there
being but one law of obedience for all. And Christ has not appointed anyone to be more ignorant than another, and to everyone that asks alike, he
gives alike, and they that seek alike, shall find alike. (Matthew 7:7) For
"there is no respect of persons with God." (Romans 2:11)

Now there is one ground that is most dangerously perverted to the
destruction of many souls, wherein we pray the best advised godly consideration of every reader, and that is this: if men walk uprightly in the
truth, according to that they know, and endeavor to attain to better and
more knowledge of God's truth that they may walk in it, such men though
they commit much sin through ignorance, yet repenting of all their sins of
ignorance, there is mercy with the Lord for such sins and sinners. We confess this is a most true ground, or else no flesh could be saved, if the Lord
should not accept of the willingness of men's minds in the truth, according
to that which they have. But this ground is most wickedly perverted and
brought in to excuse all unwilling minds to be informed, who willingly resist
the truth, and have no willing minds to be directed by God's Word, no
further than stands with their good (uncertain). And yet this ground must
excuse all their false worship and all false ways, and all false doctrine, and
exposition of the scriptures, and all the profanation of the holy ordinances

of God, which they do through ignorance, although they repent not thereof, but justify themselves to do well therein. Can any godly heart thus conceive that because God in mercy does pardon the sins of ignorance, men repenting of their ignorances, that therefore God will pardon men that through ignorance commit sin and justify themselves in those their sins, either by word or practice? Cannot men see the great difference which is between repenting of their sins of ignorance and justifying of their sins committed through ignorance? But will they make it all one, to confess sin and to justify sin? Can the just God, contrary to his own Word and law, forgive anyone sin that is not repented of? "If we acknowledge our sins he is faithful and just to forgive us our sins, and to cleanse us from all unrighteousness." But if when we have sinned in any particular thing, we say, therein "we have not sinned, we make God a liar, and his word is not in us, and we cannot be forgiven nor cleansed." (1 John 1:9-10) Can the holy and just God forgive such sinners and sins, as when they have through ignorance sinned in divers things against the Word of God, they will justify themselves that they are not ignorant and that they have not therein sinned, and so make the Word of God a lie? The Word of the Lord is plain that they which are ignorant and sin, and say therein they are not ignorant, their sins remain upon them. They are the words of Christ (in) John 9:41, "If you were blind, that is, if you did see and acknowledge your blindness, you should not have sin. But now you say, we see, therefore, your sin remains." Thus does our Savior Christ show in as plain words as the heart of man can desire that all and every sin men commit through ignorance, and say therein they do not sin, all those sins are not pardoned, but remain upon them. And the judgment of the Lord is against them that so sin, as the wise man further shows (in) Proverbs 28:13, saying, "He that does not confess and forsake his sin shall not have mercy at God's hands, but that confesses and forsakes them shall have mercy." How shall men yet vainly persuade themselves that God will pardon their sins of ignorance, which they neither confess nor forsake, but justify themselves in many grievous sins, and say they have not sinned, and that they do not commit evil in doing them, but that they do that which is good and just in the sight of God? What sin shall be condemned if this sin is pardoned? Shall not the adulterer that confesses he does evil in committing adultery, and the drunkard that confesses he sins in his drunkenness, and the blasphemer that confesses he does evil in blasphemy, shall not all these be much rather pardoned (although they forsake their sins in that they confess them) than they that neither confess nor forsake their sins but justify themselves in their sins? Does this cause God to pardon their sins because they are fully persuaded in their minds that they sin not? Why then if the adulterer, drunkard, blasphemer, idolater, and covetous man fully persuaded in their minds that they sin not in doing those things, they shall also be pardoned. Thus must the Lord accept of ignorant, strong persuasions of men's minds in error and disobedience, for true knowledge, faith, and obedience. For if they that through ignorance, being fully persuaded in their minds or consciences, obey unrighteousness and justify error, shall be saved and through Christ be accepted with God, as they that of true knowledge and faith obey righteousness and justify the truth, so then is there salvation by Christ through ignorant persuasion of mind and disobedience as well as through true knowledge, faith, and obedience. What will men make of God? How has the mystery of iniquity prevailed? First, to take from him his power and government in his kingdom, as we have showed, and then to take from him his justice and judgement. For if the Lord shall not in his justice judge those that ignorantly pervert his laws, statutes, and ordinances, who "call light darkness and darkness light, sour sweet and sweet sour," (Isaiah 5:20) speaking evil of that they know not, teaching for doctrines men's precepts, overthrowing the doctrines of the foundation of the beginning of Christ, following the imaginations of their own hearts, and setting up the traditions of men instead of the holy ordinances of God, and because in all these things they are ignorant and walk as far as they see, and do as they are persuaded in their minds, thinking they do God good service, therefore they shall be accepted with God, if the Lord shall not in his justice judge these that thus sin and transgress against him, then is the righteous judgement of the Lord overthrown, and the ordinances of Christ under the Gospel made of none effect. And if men know them and do them, they shall do well. But if they be ignorant and walk in false ways, maintaining divers errors, they being persuaded in their consciences that it is the truth, they also shall be accepted. Of what use then are the ordinances of Christ? Then is truth and error all one, if men be as well persuaded of the one as of the other. This destroys all the religion of God, if everyone may take liberty to themselves to walk according to the persuasion of their minds though it be error. Yet if they know better, so long as they confess the name of Jesus, all is well. If they be so persuaded, they shall be saved. Then not only they that walk in the way of life but they that are persuaded they walk in the way of life, shall also be saved, though they walk in error.

Thus, as you have set open the door of the kingdom of heaven, and let all in that confess the name of Jesus with their infants, making them (as you think) members of the body of Christ, so now, you will also set open the gates of the kingdom of glory, and let in all that confess the name of Christ, though through ignorance they walk in much darkness, and make them, as you imagine in your foolish minds, fellow heirs with Christ in his glorious inheritance. And yet the Holy Ghost says, "If we walk in darkness and say we have fellowship with Christ, we lie and do not truly." (1 John 1:6) Therefore you shall all be deceived with the foolish virgins who were overtaken in their foolishness, who, though they hoped and were persuaded they should have been let in, yet were shut out. And so shall all you be that through ignorance justify false ways, although you should begin to say, "We have eaten and drunk in your presence, and you have taught in our streets, and we thought we had done well, and we knew no better." Yet the Lord shall say unto you, "I tell you I know you not. Depart from me, you workers of iniquity."[31] Then shall you see (if you will not learn before) that though you should plead you had done it ignorantly, it will not serve the turn. Yea, though you should say you had sought to enter in at the straight gate, but through your ignorance you were not able, notwithstanding your seeking, in that you have not sought aright, the door shall be shut upon you. And when you should knock and say, "Lord, Lord, open to us," the Lord shall answer, "I know you not, whence you are." (Luke 13:27) Then shall you see that your deceitful hearts have seduced you, and that your good meanings were not according to godliness, but according to your own minds and persuasions. Then shall you see that you casting down, destroying, and rejecting the holy ordinances of God, and setting up the vain inventions and traditions of your elders (as you do), thinking you do God good service, you shall no more be excused therein than they that have rejected and killed the disciples of Christ, and think they have done God good service,[32] your sins being much greater than theirs. For they ignorantly kill, destroy, and reject the disciples of Christ for keeping the ordinances of Christ, and yet ignorantly destroy, and reject the ordinances of Christ, that none should keep them, and set up other ordinances abolishing Christ thereby. Will the Lord think you, hold you guiltless for these things, although you do them

---

[31]Matthew 7:23.
[32]John 16:2.

ignorantly, especially you justifying yourselves and saying you do that which is good in God's sight, and that you sin not therein. Hear what the Lord says to his own people, who justified themselves in their ways of wickedness, saying, they are guiltless. "Behold, says the Lord, I will enter with you into judgment because you say I have not sinned." (Jeremiah 2:3) Even so will the Lord enter into judgment with every one of you that say you see when you are blind, and continue in the works of darkness, and say you sin not therein. Hear us with patience and consider what we say. The judge of all hearts knows that we earnestly desire the salvation of your souls. Will the just God forgive any one sin unrepented of? Or can he justify them that justify themselves in any one evil? Whoso knows God knows this cannot be, for he that is guilty of one sin, being guilty of all. (James 2:10; Ezekiel 18:11-13) If God should forgive any one sin unrepented of, he must needs forgive all sins unrepented of. But there can no sin be pardoned without repentance. Ignorance shall not excuse any. For a further full proof whereof, take the words of our Savior Christ, who says, He that is ignorant and knows not his master's **will** and sins, or "does things worthy of stripes," shall be beaten **(uncertain) receive** punishment.[33] Therefore let the ignorant never plead their ignorance more. The Lord has judged them. They shall all perish except they repent and come to the knowledge of the truth. And is it not just with the Lord to condemn all the ignorant, seeing the Lord has given them all means of knowledge, and they will not seek for it, nor ask after it, no further than they themselves think good?

What think you with yourselves? If a king make laws just and good, and bind himself by oath that without respect of persons whososever shall break any one of those laws he shall certainly die, except he acknowledge his fault and repent, and whosoever shall keep them shall be advanced to great dignity and honor, and these laws the king causes to be written so that all men may have them, and yet further the king in his great mercy, because he would have none of his subjects perish for want of the right understanding of his laws, the king to prevent them of that danger appoints in every place such a one as shall always be ready truly to inform his people in the right understanding of every one of those laws and statutes, and charging them to be directed by no other for the understanding thereof, if not withstanding the commandments, and all this love and care of their lord and

---

[33]Luke 12:48.

king over them to preserve them from falling under the judgment of death, his people and subjects shall either carelessly neglect to be informed, or shall think themselves wise enough to inform themselves, or go to be informed for the understanding of those laws to any other than the king has appointed, and resting upon their information break any one of those laws of the king, and do not acknowledge their fault and repent, shall their ignorance excuse them, when they had one ready at hand always to inform them before they offended, and yet ready to inform them that they might repent if they would but ask to be informed? **(uncertain)** they would not be informed before they break the commandment of the king, neither after they have offended will be informed to repent thereof, but justify themselves that they have not offended. Can a just king break his oath, and pardon and forgive the willful ignorance of such careless subjects, and advance them to the same honor whereunto he advances his dutiful subjects, but he shall dishonor himself, and make his oath and law of no effect? No wise and just earthly king will ever dishonor himself.

Now shall then the most glorious King of Kings who is most wise, just, and holy, having made most righteous, holy, and perfect laws, and "to show **stableness** of his counsel has bound himself by oath and promise" (Hebrews 6:18), without respect of persons, that whosoever shall break any one of those laws he shall certainly be damned, except to confess his sin and repent (Mark 16:16:Luke 13:3), and whosoever keep them shall inherit glory and honor and immortality. And these laws has he caused to be written by inspiration that all men may have them, and yet to make his mercy further to appear that he would not any of his people should perish for want of the right understanding thereof, has sent "the Comforter, and gives the Holy Ghost to everyone who asks them, to reach and lead them into all true understanding," (John 14:26; Luke 11:13) charging them to be directed by no other (James 1:5) for the understanding thereof. If notwithstanding the commandment and all this love and care of the King of Heaven over his people to preserve them from falling under the just judgment of eternal death, his people and subjects shall either carelessly neglect to be informed, or shall think they are wise enough to inform themselves, or shall go to any other to be informed of the understanding of those laws than the Lord has appointed, and relying and trusting on their information, break any one of the laws of the King of Heaven, and do not acknowledge their sin and repent, shall their ignorance excuse them? When they might always have had the Holy Ghost for asking to have informed them before they offended, as also after they have offended, that they might repent, can the most holy and just God and King, contrary to his oath, pardon and forgive the willful ignorance of such careless subjects as break his laws, and will not acknowledge their sin and repent, and give them eternal glory and honor with his servants (who though they have offended yet they have repented), but he shall dishonor himself, and make his oath and law of none effect? Oh, that men would consider that the most holy, wise, and just God cannot do so against his oath, and make himself unjust and untrue. If men would consider what God is, as he declares himself to be, that is, "a jealous God, not making the wicked innocent, visiting iniquity to the third and fourth generation of them that break his commandments, a God of severity against them which fall through unbelief," (Romans 11:22) a God that will certainly "take away their part out of the book of life that takes anything away from his Word, and that will add all the plagues written in his Word under them who add anything unto his Word." (Revelation 22)

If men would believe God to be such a one as he declares himself to be, they could not be so vain as to persuade themselves that God would forgive them their sins of ignorance, their ignorance being through their own wilful neglect, and when through such their ignorance they overthrow the ordinances of Christ, and abolish the laws of his testament, and repent not, but justify themselves in those their sins, saying they sin not therein.

What were sufficient to say in this great deceivableness of unrighteousness, wherewith men are seduced to think that if through ignorance they justify sin it shall be forgiven them, they knowing no better, although they repent not, which they cannot do, in any sin wherein they justify themselves? For men cannot both justify and repent of one and the same sin at one instant. If men will be so far void of all grace and understanding as to hold and think that any sin committed through ignorance, and through ignorance justified, (because they know no better) shall be pardoned, then it cannot be denied but that they that put Christ to death through ignorance, and through ignorance justified they had not sinned, but that they had done well, and according to the Word of God, in putting a blasphemer to death, that said he was the Son of God, they shall also be pardoned, for they did it ignorantly, and knew no better, as our Savior Christ testified, when he said, "Father, forgive them. They know not what they do." (29) And the apostle Peter acknowledges the same (Acts 3:17) saying, "Brethren, I know you did it through ignorance, as also your governors."

Now let us compare things together, so shall we through the grace of God the better see the **(uncertain)** of this ground, as it is misapplied. The ground we are to remember is this, that if men walk conscionably as far as they know, and desire better knowledge, yet through ignorance commit much sin, there is mercy with God, and they, acknowledging and repenting of their ignorances, shall be pardoned by grace through faith and repentance. (Ephesians 2:8) This ground is misapplied, as we trust will easily appear, being brought to prove that if men walk conscionably as far as they know and commit some sins through ignorance and through ignorance justify the sin, thinking they do well, and knowing no better, their sin shall be pardoned, which if they be, it must be by grace through persuasion and ignorance, for there is no faith in ignorance. Where is there any warrant for such a ground? Who is so blind that cannot see the grievous error of this ground thus misapplied? This is to excuse sin by sin, that **is,** by ignorance. We conclude this point by the word of truth that none can deny that have any knowledge of the means of salvation: there is no salvation, but by grace in Christ, through faith and repentance. So is there then no pardon for any sin, but by the grace in Christ through faith and repentance. This being an undeniable ground, none then can be saved, nor have their sin pardoned by grace in Christ through ignorance, justifying any one sin. For there cannot be either faith or repentance in ignorant justifying any sin. Therefore no such sin can be pardoned, but all such sinners must be condemned. And for this end and purpose have we spoken all that we have spoken in this point to show unto all men that if they justify any one sin or evil, **though it be** of ignorance, they can never be saved, but **shall perish** to everlasting destruction. Such sins cannot come within men's general repentance of all their ignorances, seeing they justify themselves in them, and say they sin not, therefore their sin remains, and cannot be taken away by Christ. As for example: you will justify the baptizing of infants. Now when you repent of all your sins of ignorance, have you any thoughts to repent of that? And if you were asked, would you not with your last breath justify that you have done well therein, and that the baptizing of infants is a holy ordinance of Christ? But if it be no ordinance of Christ, and that you sin therein, can you be so simple as to imagine **that this** sin shall come within your general repentance, wherein you **bless** and justify yourselves? You can no more be forgiven at God's hands than they that ignorantly set up a false Christ, and justify him to be the true Christ, or than they that put the true Christ to death, and justify he is a false Christ. We know your answer in this will be that if you could see it to be your sin to baptize infants, and to maintain it to be a holy ordinance of God, you would repent of it, but before you cannot. Will not God answer you that when he can see you repent he will forgive you, but before he cannot? (Ezekiel 18:21-27)

Will not the pope make the same answer for all the bloody persecutions wherewith he has, and does persecute all Protestants, so called? Will not the lord bishop make this answer for all their wicked and cruel persecutions against the Puritans and Brownists (so called). But shall they be pardoned, they justifying themselves in all these wickednesses (wherein they think they do God service) because they repent of all their sins of ignorance, whereof they justify these to be none? Will God pardon them in all this their wickedness, because they cannot see it to be their sin? You all will grant they cannot be pardoned of these sins, they justifying themselves therein. Neither can any be pardoned of any sin, they justifying themselves therein.

If this were duly considered it would make men take heed what they profess or practice in the profession of Christ, seeing if they profess or practice any thing that is not according to the Word of God, and justify it for good, they must perish and cannot be saved. It stands therefore all men upon the peril of their souls to look to their ways, and to be upon a sure ground from God's Word, what they condemn for evil or error, **and** what they maintain and justify for truth. For if "they that justify the wicked, and they that condemn the just be an abomination unto the Lord," (Proverbs 17:15) then they that justify error and wickedness, and condemn truth and righteousness, call light darkness and darkness light, such must needs be an abomination to the Lord. If all the learned scribes and Pharisees and false prophets in the world had hearts to believe this, and confess it, it would make them take heed what they justified for truth, and what they condemn for error, and how they taught others to do so. If all the careless professors of Christ that profess him in word would believe this word of the Lord to be true, it would make them look more circumspectly to their ways, and not think that any profession of Christ is sufficient, and that they may profess Christ after that manner that is best pleasing to their own minds, making the way large that they walk therein at liberty according to the vanity and excess of their own hearts. If the simple hearted, who in many things are **weaned** from the world and who have many zealous desires in them, did faithfully believe the Lord herein, that if they justify any false ways, untruth, or error, and condemn any way of light and truth, their sin remains, and they are an abomination to the Lord, if they did believe God herein, it would make them take heed how they went on in their ignorant zeal, being led by their teachers, approving and justifying what they teach them, and disapproving and condemning what they teach them to disapprove and condemn, forsaking the teachings of God's Spirit, not thinking it possible for themselves to attain to the understanding of the scriptures but by the teaching of their learned and good men (as they falsely call them). But if they did believe this word of the Lord, that they must perish if they justify any one error or false way, and condemn any one truth, it would make them with fear and trembling to seek wisdom, knowledge, and understanding of God, that they being taught of God might be able of themselves, by the help of the Holy Spirit (the only true teacher and leader into all truth) to discern and judge between good and evil, light and darkness, truth and error, lest they, relying upon men, be seduced and led to justify false ways, and condemn the way of truth in any particular, and so fall under the just judgment of the Lord, even the judgment of eternal death and condemnation, a right recompense of reward for all that will of ignorant simplicity out of their good meanings and zealous affections (falsely so called) submit themselves to be led and taught only of men, seeking for knowledge at their mouths, and not wholly depending upon the scriptures for instruction, and the Spirit of God to teach them the understanding there, neglecting (of faith) the reading and searching and meditating of the scriptures day and night, and earnest praying without doubting that the Lord would give them the Spirit of wisdom to direct them to the true understanding and meaning of God in the scriptures, that they might be able, if an angel from heaven should come and teach them any other doctrine than Christ and his apostles have taught, to judge him accursed. When this way shall be once truly learned and faithfully practiced of God's people to attain to true knowledge, then shall all that seek after Christ strive to enter into his kingdom by repentance and new birth, being born again of water and the Holy Ghost. Then shall men learn to know the true baptism of Christ, which is the "baptism of repentance for the remission of sins," and be therewith baptized and "put on Christ," and not satisfy themselves with childish baptism, in which baptism they have not, nor could not put on Christ, and without which baptism of repentance for the remission of sins they cannot put on Christ. And then shall the elect of God not be deceived by the multitude of false prophets, with all their lying wonders, that say, "Lo, here is Christ, lo, there is Christ." But they shall take heed to the glorious brightness of his coming, which shall be in the shining light of his truth, unto the which the chosen of God shall flee, and come from far, as eagles to their prey. And to this clear light of truth the Lord that has bought you all with his blood. Raise up your hearts that you may seek his face, and be filled with the fullness of his presence.

Amen.

Appendix

We hold ourselves bound to acknowledge, and that others might be warned, to manifest how we have been (through our great weakness) misled by deceitful hearted leaders who have and do seek to save their lives, and will make sure not to lose them for Christ. And therefore they flee into foreign countries and free states, and draw people after them to support their kingdoms, first seeking their own safeties, and then publishing (as they pretend) the Gospel, or seeking the kingdom of heaven, as far as they may with their safety. And this they justify by perverting and misapplying the words of our Savior Christ, where he says, "When they persecute you, or drive, or thrust you out of one city, flee into another." (Matthew 10:23) These words have they picked out for their purpose, casting away or leaving forth divers rules of Christ going before and following in the same scripture, which cannot permit of their exposition and practice. But we will only instance the reason why our Savior Christ bids them, when they are persecuted in one city, go to another, and his reason is this: "For verily, I say unto you, you shall not go over all the cities of Israel till the Son of Man come." This shows that our Savior Christ's meaning was that when they were driven or expelled out of one city, they should go to another city in Israel to preach the Gospel unto it. But these men flee to cities to the which they cannot preach the Gospel, being of a strange tongue, neither have they any intent or meaning to preach the Gospel to those cities. Their fleeing is not to that end, but to save themselves, for being as "sheep in the midst of wolves," and for being "delivered up to councils, and for being brought to governors and kings, for Christ's sake, in witness to them and to the Gentiles."[1] These men need not this advice of our Savior Christ, who counsels his disciples to "take no thought what they shall speak, or what they shall answer" when they are brought before princes and governors. For

---

[1]Acts 11:19.

they flee to such places where they make sure they shall never come in question before them.

The disciples of Christ unto whom he speaks these words ("when they persecute you or drive you out of one city, flee to another") did not understand our Savior Christ as these men do. If they had, they would not have believed the angel (Acts 5:19-20) that bade them, when he delivered them out of prison, "Go, and stand in the temple, and speak to the people all the words of this life." They would have said, "We have been imprisoned and persecuted, therefore we are to flee. Our Lord told us so." But they obeyed the voice of the angel, knowing it did not contradict that rule of Christ. Neither would they (if they had understood Christ as these men do), after they had been beaten and commanded to speak no more in the name of Jesus, still have stayed in that city, "daily in the temple and from house to house, teaching and preaching Jesus Christ." (Acts 5:40, 42) But these men flee before they feel either strokes or bonds, and teach men so. The whole scriptures are against them in this their understanding. Acts 8:1-4 might suffice to satisfy them in this point, and to discover their error fully, where it is showed that there was great persecution against the church at Jerusalem, and "they were all (except the apostles) scattered abroad through the regions of Judea and Samaria." And Acts 11:12, "They that were scattered abroad, went throughout till they came to Phoenicia and Cyprus, and Antioch, preaching the Word."[2] Here we see that, notwithstanding the great havoc Saul made of the church, and entered into every house, and drew out both men and women, and put them in prison, yet the apostles did not flee. And they that did flee went to cities to the which they could and did preach the Gospel. But neither the example of the apostles that did not flee, nor of them that were scattered, who went to cities to which they preached the Gospel, will serve these men's turn, but they flee to cities most commodious for their safety and profit, to which they cannot preach the Gospel. Furthermore (in) Acts 14, although there was an assault made both of the Jews and Gentiles against Paul and Barnabas, to do them violence at Iconium, and although Paul was stoned and left for dead at Lystra, yet they returned again to Lystra and Iconium to confirm the disciples' hearts, preferring that duty before the fear of persecution.

---

[2]Matthew 10:18.

For further overthrowing of this misunderstanding of these words of our Savior Christ, "when they persecute you in one city, flee to another," let all hearts consider how the apostle Paul commended and rejoiced in the church of the Thessalonians because of their "patience and faith in all their persecutions and tribulations that they suffered." (2 Thessalonians 1:4) And in 1 Thessalonians 2:14, "Brethren, you are become followers of the churches of God in Judea which are in Christ Jesus, because you have also suffered the same things of your own countrymen, even as they have done of the Jews." Thus does the apostle commend to the churches of Judea, and of Thessalonica, for their constant suffering of persecution in their own countries, not once advising or teaching them to flee out of their countries to avoid persecution. This is a new doctrine of devils brought in by men, that were never found in the faith.

Further, hear what the Spirit says to the church of Pergamus. "I know you dwell where Satan's throne is. And you have kept my name and have not denied my faith, even in those days when Antipas, my faithful martyr, was slain among you, where Satan dwells." And to the church of Smyrna the Spirit says, "Fear none of those things which you shall suffer. Behold, it shall come to pass that the devil shall cast some of you into prison that you may be tried, and you shall have tribulation ten days. Be faithful unto the death, and I will give you the crown of life." (Revelation 2) Who will not be blind may see here how the Spirit of God commends the **saints** for holding the faith, and dwelling where there was bloody persecution and where Satan dwelled, and does not exhort them to flee, but not to fear what they should do unto them. Let then the simple hearted be no more troubled by these men who have rent the words of our Savior Christ ("when they persecute you, or drive you out of one city, flee into another") from the true sense and meaning wherewith they stand compassed round about in. (Matthew 10) And whereas our Savior Christ in these words gave a rule of direction unto his disciples, how they should proceed in the publishing of the Gospel, appointing them, when they were expelled or persecuted in one city, that they should go to another to preach, because there were many cities of Israel to go through, these men of corrupt minds, lovers of themselves, utterly pervert the meaning of our Savior Christ in these words, and say, he gave it for a rule to his disciples to teach them to flee to save themselves from persecution. And so by this their understanding, when the disciples of Christ had found a city of most safety, there they should hide themselves as these men do, and let the publishing of the Gospel alone, except any would follow after them, or come to them where they might be in safety.

Now do the ignorant, blind, corrupt hearts and tongues of these men conceive and speak against God and his truth, and pervert it to their own destruction, overthrowing the whole doctrine and meaning of Christ in this place (Matthew 10:16-39), where Christ with all the wisdom of the Spirit does set himself to teach his disciples to suffer persecution, showing them what persecutions they should suffer, and what persecutions they should have, and how far they should suffer persecution, exhorting them not to fear them that kill the body, and declaring unto them for their unspeakable comfort his providence and protection over them, telling them that all the hairs of their heads are numbered in his sight. And these deceivers, they teach their disciples to flee persecution and persecutors and to spare and save themselves that it may not come so unto them. But when the worthy disciple of Christ, Peter, advised his master so, Christ bade him, "Come behind me, Satan. Thou art an offense to me." (Matthew 16) Judge then what Christ will say to these false prophets that are the disciples of the man of sin, supporting and perverting his kingdom by this their doctrine. For the disciples of Christ cannot glorify God and advance his truth better than by suffering all manner of persecution for it, and by witnessing it against the man of sin, with the blood of their testimony. We must leave this point to godly consideration. (It had been much better, we confess, to have been part of a book than such an addition.) And we leave these men with all their disciples (if they will not be informed herein) to be a reproach to all men, who shall say unto them, Where have you learned to flee into foreign countries and not to suffer persecution for Christ of your own countrymen? Where have you learned for fear of men to flee from your own country, and fathers' houses to whom you ought, and where you might best publish the Gospel? And where have you learned to draw parents from children, and children from parents, to whom they are especially bound to witness God's truth, and to be lights unto them? You have not learned it of Christ, who would not suffer him that had been possessed when he prayed him that he might be with him, but Christ said unto him, "Go your way to your friends, and show them what great things the Lord has done unto you. And he went and published them." (Mark 5:18)[3] Yea, all men shall say unto them, Where

---

[3]Mark 5:19.

have you learned to set up your light in secret places? And where have you learned to pull your shoulder from the yoke and to seek to save your lives? But therefore, says Christ, surely you shall lose them, except you repent.

Furthermore, if Christ gave this for a rule or precept to his disciples to flee persecution to save themselves, then was it an absolute commandment, and so did all the apostles and disciples of Christ break his commandment and sin, in that they did not flee to save themselves always when they were persecuted. And thereby do these men condemn all their brethren that flee not as they do, except they will add error to error, and affirm as some of them do, that it is indifferent to flee or not to flee, making thereby this precept of Christ indifferent to be obeyed or not to be obeyed, which cannot be affirmed or any one precept of Christ. For nothing can be both commanded and indifferent to be obeyed or done. And those words of Christ will no way permit such indifference. For they are an absolute precept for that end for the which they are given, which is not to flee to save themselves, but to flee or go to another city to preach the Gospel. And we put these seducers in remembrance that our Savior Christ gives this rule also unto his disciples, that if they shall "enter into any house or city that shall not receive them, nor hear his word, when they depart thence, they shall shake off the dust of their feet for a witness against that house or city."[4] But when will these men, according to this rule of Christ, shake the dust off their feet for a witness against Amsterdam or Leyden, which cities neither receive them nor the word they bring, otherwise than they receive Turks and Jews, and all sorts who come only to seek safety and profit? It should seem this rule of Christ appertains not to these men. But let them and all men see that this rule appertains to whomsoever the other appertains, they being both given at one time, and upon one and the same occasion, and to one and the same persons. And when these great deceivers have learned not to divide Christ, they will learn also not to divide his precepts and ordinances, taking what is agreeable to their corrupt minds, and forsaking what is contrary to them. We will pass by the lamentable fruits and judgments that we have, and do see with our eyes, follows this damnable error, when many, yes, the most men that had in a great measure forsaken the love of the world, and began to be zealous of some good things, being drawn by this opinion and these seducers into foreign

---

[4]Matthew 10:14.

countries, not knowing which way to support their outward estate, have turned again unto the world, and are fain to hunt to and fro, far and near, after every occasion. And all is too little to satisfy most of their wants, and nothing will satisfy some of their desires. All these things and many more, these hirelings, their shepherds, can well bear withal, so that they return to the **hive**, that their portion may not be reproved. And those of best hearts, and some of best quality that cannot run and rove, and set their hearts to seek the world, consume that they have and fall under hard conditions, and by little and little lose their first love also. It is the general judgment we **arrive at** in all this, in that by these means, former zeal and the best first beginnings that were in these men do vanish, fade away, and come to nothing, to the unfeigned grief of our souls to see it. How much better had it been that they had given their lives for that truth they profess in their own countries. Now as we, through the grace of God, and by the warrant of his Word (as we have manifested), cast away these perverters of the holy scriptures and their doctrines, so we wish all to do that fear God and seek the glory of his name, and come and lay down their lives in their own country for Christ and his truth. And let none think that we are altogether ignorant, what building, and warfare we take in hand, and that we have not sat down and in some measure thoroughly considered what the cost and danger may be. Also let none think that we are without sense and feeling of our own inability to begin, and our weakness to endure to the end, the weight and danger of such a work. But in all these things we hope and wait for wisdom and strength, and help from the Lord, "Who is able to establish us that we may stand, and by weakness to confound mighty things." (1 Corinthians 1) Let none therefore "despise the day of small things," (Zechariah 4:10) nor be grieved and say with that scorner (Nehemiah 4:24), "What will these Jews do?" Thus commending all our poor endeavors to the best acceptance of every well disposed reader, beseeching the Lord to make his grace to abound to you all, for the glory of his name, and the salvation of every one of your souls.

Amen.

Indexes

Topics

CPSIA information can be obtained at www.ICGtesting.com
Printed in the USA
238551LV00004B/42/A